DATE DUE			

WEST CAMPUS

GAYLORD

Dr. Seuss and Philosophy

Oh, the Thinks You Can Think!

edited by
Jacob M. Held

ROWMAN & LITTLEFIELD PUBLISHERS, INC.
Lanham • Boulder • New York • Toronto • Plymouth, UK

Published by Rowman & Littlefield Publishers, Inc.
A wholly owned subsidiary of The Rowman & Littlefield Publishing Group, Inc.
4501 Forbes Boulevard, Suite 200, Lanham, Maryland 20706
http://www.rowmanlittlefield.com

Estover Road, Plymouth PL6 7PY, United Kingdom

British Library Cataloguing in Publication Information Available

Library of Congress Cataloging-in-Publication Data
Dr. Seuss and philosophy : oh, the thinks you can think! / edited by Jacob M. Held.
    p. cm.
  Includes bibliographical references.
    ISBN 978-1-4422-0311-2 (pbk. : alk. paper) — ISBN 978-1-4422-0312-9 (electronic)
  1. Seuss, Dr.—Criticism and interpretation. 2. Literature—Philosophy. 3. Children's stories, American—History and criticism. I. Held, Jacob M., 1977– II. Title: Doctor Seuss and philosophy.
  PS3513.E2Z65 2011
  813'.52—dc22

                                                                    2011006488

Printed in the United States of America

Dedicated to those teachers who impressed upon me through their words and deeds that learning is about growing as an individual, and who helped me grow immensely—especially Dr. James B. South and Ken Fought

~

Contents

~

Preface

When I first started college I was ecstatic. I was finally in a learning environment where I could take a class on anything I could imagine; where I was in control of my educational destiny. So I started looking for courses on topics I hadn't had before, courses beyond the simple English, history, and various sciences I had been instructed in since I was five. I saw Philosophy 151 and thought I'd try it out. While discussing my future class schedule with my dad, I asked him what philosophy was. He replied, and I paraphrase, "The only people who study philosophy are future philosophy professors." It wasn't hard to read between the lines: philosophy was a waste of time. I took it anyway. What I found was eye-opening. I discovered the history of humanity's collective attempts to understand, contextualize, and discern the meaning of existence, from politics, law, and ethics to God, art, and science. I could not think of anything more profound or important. But at the same time, I noticed no one else was taking these classes. On a campus where an introductory zoology lecture may have upward of two hundred students, my philosophy courses would max out at about fifteen. Philosophy was also the butt of jokes. It was treated as a flaky, irrelevant pastime, not a legitimate area of study. So it did seem as if only those interested in becoming philosophy professors took philosophy courses, and what a shame. It was in those classes that I found an appreciation of and engagement with ideas that have defined and continue to influence our culture and our very existence as a human race. So I decided to become one of those philosophy students who wanted to teach philosophy. But it wasn't out of necessity; it's not that all you can do with a degree in philosophy is teach. Philosophy is a love of wisdom, and with wisdom you can do anything, usually better than most, including the most important thing of all, live well. I decided to teach because I had concluded at the end of my first semester at college that I was never going to leave campus. I loved being surrounded by curious, bright people discussing everything under the sun. Regardless of what I had majored in, I would have become a professor of it. Philosophy just struck my fancy. It covered every facet of the human experience. My enthusiasm translated into a desire to open up the world to others in the way it had been opened to me. I have been lucky enough to be in the position for some years now to do just that. But I still have to fight against the prevailing attitude that philosophy is worthless. It's not my dad with whom I have to deal, but students and their parents, who want to know, "What can you do with a philosophy degree?" I can't answer this question. Or rather I can, but no answer will satisfy those who ask this question. Whoever asks this question already presumes that an education is only as good as the job it secures, and whatever isn't a hirable skill isn't worth developing. But college isn't about getting a job; it's about getting an education, and an education is about developing the whole person. Music, art, history, philosophy, religion, as well as sciences, math, and whatever job training you get in Business 101 are all part and parcel of your growth as a person. Philosophy trains you to be open, thoughtful, and resourceful—a genuinely sharp, bright, and creative human being. This is valuable whether you get a job or not. Thankfully, there has been a recent trend in philosophy to popularize the discipline and bring it to a general audience. This trend is almost exclusively due to William Irwin and his wildly successful series on philosophy and popular culture, to which I have contributed previously. This use of popular elements to disseminate philosophical wisdom is useful both as a public relations move for my discipline but also in promoting the goal of philosophy, which is living well through a critical and reflective attitude. This book was produced in the same spirit. However, it is markedly different than other similar volumes in one regard—it is meant to be an introduction to philosophy in general. This is why I chose to focus on Dr. Seuss. From the outset I wanted to offer an accessible and fun introduction to that tradition that inspired me so many years ago. What I have sought to produce, with many thanks to my wonderful, helpful, and accommodating contributors, is an introduction to major themes and traditions in philosophy through an aspect of popular culture with which almost everyone is familiar, Dr. Seuss. This introduction isn't exhaustive, it's merely a window into a discipline, but hopefully opening that window will let in a breath of fresh air and open the reader's eyes to the fact that it truly is "opener there in the wide open air" ("Oh, the Places You'll Go").

~

Acknowledgments

I would like to acknowledge all of those who supported me during the completion of this project, from my loving family to all of my contributors. I would also like to thank those colleagues/friends who have kept me sane over the years by being supportive, helpful, and always willing to lend an ear not only for my ideas but also my gripes. They remind me daily why we do what we do, and their company and support are appreciated more than they will ever know. Thank you, Ron and Tanya. In addition I'd like to acknowledge the University Research Council at the University of Central Arkansas for awarding me a summer stipend during the summer of 2010 to assist in completing this volume.

~

Editor's Note

Many of Dr. Seuss's works are not paginated, which can make citing them tricky. Luckily, the books are quite short, so if anyone wants to know on what page a reference occurs they merely have to flip through until they find it. So in order to make things simpler and to avoid vast amounts of endnotes, all references to Seuss's works will be parenthetical according to the key below. All works are published by Random House.

And to Think That I Saw It on Mulberry Street (Mulberry)
Bartholomew and the Oobleck (Oobleck)
"The Big Brag" in *Yertle the Turtle and Other Stories* (Brag)
The Butter Battle Book (Butter)
The Cat in the Hat (Cat)
Daisy-Head Mayzie (Daisy)
Did I Ever Tell You How Lucky You Are? (Lucky)
Dr. Seuss's Sleep Book (Sleep)
"Gertrude McFuzz" in *Yertle the Turtle and Other Stories* (McFuzz)
Green Eggs and Ham (Eggs)
Happy Birthday to You (Birthday)
Horton Hatches the Egg (Hatches)
Horton Hears a Who! (Horton)
How the Grinch Stole Christmas! (Grinch)

I Had Trouble in Getting to Solla Sollew (Trouble)
If I Ran the Circus (Circus)
The Lorax (Lorax)
McElligot's Pool (Pool)
Oh, the Places You'll Go! (Places)
On Beyond Zebra! (Zebra)
Scrambled Eggs Super! (Scrambled)
"The Sneetches" in *The Sneetches and Other Stories* (Sneetches)
Thidwick the Big-Hearted Moose (Thidwick)
"What Was I Scared Of?" in *The Sneetches and Other Stories* (Scared)
"Yertle the Turtle" in *Yertle the Turtle and Other Stories* (Yertle)
You're Only Old Once! (Old)
"The Zax" in *The Sneetches and Other Stories* (Zax)

~

Unsettled Meddling:
An Introduction in Verse

It started way back, when I was quite small
I would simply ask "why?"
one question, that's all.
I would wait for an answer, sometimes it would come
"Because," "I Don't Know," "Ask your father or mum."
But it never stopped there
The questions kept coming.
And answers were lacking, adults kept "ho-humming."
It would start out quite simply and then get all muddled
I'd ask just one question and end up befuddled.
Why is the sky blue? or Why are plants green?
Why are they poor? and Why is he mean?
Why should I be good?
Who put you in charge?
My mind would start racing as questions loomed large.
Why are we here?
What ought I do?
Is there a rhyme, or a reason, or two?
Can it be learned, can I learn it, from who?
Will the answers be certain, or guesses, who knew?
My mind was unsettled, my brain never rested
But everyone moaned when their answers were tested.
I meant them no harm, I truly did not,

But I wanted some reasons for "why," "which," and "what?"
Their moaning made sense when I learned that adults
Although bigger and stronger, respectable folks
Were confused just like me, but had stopped asking "why?"
They just didn't care, so they just didn't try.
Or maybe they cared and that's why they had ceased
When you care about answers, doubt leads to unease.
The questions I asked were very unsettling
And unsettled folks don't appreciate meddling.
But questions are things that are meant to be asked,
Meddling's our nature, unsettling's our task.
When I got older I went off to school
To college to learn from professors who knew.
I learned about dinosaurs, classics, geology
African poetry, gods, and psychology.
But philosophy, that was the first course to show me
That questions, not answers, are how we keep growing.
We ask them because we're inquisitive beings
We're naturally wonder-full, curious things.
I decided that asking is what I *should* do
And I'd help others get good at it too!
A philosopher, that's what I wanted to be
I'd never leave college, I'd stay here and teach.
My parents were less than excited, you see
College for them was about a degree
And degrees are just things for getting good jobs
And good jobs pay lots, oh yes money in gobs.
But philosophy isn't that kind of position
It won't earn you fame and there is no commission.
And some don't think teaching's a worthwhile job
"Those who can't do . . ." say the ignorant mob.
For people like this life is just about stuff,
Having more than your neighbor and never enough.
For these types of folks it's all fortune and fame
What pays off is good, what does not is lame.
So they don't, and they won't, and they can't understand
It's wisdom, not money that makes a life grand.
So I kept on pondering year after year
Up to this point with me sitting right here
A professor, philosopher, questioning guy
Seeker of answers, asker of "Why?"
For questions are things that are meant to be asked,
And answers are things that are meant to be passed . . .

Passed on to the next generation of Why-er
Passed by when they're old, outdated, and tired.
I've met many strange birds as I've travelled this road
And some of them helped write the book that you hold.
These doubters and why-ers these fabulous scholars
Address some big questions and offer some answers.
We begin with a huge, spectacular query
One for which all thinkers have their own theory.
The meaning of life, now we are talking
A question so big it leaves everyone gawking.
A question so big it can't fit in one mind
So I've gathered a few to help with this bind.
But the number of answers is too great to count
And the answers we've counted are too great to mount
In the pages that follow, you'll just have to deal
with a brief introduction to a very large field.
Ancients and Moderns, Greek, German, and French
All play the game, no one's left on the bench.
They'll tell you to flourish, live well free of pain.
Or perish and suffer, and struggle in vain.
They might be quite playful or doleful and dry
But at least these dear fellows do give it a try.
We have theories and guesses and tries by the oodle
Enough twisted fellows to twist up your noodle
And when thoroughly twisted we'll keep right on going
We'll ask about knowledge our minds over-flowing.
Epistemology! "What can I know?"
And why does it matter and how does it go?
This stuff is important for one cannot travel
The road of the wise if one can't unravel
The true from the false, the sense from the babble
The solid and firm from the dribble and drabble.
And once we begin to get smarter on smarts
We can move ourselves on to the ethical arts.
There's so much one can think o'er the good and the bad
And so many dear thinkers and thoughts that they've had.
We'll do our best to give you a view
A snapshot or glimpse o'er a theory or two.
We've got Greeks once again, and our German friend Kant
As well as a Scotsman, that's more than you'll want.
We'll do all the theory, apply it as well
To issues like nature and business pell mell.
We'll give you a history as well as some praxis

And then we'll move on to grind other axes.
It's off to the realm of political thought
Where it isn't just personal questions of "ought."
Now we will wonder about our relations
How people should be and what of their nations.
Contracts and property, how to divide it
Diversity, needs, all the ways to contrive it
And once we've wound through these odd wiggled roads
we will find that our story has not all been told
there are questions that still have yet to be asked
but this book isn't big enough for such a huge task.
Clearly one book can't hold all the big thoughts
So we haven't discussed all the whys, whats, and oughts.
This book offers a glimpse
It's merely one look
If you seek understanding you'll need more than one book.*

---

*Thanks to Kim Newman for her suggestions on the rhyme.

CHAPTER ONE

~

Oh, the Places You'll Go! The Examined, Happy Life

Benjamin Rider

You have brains in your head.
You have feet in your shoes.
You can steer yourself
any direction you choose.
You're on your own. And you know what you know.
And YOU are the guy who'll decide where to go. (Places)

On the journey of life, we face many choices: What career should I pursue? Where should I live? What should I do with my money and time? What kind of person should I be, anyway, and what should I stand for? As we make these choices, large and small, we chart the courses of our lives, creating our unique selves and making an impact on the world and the people around us. And whether we think about it consciously or not, we want these choices to turn out well. We want to live good lives and be happy. Of course, people have different ideas about what it means to live a good life. One person might think her life is good when she has lots of money; another when he has a large family; another when she contributes to making the world a better place. Nevertheless, each of us seeks the paths that will bring us happiness and success while navigating the inevitable Bang-ups and Hang-ups, Lurches and Slumps, that get in our way. There is a reason that Dr. Seuss's *Oh, the Places You'll Go!* is popular as a graduation present. In this book, Dr. Seuss's protagonist faces the challenges, opportunities, and unexpected joys that life offers and responds to them with courage and imagination.

So what is the best way to make all these difficult choices well? How do you make your way successfully through the maze of life? How should you deal with the Hang-ups and Slumps, the lonely games and the confusing wiggled roads, the Hakken-Kraks and other real and imagined monsters you'll encounter along the way? Dr. Seuss assures his reader that he'll succeed ("98 and ¾ percent guaranteed"!) but what does it mean to succeed, anyway? What is a good and worthwhile life? And how do we achieve it?

Questioning Life's Big Questions

For ancient Greek and Roman philosophers questions about the good life were fundamental not only to philosophical inquiry but also to human life in general. The first philosopher to ask these questions prominently was Socrates (469–399 BCE), who referred to them as "the most important matters" in life.[1] Socrates assumed (and subsequent ancient philosophers agreed) that all humans desire good and happy lives.[2] Although we're often shortsighted or confused about what that means—sometimes, perversely, we even do things we know will make us miserable—nevertheless, deep down, we do want to be happy and flourish. Indeed, many ancient philosophers went further and argued that, ultimately, the desire for happiness underlies every choice we make, even the most stupid and impetuous ones. Suppose a teenager gets drunk and is arrested driving home from a party. Socrates would say that, as stupid and thoughtless as his actions might seem, his choices must have made sense, at least in terms of what seemed right to him at the time.[3] Perhaps he wanted to be accepted by his friends, or he didn't want to have to call his parents and get in trouble. To be sure, he wasn't thinking clearly or well. All the same, he did what he thought was best. So even if he never stops to think about the "most important matters" in life—happiness, virtue, what it means to be human, or in general, as Socrates puts it, the "condition of his soul"[4]—nevertheless his actions and choices reflect his unexamined values, assumptions, and beliefs. He makes his decisions based on what, deep down, he believes is good and worthwhile, and if his beliefs are shoddy, so will be his life.

Dr. Seuss's books often feature characters whose unexamined and false beliefs prevent them from being happy or satisfied with their lives. For example, "The Sneetches" tells the story of two kinds of Sneetches who share the beaches—Star-Belly Sneetches and Plain-Belly Sneetches. The difference between the two is not significant: "Those stars weren't big. They were really so small / you might think such a thing wouldn't matter at all"

(Sneetches). Yet Star-Belly Sneetches look down upon Plain-Belly ones, exclude them from their games, and leave them out in the cold during their frankfurter roasts and marshmallow toasts. The Sneetches on the beaches are miserable and divided, all because of their silly belief that little belly stars make some Sneetches better than others. Then, a "Fix-It-Up Chappie" arrives with a wondrous machine that—for a price—can add stars to unstarred Sneetch bellies. The Plain-Bellies eagerly line up, thinking that once they have stars, they'll be able to participate fully in Sneetch society. However, when the original Star-Belly Sneetches see what has happened, they want to maintain their distinctive status, so they pay the Fix-It-Up Chappie to take their stars off. And as every child knows, the situation soon spirals out of control. Sneetches run in and out of the machines, putting on stars, taking them off, all the while paying more and more to the Fix-It-Up Chappie, until they have nothing left and no one can even remember who had a star or not in the first place. Only after Sylvester McMonkey McBean drives off laughing, taking a huge pile of Sneetch cash, do the Sneetches learn their lesson: "They decided that Sneetches are Sneetches / and no kind of Sneetch is the best on the beaches" (Sneetches). They finally realize that the beliefs that had divided them were false and meaningless. Until that point, no one ever thought to question them.

According to Socrates, we have many of these false and happiness-destroying beliefs, but the problem is that most of the time, like the Sneetches, we don't even think to examine or question them. We just accept the prevalent worldview uncritically, often for no better reason than that it's what "everybody" thinks. As we grow up, we absorb and internalize from our parents and culture a whole slew of beliefs and prejudices about how the world works, what life is about, and what is important. However, most of these unexamined opinions are confused, contradictory, hopelessly simplistic, or just plain wrong.[5] So we blunder mindlessly through life, treating each other badly for no good reason, limiting our horizons, and wasting effort on things that don't matter and may even make us positively miserable, all the while wondering why our lives feel so meaningless and unsatisfying.

Socrates confronted this problem head on. Like Dr. Seuss, he dared to ask the questions that most people ignored, to challenge conventional wisdom, and to force people to think about what they were doing with their lives and why. Dr. Seuss's stories are fanciful, but they often pose for children and their parents problems and questions that many of us as adults have learned to ignore or forget, to our detriment. When we read "The Sneetches," we wonder, am I acting like them? Do I judge and exclude others because of superficial and meaningless things like belly stars? The same with Socrates, as he is depicted in Plato's dialogues: His questions force people to think about and defend their beliefs and assumptions, and if—as often happens—they can't answer his questions or respond adequately to his criticisms, he exposes their ignorance and complacency and takes them to task for not paying more attention to how they are living their lives. In Plato's *Apology*, while defending himself in a trial for his life, Socrates tells the jury, provocatively: "I say it is the greatest good for a human being to discuss virtue every day and those other things about which you hear me conversing and testing myself and others, for the unexamined life is not worth living for a human being."[6] According to Socrates, to fail to examine and discuss your deepest beliefs and values is to fail as a human being! Because of his conviction about the importance of living a thoughtful, examined life, Socrates made it his mission to put people's lives to the test. As one character in Plato's dialogues explains:

> Whoever comes into close contact with Socrates and associates with him in conversation must necessarily . . . keep on being led about by the man's arguments until he submits to answering questions about himself concerning both his present manner of life and the life he has lived hitherto. And when he does submit to this questioning, you don't realize that Socrates won't let him go before he has well and truly tested every last detail.[7]

A Socratic cross-examination is often a painful experience. It is not easy having your beliefs and values called into question, your whole "manner of life" lain bare and scrutinized. But once you have submitted to Socrates' test—whether talking to the man himself or, today, by reading Plato's dialogues—it's hard not to be changed by the experience.

Things That Scare You Right Out of Your Pants: Socrates and Seuss on Courage

> You will come to a place where the streets are not marked.
> Some windows are lighted. But mostly they're darked.
> A place you could sprain both your elbow and chin!
> Do you dare to stay out? Do you dare to go in?
> How much can you lose? How much can you win? (Places)

One major theme of *Oh, the Places You'll Go!* is the importance of having *courage* when facing life's challenges. In his adventures, the young protagonist of the story faces many dangerous and uncertain situations—unmarked streets; darked windows; confusing, wiggled roads; foul weather; prowling monsters. If he failed to face these problems courageously, to "dare to go in," he would have missed out on most of his opportunities and adventures. He's able to succeed and "move mountains" in large part because he dares to go on, take chances, and face his fears.

So what is courage, and how do you get it? Socrates' main discussion of courage occurs in Plato's *Laches*, where Socrates talks to two Athenian generals, Laches and Nicias. Although the dialogue itself is probably fictional, the characters in it were real people: Both generals were well-known Athenian military and political leaders during the long, bloody Peloponnesian War against Sparta in the latter half of the fifth century BCE. As generals, their primary duties included training and rallying soldiers to face death in battle. So if anyone should be able to define or explain courage, it would be them. Socrates begins by asking Laches to explain courage to him. Laches answers confidently: "Good heavens, Socrates, there is no difficulty about that: if a man is willing to remain at his post and to defend himself against the enemy without running away, then you may rest assured that he is a man of courage."[8]

What Laches has in mind here is the kind of courage typically required of Greek hoplites (armored foot soldiers) facing an enemy charge. At the time, hoplites typically fought in a tight formation called a phalanx. By fighting close together, they could interlock their shields to form a solid wall of protection, with the spears of men behind projecting over the top. Such a formation made a frontal assault by the enemy difficult—but only if each man held his ground and protected his fellow soldiers! The tight formation could fall apart disastrously if any soldier lost his nerve and ran away. A soldier who did not "remain at his post" and protect his comrades therefore put everyone in his unit in greater danger.

This kind of "remaining at your post" courage is exemplified nicely by the noble elephant Horton in *Horton Hatches the Egg*. In the story, Mayzie (the lazy bird) is bored. She doesn't want to sit on her nest hatching her egg anymore, so she convinces the kindhearted Horton to give her a break, and he agrees to sit on the egg for her. However, she immediately flies off on vacation to Palm Beach, leaving poor Horton alone on the nest, sitting on her egg (for months, apparently). But Horton refuses to give up, enduring thunder, rain, ice, and even mockery from the other animals as he remains at his post and keeps his word. Eventually, Horton is even threatened by hunters, who aim rifles straight at his heart! But "did he run? / *He did not!* / HORTON STAYED ON THAT NEST! / He held his head high / And threw out his chest / And he looked at the hunters / As much as to say: / 'Shoot if you must / But I *won't* run away! / I meant what I said / And I said what I meant. . . . / An elephant's faithful / One hundred per cent!'" (Hatches). The hunters are amused and decide to take Horton back home as a circus exhibit rather than shooting him. Horton's courage and faithfulness make the story's happy ending possible: If he had run away, he would not only have abandoned the egg and his duty but also put himself in greater danger.

Remaining at your post, therefore, is sometimes very courageous indeed. But as Socrates points out, Laches' definition covers only *one type* of courageous action. What about when military units perform other tactical maneuvers, such as a feigned retreat to draw the enemy in for a counterattack? What about the tactics of cavalry units, which swoop in for quick strikes and withdraw before they can be hemmed in? What about the courage shown by an army that has to retreat to fight another day? This is when a soldier most needs courage to protect his friends, when the army is demoralized and the enemy is bearing down on them.

Socrates also wonders, quite rightly, about all the ways courage can be shown in situations other than battle. What about the bravery people show in the face of dangers at sea, or illness, or poverty? Horton, after all, shows courage not only when he stares down the hunters' guns but also when he confronts bad weather, the skepticism and mockery of the other animals, and the indignity of being caged up and shipped around the country in the circus. Also, Socrates asks, what about people who courageously stand up against injustice and evil? In short, the problem with Laches' first definition is that it is too narrow—it applies well to one set of circumstances but fails to account for many other instances of courage.

Laches sees the force of Socrates' arguments, and so he next tries a new, broader definition. Courage, he now says, is "a sort of endurance of the soul."[10] A courageous person is one who has the strength of mind to endure fear and threats, in any circumstance.

Once again, Socrates finds problems with Laches' answer. This time, his definition is too *broad*, because there are many cases where "endurance of the soul" is not genuine courage. For example, suppose that, on a dare, a person "endures" danger and lies down on the yellow line in the middle of a busy street. Or suppose a racist "endures" criticism and holds stubbornly to his hateful beliefs. Both of these people display "endurance of the soul," but neither shows genuine courage. If courage is a virtuous and good quality to have, Socrates argues, an action should count as courageous only if it is noble and good.[11] Endurance motivated by foolishness and stupidity isn't courage but recklessness or stubbornness.

King Derwin in *Bartholomew and the Oobleck* offers a good illustration of the danger posed by the foolish, stubborn endurance of the soul. King Derwin rules the Kingdom of Didd, but despite his power and the happiness of his kingdom, he's bored with the four things that naturally come from the sky—rain, sunshine, fog, and snow. He wants something different and exciting. So he summons his royal magicians and orders them to cast a spell to make something new fall from the sky, "oobleck." The king's page, Bartholomew Cubbins, presciently warns him, "Your Majesty, I . . . think that you will be very sorry. . . . They'll do something crazy!" (Oobleck). But the king won't listen, stubbornly persisting in his desire to be "the mightiest man who ever lived" and have "something fall from the skies that no other kingdom has ever had before" (Oobleck). The results are predictably disastrous—the kingdom is inundated by the sticky, green oobleck, which covers everything and makes life impossible. But even at the lowest point of the disaster, King Derwin continues to resist Bartholomew's suggestions. He finally shows genuine courage only when, at the end of the story, he admits his mistake and says he is sorry.

These examples show that a courageous person needs not only to be able to endure fear, danger, and opposition but also to endure them *wisely*, at the right time, for the right reasons. True courage is about facing fear and danger and enduring risk for the sake of an important and worthy goal. A soldier who stands his ground in order to protect his comrades is courageous. Horton shows courage when he refuses to abandon the egg; similarly, in *Horton Hears a Who!*, the elephant again displays courage when he stands up for and protects the *Whos*, a civilization of tiny people living on a dust speck whom none of the other animals can hear. So what kind of wisdom does a courageous person need? The second general, Nicias, proposes that courage is "knowledge of the fearful and hopeful in war and in every other situation."[12] In other words, a courageous person has the knowledge to be able to determine correctly which risks are worth facing and which are not. A courageous soldier has enough knowledge and wisdom to be able to determine when it's appropriate to have hope and stand his ground against the enemy and when it's better to retreat. A courageous citizen knows when to actively resist a tyrannical regime and when to bide his time for a better opportunity. This is the courage displayed by Bartholomew Cubbins. He may be a simple page boy, but he alone is wise enough to foresee the terrible consequences of the king's arrogance. And, sure enough, when the oobleck disaster happens, he is the only one who keeps his head and recognizes what needs to be done. He defies the king, telling him what he needs to hear:

Bartholomew Cubbins could hold his tongue no longer.

"And it's going to keep on falling," he shouted, "until your whole great marble palace tumbles down! So don't waste your time saying foolish *magic* words. YOU ought to be saying some plain *simple* words!"

"*Simple* words . . .? What do you mean, boy?"

"I mean," said Bartholomew, "this is all *your* fault! Now, the least you can do is say the simple words, 'I'm sorry.' . . . And if you won't even say you're sorry, *you're no sort of king at all!*" (Oobleck)

Amazingly, this lowly page boy has the courage to berate a king who claims repeatedly to be "the mightiest king in all the world," and he manages to shame the king into apologizing.

In the end, however, even Nicias' definition fails to explain courage adequately. The problem is that *all* virtue seems to rest at least in part on knowledge of what is good and bad. Therefore, Nicias' definition fails to explain what is distinctive about courage, as opposed to other good qualities that a person might have.[13] By the end of the dialogue, Socrates and the two distinguished generals have failed to find a complete and adequate definition of courage.

Now, one might wonder about the point of this exercise. Socrates wants a definition of courage. But if Laches and Nicias can do their jobs, why should it matter whether they can define it? But consider: Laches and Nicias are supposed to be two of the best generals Athens has to offer—and it's their job to *teach* the young men of the city how to be courageous. Moreover, in battle, they're the ones who make decisions about when to press forward, when to fall back, and when to cut losses and run. A general who is fundamentally confused about courage—the central martial virtue—won't be able to make these decisions well. How can he lead armies and teach his soldiers to be courageous when he doesn't even know what it is himself? And more importantly, how much do any of the rest of us know, when these men who have spent their lives facing death and risk know so little? It's worth mentioning that, although the historical Laches and Nicias both had some successes during the war, they are best known for their failures, for battles in which they led the Athenians to defeat. Given this history, we have to wonder: Did their simplistic and unexamined ideas about courage contribute to their failures?

Even as he challenges the generals' unexamined beliefs, however, Socrates nevertheless helps us—the readers of the dialogue—to develop a deeper understanding. After reading the dialogue and thinking about the examples, we realize that courage does often involve standing firm, and, like Horton, having endurance of soul and not abandoning your "post" in the face of obstacles and fear. But it also requires a sort of wisdom or knowledge to understand when it is worth holding firm and when it is better to change course. We can see this clearly in the contrast between the stubbornness of King Derwin and the wisdom and foresight of Bartholomew Cubbins. Even if we still can't define courage precisely, we nevertheless come to have a clearer idea by examining our beliefs and thinking about these kinds of examples.

Simple It's Not, I'm Afraid You'll Find

Should you turn left or right . . .
or right-and-three-quarters? Or, maybe, not quite?
Or go around back and sneak in from behind?
Simple it's not, I'm afraid you will find,
for a mind-maker-upper to make up his mind. (Places)

It's pretty rare for most of us to undergo the kind of intense cross-examination of our beliefs and values to which Socrates submits the characters in Plato's dialogues—we're usually too lazy, complacent, or polite to "test every detail" of our lives, let alone someone else's. So why does Socrates think it is so important? How does subjecting yourself to philosophical examination help you to live a better life?

According to Socrates, our biggest problem is that, most of the time, we just don't realize how stupidly ignorant we actually are about the things that matter. Dr. Seuss puts it nicely in the passage above: We have to "make up our minds" about how to live and what paths to take, but it's hard, harder than we realize. In Plato's *Apology*, Socrates explains how he has devoted his life to talking to anyone he meets, young or old, rich or poor, and asking them questions about virtue and happiness, about what is good and worth pursuing in life. And he's discovered that, although people almost always *feel* confident, for the most part they understand very little.[14] They think they already know everything they need to know—in many cases, as we saw with Laches, they can't imagine that there could be any doubt! But, when Socrates puts their ideas to the test and challenges them to explain or support their claims, or to show how their beliefs fit with other things they believe, they can't do it. Like the Sneetches, Mayzie the lazy bird, and King Derwin, it turns out that they don't know as much as they think they do, and they often have to learn the lesson about their intellectual arrogance the hard way.

This wouldn't be a serious issue if the things about which people are ignorant were trivial or if we could muddle along well enough with our half-truths and conventional clichés. But, according to Socrates, our situation is much worse than that. The matters upon which people are the most ignorant are, at the same time, the most important and fundamental questions about life. Moreover, the beliefs people have about these matters are often not just ill considered, incomplete, and inconsistent, but disastrously false, so that they end up wasting or ruining their lives. As Socrates says, they come to "attach little importance to the most important things and greater importance to inferior things."[15] In other words, our priorities wind up being the opposite of what they should be.

For example, many people with whom Socrates talks believe that happiness comes from wealth, possessions, and social status. They think that the more you have—the bigger your estate, the fancier your chariots, the more power and influence you wield—the better off you are. We see this attitude (and its consequences) in Dr. Seuss's story "Gertrude McFuzz." Gertrude is "a girl-bird" with "the smallest plain tail there ever was. One droopy-droop feather. That's all she had. And oh! That one feather made Gertrude so sad" (McFuzz). She is sad because she defines her self-worth by the quality and quantity of her tail feathers, and when she sees another bird with *two* fancy feathers, she wants more. She thinks that if she had more and prettier feathers, she would some-how be better than the other birds. She therefore eats pill-berries from the pill-berry bush until she has so many tail feathers that she can't fly.

Yertle the Turtle, the king of the turtle pond, makes a similar mistake. Life on the island of Sala-ma-Sond is warm and happy for the turtles, but Yertle wants more. He decides that he needs a higher throne: "If I could sit high, how much greater I'd be! / What a king! I'd be ruler of all I could see!" (Yertle). Yertle defines his worth as king not by the wisdom of his decisions or the well-being of his subjects but by how high he sits and how much he can see. In pursuit of his goal, he calls in hundreds of turtles for him to sit on, to make his throne higher and higher so that he can see and be king of more and more things.

Why do people define themselves and their self-worth in this way? In part, it's because they believe (in a vague, confused way) that the goal of life is to outdo or get more than others. They decide how worthy or happy they are, not by looking at the real conditions of their lives, but by comparing them-selves (superficially) to others. Money, social status, and power thus provide ways of keeping score and figuring out if you are getting more or doing better than others. According to this way of thinking, the political, social, and eco-nomic community exists primarily as an arena for the cutthroat competition for wealth and status—the winners use guile, brashness, and luck to get more; the losers are too weak or stupid or gutless to compete.[16]

Now imagine how a person with this worldview would approach his life, choices, and relationships. Because he believes that happiness results from outdoing others, he would focus on doing whatever he thought would get him more, regardless of the consequences. He'd ignore or devalue anything that didn't appear to help him get ahead. More importantly, he'd have no scruples about doing anything it takes to get an edge—whether it be eating pill-berries, cheating, taking steroids, tyrannizing other turtles, pawning off worthless credit default swaps, or something even more sinister. Dr. Seuss's *The Lorax* is a powerful cautionary tale about the tragic consequences of the blind and unscrupulous pursuit of profit. When the Once-ler arrives in the beautiful land of the Truffula Trees, populated by singing Swomee-Swans, frolicking Brown Bar-ba-loots, and splashing Humming-Fish, he sets up business cutting down the Truffula Trees to make and sell Thneeds. His sole desire is to "bigger" his profits: "I meant no harm. I most certainly did not. / But I had to go bigger. So bigger I got. / I biggered my factory. I biggered my roads. / I biggered my wagons. I biggered the loads [. . .] I went right on biggering . . . selling more Thneeds. / I biggered my money, which everyone needs" (Lorax). The Lorax repeatedly warns him about what he's doing, but he doesn't listen, and eventually his greed destroys the entire Truffula forest and drives away all the wonderful creatures, so that he is left alone in an empty factory in a toxic wasteland. The Once-ler's unquestioned desire for money—"which everyone needs"—blinds him to the terrible consequences of his actions.

In Plato's dialogues, Socrates consistently argues that any person with this approach to life has no chance of finding true happiness. As the characters in Seuss's stories eventually discover, it isn't wealth, possessions, or power that make life happy and good. According to Socrates, what really matters for happiness is the condition of your soul (*psychê* in Greek)—that is, your mind and character, the kind of *person* you are. If you lack wisdom and integrity, if you value your own profit and self-interest over what's just and right, if your guiding motivation is a hubristic desire to outcompete and overpower others, you won't live a good life. You may well succeed in getting the money or power or whatever it is you thought you wanted, but it won't make your life genuinely satisfying or worth living. And, because you are so fundamentally ignorant, you often won't even realize what's wrong! You'll feel in conflict with yourself, deeply unsatisfied with your material gains, but you won't see that the problem lies in your own ignorance about and lack of concern for what really matters in life.[17]

Most people are not as blatantly dishonest, selfish, and opportunistic as Yertle or the Once-ler. All the same, we do have unexamined, contradictory, and false beliefs that tend to undermine our happiness in less obvious but no less real ways. For example, since the fifties, the United States has seen a trend toward working harder, longer hours in order to afford bigger houses farther from our workplaces, requiring us to spend more and more time in traffic. Like the Once-ler, we've biggered our houses, biggered our cars, biggered our hours at work, biggered our productivity and GDP. We have more material wealth than any country in the history of the world! But as a result, Americans increasingly have less and less time left over to spend with family and friends or to devote to nonwork activities, such as hobbies or community service. Has it made us happier?

Looking at the evidence, the answer seems to be—emphatically not! Despite increasing material wealth, Americans are not happier. Research consistently shows that the factors that most contribute to an individual's happiness include spending time with family and close friends, hobbies, and contributing to the community, and that the thing that people most hate is spending time in traffic.[18] Yet people keep making choices that result in them spending more time at work and in traffic and less time with family and friends! But still they wait, thinking that someday, somehow, things will get better. They are waiting for a better job, a promotion, a new office, a new car, or maybe just a bigger television or fancier smartphone—something new to relieve the stress, disharmony, and boredom they have created in their own lives through their choices. These people are stuck in, as Dr. Seuss says, "a most useless place":

> The Waiting Place . . . for people just waiting.
> Waiting for a train to go / or a bus to come, or a plane to go
> or the mail to come, or the rain to go / or the phone to ring, or the snow to snow
> or waiting around for a Yes or No / or waiting for their hair to grow.
> Everyone is just waiting.
> Waiting for the fish to bite / or waiting for wind to fly a kite
> or waiting around for Friday night / or waiting, perhaps, for their Uncle Jake
> or a pot to boil, or a Better Break / or a string of pearls, or a pair of pants
> or a wig with curls, or Another Chance.
> Everyone is just waiting. (Places)

Socrates and Seuss would agree that, when someone gets stuck waiting like this, something has gone fundamentally wrong with his way of thinking about "the most important matters" in life. Someday, he says to himself, I'll be happy! The problem is that someday never comes, and he doesn't have the courage or imagination to try something different. He needs to reexamine what he really values and what really makes him happy rather than just accepting the same old ideas about what he ought to value. Perhaps we need to leave the old, well-worn paths behind, and, like Seuss's protagonist, "head straight out of town!" (Places)

The Places You'll Go: The Journey of Life

> You'll look up and down streets. Look 'em over with care.
> About some you will say, "I don't choose to go there."
> With your head full of brains and your shoes full of feet,
> you're too smart to go down a not-so-good street.

And you may not find any you'll want to go down.
In that case, of course, you'll head straight out of town. (Places)

If, as Dr. Seuss suggests, life is a journey, a fantastical adventure or game, how do we decide where to go, what paths to take? Once we strike out away from the well-worn paths of conventional wisdom—once we challenge what "everyone" believes and start asking questions—we'll find that there are no easy answers. So how do we deal with what life gives us so that we can live the good and happy lives that we want?

According to Dr. Seuss, the answer is clear: You have brains in your head, feet in your shoes, so you need to *use* them and do the best you can with what life gives you. In other words, humans are rational beings, and we need to use our rational capacities to make the best decisions we can. In Plato's *Crito*, as Socrates is facing a difficult decision about whether or not to escape from prison and avoid his execution, he tells his friend Crito: "We must therefore examine whether we should act this way or not, as not only now but at all times I am the kind of man who listens to nothing within me but the argument that on reflection seems best to me."[19] Socrates faces an ethical dilemma. If he escapes from prison, he'll be breaking the law and betraying all that he's stood for in his life. But if he stays, he'll be executed and leave his children without a father to care for and protect them. Either choice is ethically problematic. But because he's spent his life examining himself and others and thinking about happiness, virtue, and other ethical issues, he is able to make a better decision and choose a better path.

In the *Phaedo*, Socrates' friend Simmias provides a very Seussian metaphor for the situation we face as we navigate the journey of our lives: "One should achieve one of these things: learn the truth about these things or find it for oneself, or, if that is impossible, adopt the best and most irrefutable of men's theories, and, borne upon this, sail through the dangers of life as upon a raft . . ."[20] As we sail through life, we're going to face new situations and challenges that our previous life and experiences haven't prepared us for. We're going to have setbacks and failures, slumps and loneliness, hazards and dangers that we'll need courage and wisdom to traverse. And "when you're in a Slump, / you're not in for much fun. / Un-slumping yourself / is not easily done" (Places). Especially in a rapidly changing world, we'll continually face new challenges and new "games" that we need to learn to play in order to succeed. Sometimes things will go our way, but often, they won't. The person who is able to live best and most successfully is someone who has developed the ability to think rationally and thoughtfully about what really matters, who can learn from her mistakes and continually improve the raft upon which she sails the seas of life, and who can make wise decisions. As Seuss says, "Life's a Great Balancing Act" (Places). The key is to find the right balance.

Perhaps more importantly, for Socrates, living rationally constitutes a distinctively human way of life. Even before Socrates, Greek philosophers agreed that what makes humans special and different from other animals is our ability to reason. To say that humans are rational beings means, among other things, that we can weigh options and choose the path for ourselves that we judge best. A human being is not a mere thing, carried passively along the currents of life. In order to flourish and excel in a human life, we must use the brains in our heads to decide what our lives will be.

Kid, You'll Move Mountains!

Step with care and great tact
and remember that Life's a Great Balancing Act.
Just never forget to be dexterous and deft.
And never mix up your right foot with your left.
And will you succeed? Yes! You will, indeed! (98 and ¾ percent guaranteed.)
(Places)

The ending of *Oh, the Places You'll Go!* is thoroughly positive. Dr. Seuss assures us that, if we take his advice and set off boldly along the journey of life, we'll do great things. But how can Seuss be so confident of success? Aren't some setbacks and slumps just too much to overcome? Don't even the best choices sometimes fail to work out?

Once again, I think Dr. Seuss's answer to these questions is similar to the ones Socrates and other ancient philosophers would give. Socrates and most ancient philosophers argued that, in the final reckoning, the external events of life aren't what matter most. If you don't actually fly ahead of other people or win games or manage to move a mountain, that's not important. What matters is the attitude that you have about life, the choices you make in the face of what life gives you. Seuss and the ancient philosophers agree that someone who has the courage to question and find her own path and the wisdom to face problems and challenges with equanimity, who develops rational abilities to make good decisions about her life, *will* almost certainly succeed in life. So, as Dr. Seuss says, "be your name Buxbaum or Bixby or Bray / or Mordecai Ali Van Allen O'Shea, / you're off to Great Places! Today is your day! Your mountain is waiting. So . . . *get on your way!*" (Places).

CHAPTER TWO

~

My Troubles Are Going to Have Troubles with Me: Schopenhauer, Pessimism, and Nietzsche

Jacob M. Held

Philosophy is the love of wisdom, and we seek wisdom in order to live well. And to live well is to excel at being human; to be exemplary. Those who seek to live well want to live praiseworthy lives; they want this life to mean something, to be "worth it." And so in dealing with the human condition and in trying to explain why this life is "worth it," philosophy often must focus on those aspects of life that seem to detract from its meaning and fullness, that seem to make it not worth living; namely, pain and suffering. After all, as much as we'd prefer it were not so, a great deal of life is painful. Dr. Seuss was well aware of this fact, and several of his books dealt with pain and suffering and what type of response to our existence as suffering beings was appropriate. At first blush we might find it odd that a children's author would focus on pain and suffering, but upon reflection I think there is no more suitable topic. What lesson could be more important for a child to learn than how to deal with the inevitable bang-ups and hang-ups, the lurches and slumps of which this life is invariably constituted? As anyone with children can attest, one of the most important lessons a child can learn, and one of the most difficult—for both the children learning it and the parents watching—is that life will be full of obstacles, disappointments, and basically pain. What good parents do for their children is not remove pain and obstacles from their children's lives but provide them with the tools necessary in order to deal with the inevitable suffering that life entails.

The lessons in Dr. Seuss's stories about suffering are varied, but each is fundamentally about the recognition that life is full of discomfort and dealing with it is one of our principal tasks in this life. For example, in *Oh, the Places You'll Go!*, the child is guaranteed success, at least with a 98 and ¾ percent chance. One response to life's pain is (naïve?) optimism; we pat our children on the head and say "It'll be okay." But will it? Perhaps we shouldn't promise success. Instead maybe we ought to offer only contentment. Such a response appears to be offered in *Did I Ever Tell You How Lucky You Are?* Here the child learns that plenty of people have it much worse off than he. The ultimate lesson being, "Some critters are much-much, oh, ever so much-much, so muchly much-much more unlucky than you!" (Lucky). So we might tell children: "It could be worse, you could be . . ." But just because it could be worse doesn't mean that your suffering is acceptable. Things could always be worse, that doesn't mean that how they are now is okay. And should the suffering of other people make me feel good? So what other options are we left with? Well, what about sheer resignation. We might just respond, "Deal with it!" Don't lie about how they'll win in the end. Just simply say, "Suck it up." Dr. Seuss says about as much in *You're Only Old Once!*, a book whose title is oddly ambiguous. It could mean, "You're only old once, so enjoy it. Make the most of it," or it could mean, "Thank goodness, you're only old once. It'll all be over soon." Maybe we ought to just resign ourselves to the fact that life is painful, but at least it ends. But these are all unsatisfying responses to the human condition, and surely a playful, fun-loving author like Dr. Seuss can offer us more. Thankfully, the answers above don't exhaust Dr. Seuss's repertoire. There is one last possibility, and one story I haven't yet mentioned, *I Had Trouble in Getting to Solla Sollew*.

And that's how it started.

In *Solla Sollew* we are introduced to our protagonist, who by his own admission has had a pretty easy life up to this point. "Nothing, not anything ever went wrong" (Trouble). So he has been fortunate enough to have a carefree life, one of ease and contentment; a life that resembles many children we may know. When we think of children who are well taken care of we think of them as problem free. They don't have mortgages and debt, illness or debilitation, a lifetime of piled up failures, stress, anxiety. . . . Most children's lives are not full of the pain we all experience. They have yet to suffer the spiritual death by the proverbial thousand cuts of life's disappointments. Yet things quickly change for our protagonist. He attributes his bad fortune originally to carelessness. He wasn't paying attention and then . . . he stubs his toe, flies through the air, and lands on his bottom, spraining the main bone in the tip of his tail. This is unfortunate, but not devastating. But things go from bad to worse. Even though he keeps his eyes open, a green-headed Quilligan Quail comes from behind to nip his tail. A Skritz goes after his neck, while a Skrink goes after his toe. No amount of vigilance can save him. He is surrounded by troubles, and so life creeps up on our poor young and naïve protagonist. He realizes that life is full of troubles and perils, and no matter how much you pay attention and how good you are at avoiding some, you are bound to be bit, poked, tripped, and nibbled. Luckily, he comes across a traveling chap who mentions to him a place, Solla Sollew, on the banks of the River Wah-Hoo, "Where they *never* have troubles! At least, very few" (Trouble). His prayers have been answered. If he can't avoid the troubles here, he'll go to a place where there are none.

Our protagonist is plagued with problems and is offered a chance to leave them behind for the promise of an idyllic life in a faraway land. He has realized that life is suffering, either degrees of pain or its momentary absence that we experience as joy or, more accurately, relief. But no matter what we do we are bound to experience setbacks and disappointments; life is a series of problems. Things look bleak. Our protagonist may even be on the verge of becoming a pessimist.

The Pendulum Swings from Skritz to Skrink

In everyday language, when we talk about a pessimist we think of someone who always thinks things are going to get worse, even though they are already quite bad; as the saying goes, someone who thinks the glass is half empty. If this is all there was to philosophical pessimism, it'd be very uninteresting. After all, life is full of problems; we all know that. We also know life will always contain these difficulties. But the difference between even the most morose of everyday pessimists and a true, philosophical pessimist is that even those people who see life as fraught with troubles may still see it as redeemable. Most everyday pessimists do think that the value of life can be reevaluated and seen to be worthwhile when measured against some other good like momentary pleasures or a religious doctrine of salvation. But a true philosophical pessimist sees life as irredeemable, inherently and intractably painful with no possible way to make it worth living.

Arthur Schopenhauer (1788–1860) is arguably the first and easily the most influential philosophical pessimist. He saw the glass not only as half empty but cracked and full of poison. But his pessimism doesn't stem from a depressive personality or bad childhood. He is a pessimist because that is the response he finds most appropriate to the nature of reality. Schopenhauer's pessimism stems from his metaphysics; that is, how he understands the nature of reality to be fundamentally structured.

According to Schopenhauer, the one thing that marks the essence of human life, and all life in general, is the will to life. This will is the unconscious motive force that moves us constantly and unrelentingly onward. It is "a blind, irresistible urge."[1] Our will most apparently finds expression through our choices and attempts to meet goals, but it marks even the most unmotivated among us. Even those poor saps caught in the waiting place manifest the will to life. As they wait for a phone to ring or snow to snow or a pot to boil or a better break, the will to life is acting through them and they are still driven to something; there are always urges. We are always striving even when it looks like we're standing still. And Dr. Seuss's books always depict people this way. The characters always want something new, or different, and always better and grander than what has come before. From King Derwin's oobleck to Morris McGurk's Circus McGurkus, from the most outrageous zoo populated with the most fantastical animals known to Seussdom to the most perfect and ridiculous plate of scrambled eggs, all of his characters are striving, and the stories often revolve around the obstacles and problems that come from trying to do fabulous things. When one tries to do grand things, one is bound to stumble often and encounter grand obstacles. Striving necessarily brings failure, disappointment, and pain. But when the going gets tough Seuss never calls it quits; his characters never give in and become pessimists. Yet Schopenhauer draws a different lesson from the hang-ups and bang-ups that accompany life's challenges.

> We have long since recognized that striving . . . where it manifests itself most distinctly in the light of the fullest consciousness, is called *will*. We call its hindrance through an obstacle placed between it and its temporary goal, *suffering*; its attainment of the goal . . . *satisfaction* . . . all striving springs from want or deficiency, from dissatisfaction with one's own state or condition, and is therefore suffering so long as it is not satisfied. No satisfaction, however, is lasting . . . it is always merely the starting point of a fresh striving. . . . Thus that there is no ultimate aim of striving means that there is no measure or end of suffering.[2]

As we continually see in Seuss, as the characters strive, they will succeed at times, but these successes are short lived. They are often the beginning of a new crisis or problem that must be met with a fresh striving. And all of these small victories are temporary, leading time and again to new failures or perhaps further small victories, thus marking life as a perpetual striving punctuated with short-lived satisfaction. Or as Schopenhauer so poetically puts it: "Life swings like a pendulum to and from between pain and boredom, and these two are in fact its ultimate constituents."[3] Schopenhauer is bleak, he sees only death as the end to all of our long, painful journey. "Life itself is a sea full of rocks and whirlpools that man avoids with the greatest caution and care, although he knows that, even when he succeeds with all his efforts and ingenuity in struggling through, at every step he comes nearer to the greatest, and total, the inevitable and irredeemable shipwreck, indeed even steers right into it, namely death."[4] So thank goodness you're only old once.

Schopenhauer would've made a lousy children's author. We wouldn't want to read such assessments of life to our children, unless we wanted to drive them to heroin or suicide. So Seuss, without denying that life is speckled with failures, finds answers to these problems; that is, a way to value life positively in the face of the inevitable and unavoidable pain that marks so much of it. How can Seuss do this? How can he look at and acknowledge all the pain and suffering that accompanies so much of life and smile through it, offering sunshine and roses at the end of the day?

What Would You Do, If Your Kids Asked You?

There are several responses we tend to give to deal with the problem of suffering. Three frequently offered responses find expression in Seuss's work. In *Oh, the Places You'll Go!* we're told that despite all the bumps and slumps we will succeed. All the pain and suffering of our lives is redeemed because it leads eventually to success. In the end we'll come out on top. Really? In the end aren't we all dead, just as Schopenhauer iterated above? Won't avoiding all the whirlpools and Hakken-Kraks merely delay the inevitable? And even if success is possible, ought we to offer such a promising future to all children? When our children lament their suffering, should we promise success as if their lives will turn out all right in the end? Don't we know better? Haven't we lived long enough to know most lives don't end well; they merely dissolve into obscurity after years of disappointments? Maybe such a naïve optimism and hollow promise is delusional, a lie we tell our kids so they can cope until they realize what we already know. It seems that for a true pessimist *Oh, the Places You'll Go!* offers a less than adequate response, and perhaps an intellectually dishonest one.[5] But there are other alternatives.

"It could be worse." This is a common response we've all heard from our parents and we all still often rely on. It could be worse. And surely this is true. It could always be worse than it presently is, until you're dead. And then you're dead, so why bother. So, yes, it can always be worse. But how is this supposed to help us deal with the pain we're constantly feeling? In *Did I Ever Tell You How Lucky You Are?* Seuss offers this very answer to a complaining child. The boy, lovingly referred to as Duckie, has apparently been heard complaining about how rough his life is. A wise man sitting atop a cactus decides to set him straight.[6] The wise man's answer to the child's incessant whining is simple: "I'm telling you, Duckie, some people are muchly, oh, *ever* so muchly, muchly more-more-more unlucky than you!" In fact, "You ought to be shouting, 'How Lucky am I!'" (Lucky). And surely this is true. Duckie is much better off than those caught in traffic on Zayt Highway Eight and poor Herbie Hart, Ali Sard, or Mr. Bix, who all have considerable troubles to face. Duckie is far better off than Mr. Potter, the Hawtch-Hawtcher Bee-Watcher, Professor de Breeze, and all of the Brothers Ba-zoo. He has none of their problems, all of which would seem to make any Duckie might encounter pale in comparison. And so it is for all of us. For any trouble you might have, and it doesn't matter how serious or grave it might be, we can come up with how either it could be worse or find an example of someone who is muchly more unlucky than you. But what does this do for you? Do you feel better because you're not as bad off as someone else, or do you just recognize that everyone has it tough? This doesn't seem too helpful. What kind of life is one built off of *schadenfreude*? Should our lives become meaningful because we either realize they're not as bad as they could be, or, worse still, we take pleasure or comfort in knowing that others have it considerably worse? So what other response might we, or Dr. Seuss, offer?

In *You're Only Old Once!* we're offered another response: deal with it. In this book, we follow a poor sap who is supposed to represent the reader's inevitable old age through the Golden Years Clinic. What we witness is the infliction of numerous tests and procedures that check everything from eyes to allergies. And what does our sap get for his troubles? "When at last we are sure you've been properly pilled, then a few paper forms must be properly filled so that you and your heirs may be properly billed" (Old). But it's over now so you may leave, and be content, "you're in pretty good shape for the shape you are in!" (Old).

In this tale, the proffered response to our trials and tribulations is a mix of the previous two: pain is temporary, you'll get through it, and really it's not that bad anyway. The doctor's office is a perfect setting to teach this lesson. Doctors make us better, but we're never done being made better. They can always find something wrong, something that needs poking, prodding, pilling, and billing. And each solution leads to further problems or just postpones the inevitable, insoluble problem of total body failure, death. So is the message that it's all temporary and not really that bad supposed to make us feel better? Is life worth living, or is it like a trip to the doctor, something that for the most part can be tolerated until it's over? Our poor sap has incurred enormous debts, been given a rigorous pill regimen, and sent on his way. But we know he'll return to suffer it all again. Or maybe he won't. His next trip might be to the morgue. Ultimately, the only cure to life is its end. As Socrates mentions in the *Phaedo*, on our deathbed perhaps our most fitting action would be to sacrifice a cock to Asclepius.[7] But this attitude doesn't redeem our lives, instead it tells us to bear with it, it'll be over soon. Life is to be endured.

All three of the above responses to the pain and suffering of life seem unsatisfactory. If life is marked by pain, and pain is the direct result of our constant striving and willing, then so long as we strive we will be inflicted with the pain of existence. No matter how much we lie to ourselves that it'll be okay in the end, it won't. There will always be new troubles and failures. We can endure this by telling ourselves that it could be worse, and no matter how bad it is it's only temporary. But life is still fundamentally a problem, something to be endured, cured, or if possible, avoided. Schopenhauer offers a response as well.

For Schopenhauer's answer we need look no further than the top of the nearest cactus. Here we find our ascetic, one who has chosen to deal with the pains of existence by refusing to participate. If pain is caused by willing and striving, then quieting your will is the solution. Simply stop striving. Now this is easier said than done. After all, if we are at root will, and if will is an unconscious striving that pushes us forward, it seems to a great extent out of our control. We can try to stop, but truly ceasing to will or strive is going to be the result of nothing short of grace. So Schopenhauer's response is self-renunciation to the best of our ability. You repudiate this life of constant struggle and failure, cease to will, and thus escape the pain of life as much as possible until released through the death of this mortal body. "In fact, nothing else can be stated as the aim of our existence except the knowledge that it would be better for us not to exist."[8] Life is a disease for which the cure is to stop participating. The answer to the game of life is simply to refuse to play. Yet, Seuss never gave this response. In fact, he goes out of his way to avoid concluding that we should just stop trying. But why do so if pain is the inevitable result?

Where They Never Have Troubles

The problem we face is nothing short of determining how we ought to value a human life marked by inescapable pain and suffering. Can our lives be redeemed? In this discussion the facts are not in dispute. Although people can debate the metaphysics of will and the nature of the universe, one can't deny that our lives are characterized by constant striving punctuated with periodic successes and more frequent failures. So Schopenhauer is right on these grounds; life is striving, life is pain, and so pain and its absence seem to exhaust its possibilities. But this doesn't mean we have to find life insufferable, worthless, or a disease best cured by the sweet release of death. Life can still be loved and enjoyed for what it is. It's really a matter of perspective, or rather reevaluation. And Dr. Seuss finds a kindred spirit in Friedrich Nietzsche.

Friedrich Nietzsche (1844–1900) is infamous among philosophers. Even many professional philosophers don't know where to place him in the tradition or how to contextualize his work. And the picture of him most nonprofessionals have is more a caricature than anything else, and not a flattering one at that. The remainder of this chapter can't fix that. I can't provide a comprehensive account of Nietzsche's philosophy. What I can do is provide a window into how he saw the world and how his perspective is an answer to Schopenhauer's pessimism.

Nietzsche approaches philosophy like an artist approaches a canvas. His task is to paint a picture of life that is affirmative; a yes-saying in opposition to the asceticism, life denial of nay-saying pessimists like Schopenhauer. And in this regard his vision finds voice in Dr. Seuss, specifically Seuss's work *I Had Trouble in Getting to Solla Sollew*.

As noted above, Seuss's books often deal with life in its totality, focusing on the ups and downs. These books also often provide an answer to how we ought to deal with our troubles: optimism, denial, endurance, and so forth. But there is one response we have yet to consider, and it's the response offered in *Solla Sollew*. "I've bought a big bat, I'm ready you see. Now my troubles are going to have troubles with me" (Trouble). In this one stanza, in this powerful conclusion, Seuss communicates a message it takes many people a lifetime to learn, and one iterated throughout Nietzsche's works. In fact, one might say it's Nietzsche's primary message: affirmation.

In order to promote a positive, affirmative view of life, Nietzsche has to be able to redeem our pain and suffering. This will not include an argument based on facts and figures, since these seem to point toward Schopenhauer's pessimism. Instead, it will require a shift in perspective, a shift in how we interpret those facts and contextualize them within our lives. As Nietzsche says, "Life is no argument,"[9] and in the voice of Zarathustra indicates it's hard enough to remember his own opinions, let alone to be the "keg of memory" required to remember his reasons for them.[10] One must make a choice on how to approach and value life in light of those things we can't deny, like suffering. One can't argue one's way to the good life; one must craft it, like a work of art. Crafting one's life requires that we see life as a work of art: a serious, creative, playful endeavor. Nietzsche's writing is thus often geared toward transforming the reader, not convincing him. Beyond arguments, Nietzsche wants his work to create a shift in the reader's mentality, very much like the works of Dr. Seuss. Most of Seuss's more ethically or profound works have a powerful impact on their readers young and old, not because we can turn them into arguments that are more convincing than any alternative but because they present an image of life that gets us motivated to be better than we currently are. The works transform us, hopefully for the better. These books operate at the level of great art by inspiring and transforming the reader in a way that causes her to see and experience the world in a new way. Nietzsche's works are geared toward a specific kind of transformation. In the face of pessimism or nihilism, the idea that nothing matters, Nietzsche wants to provide us a picture of life that is laudable so that we might transform ourselves into nobler creatures who can affirm existence in all of its ugliness, who can stare into the abyss of existence and still stand tall and say "yes." Nietzsche maintains that this response is the only one adequate to Schopenhauer's pessimism. He even laments Socrates' plea in the *Phaedo* that a cock be sacrificed to Asclepius. Nietzsche ponders: "Is it possible that a man like him, who had lived cheerfully and like a soldier in the sight of everyone, should have been a pessimist? . . . we must overcome even the Greeks."[11] In order to redeem this life we must get past pessimism. We must overcome the view that life is to be cured in favor of the notion that it is to be celebrated. We can't change what life is, but we can change how we react to and interpret it.

Affirmation (with a Bat!)

Instead of renouncing life and becoming ascetics, instead of quieting our wills and giving in to the unrelenting pain of life, and instead of resigning ourselves to the inevitable pitfalls of life and just bearing through it, Nietzsche advocates self-creation and affirmation. At first blush this may seem a nonanswer. After all, if suffering is caused by striving, how can more projects and more goals solve the problem? More willing will result in more suffering. Schopenhauer is right about that. Whenever we give ourselves goals, we are bound to encounter obstacles that will frustrate us. We will often fail, and the successes we do win will be temporary, often bookended with more pain and suffering. But it's not the end result Nietzsche is concerned with; it's our disposition, our attitude. We can't escape pain; we can't escape the essential nature of our lives. But we do have a choice. We can give in and relent, or we can fight, persevere, and create a life worth living, a noble life. Pain is a fact; our evaluation of it is a choice. Pain can be valuable, and even welcome. Our trials and tribulations strengthen us and prepare us for greater deeds in the future.

Since Nietzsche isn't about offering arguments but painting a picture of life that is laudable and positive, he often wrote in aphorisms—short yet profound and dense snippets. His style also made him one of the most oft-quoted philosophers around. You probably unknowingly know a handful of Nietzsche quotes yourself. For example, on pain and suffering, Nietzsche states: "The poison of which the weaker natures perish strengthens the strong—nor do they call it poison";[12] "There is a recipe against pessimistic philosophers and the excessive sensitivity that seems to me to be the real 'misery of the present age' . . . the recipe against this misery is: *misery*";[13] "There is as much wisdom in pain as there is in pleasure";[14] and most famously, "What doesn't kill me makes me stronger."[15] Pain can be a great teacher, character builder, and often times our reaction to it, our complaining and whining that "life is hard," is more illustrative of our spoiled natures than it is the unappealing nature of our existence. We need to see pain in the right light; we need to contextualize it and develop a proper attitude toward life, one of self-mastery, creation, and ultimately a kind of playfulness. Then, each individual failure, each accident will be redeemed within the greater context of a successful life, a life of one's own making. An integrous life revalues the bumps and slumps and lurches insofar as they are part and parcel to a noble existence. Nietzsche sees himself as a redeemer of accidents. This notion is best illustrated through a thought experiment Nietzsche offers in *The Gay Science*.[16]

In aphorism 341, Nietzsche asks us to imagine the following scenario. What if some day or night, during your loneliest loneliness a demon fell upon you and decreed that your whole life up to that point, all its successes and failures, every detail would be relived by you over and over again for eternity. Herein lies Nietzsche's notion of the eternal recurrence of the same. What would your reaction be? Would you curse him, or would you praise him? Would you fall to your knees weeping, or would you celebrate your good fortune? Your response is indicative of your view of life and whether you can redeem it in its totality even in your darkest hour.

This is a brutal test, one I am sure a great many of us would fail, if we were truly honest with ourselves. But Nietzsche isn't for everyone. Although his view of life is meant for all of humanity, most people aren't ready for him. So imagine your darkest hour, your loneliest loneliness. Imagine that darkest hour when things seem not only gloomy, but hopeless. Think of that dark hour when the compassion of others feels like pity and reinforces your own self-loathing. When you truly feel useless and death isn't merely the inevitable end, but a quietude sorely longed for, if only it would come more quickly. A time when there is no room dark enough and no blanket heavy enough to make it all better. The kind of despair that results after you realize your spirit died years ago and left only a hollow corpse to carry out the mundane tasks of the day, dragged out of bed each morning by only some vague notion of duty. This is your darkest hour; this is when you see what you're really made of. Can you muscle through and burst out the other end powerful and ready to take on the day, or do you cower, whimper, and whine and like a pessimist pray for the end? Can you declare it is all worth it, and you'd gladly do it all again because life is worth it? Or do you run and hide? What is nobler? What is more praiseworthy? Who do you want to be?

Today they can "cure" this kind of despair with pills. But before our culture of self-medication predominated Nietzsche demanded that people deal with their problems, the inevitable bumps and bruises of the human condition. Our desire for constant contentment has led us to become weak and cowardly and unable to envision or deal with this scenario and life in general. Nietzsche sees this despair as instructive. If in this darkest hour you can affirm your life and declare you would do it all over again and gladly, then you redeem your life in a singular moment of affirmation. This requires a strong spirit. This is the spirit Nietzsche wants to cultivate in the reader, the ability to be a yes-sayer. Nietzsche offers a picture of life that is the remedy to the nausea and sickness of modernity, its pessimism and nihilism. And one image he uses, one apropos to Dr. Seuss, is the child.

I Was Real Happy and Carefree and Young

In *I Had Trouble in Getting to Solla Sollew*, the child does make it to Solla Sollew. After enduring obstacle after obstacle, from a Midwinter Jicker and a flubbulous flood, to Poozers and a frightful black tunnel full of billions of birds, so many troubles in fact he declares, "I wished I had never been born" (Trouble), he does arrive at Solla Sollew. Unfortunately, the doorman to Solla Sollew informs him, "There is only one door into Solla Sollew / And we have a Key-Slapping Slippard. We do! This troublesome Slippard moved into my door / Two weeks ago Tuesday at quarter to four. / Since then, I can't open this door anymore!" (Trouble). The doorman can't get in and informs the child that he will be travelling on to "Boola Boo Ball / On the banks of the beautiful river Woo-Wall, Where they never have troubles! *No troubles at all!*" (Trouble). The child has a choice to make: Should he follow the doorman and endure another treacherous journey to another supposedly problem-free town? The message is clear, there is no Solla Sollew, and there is no Boola Boo Ball. There is no place on earth or in Seussdom where you can go and escape your problems. Suffering is a fact of human existence; running is no use. There's no where you can go to avoid the inevitable pitfalls of life. So if you can't run away or otherwise remove all the problems from your life and you want to redeem your existence in the face of this intractable pain, what do you do? The child holds the key, or in this case, the bat. "Then I started back home / To the Valley of Vung. / I know I'll have troubles. / I'll maybe, get stung. / I'll always have troubles. / I'll maybe, get bit / By the Green-Headed Quail / On the place where I sit. / But I've bought a big bat. / I'm ready you see. / Now my troubles are going / to have trouble with *me!*" (Trouble).

In *Thus Spoke Zarathustra*, Nietzsche explains the need to become a child by describing it as "innocence and forgetting, a new beginning, a game, a wheel rolling out of itself, a first movement, a sacred yes-saying."[17] To become a child is necessary in order to play the game of self-creation and affirmation; that is, a playful approach to life wherein we revalue and redeem its accidents in the face of our own creative potential. How fitting that Dr. Seuss's protagonists are almost exclusively young. He writes for children using the image of a child; one who is adventurous, takes chances and risks, is not beholden by convention, demands, commands, and rules. The child is a creator, one who revalues his own life and plows through the world of wiggled roads and frightening creeks to come out the other side with a smile on his face. In fact, one common trope in Seuss's work is breaking rules, going beyond borders, and traversing new lands in an attempt to create a life worth living. All is redeemed when that child lives his life, his way. That is success, 98 and ¾ percent guaranteed. It's just too bad we forget this lesson as we grow older, complacent, and frightened.

Nietzsche's response may seem simplistic. But he is not promoting naïve optimism or self-delusion. In fact, Nietzsche's response is not only in line with pessimism but also only holds water if we presume the core of pessimism is correct—life is suffering and in need of redemption. Nietzsche recognizes the inherent suffering of life; that our existence is riddled with inescapable pain. But he refuses to give in to it and renounce life. Instead he approaches the pain joyfully, playfully, with vim and vigor. "For believe me: the secret for harvesting from existence the greatest fruitfulness and the greatest enjoyment is—to *live dangerously*."[18] Nietzsche declares we should head our ships out into uncharted seas. After all, as Seuss would say, "It's opener there in the wide open air" (Places).

Nietzsche offers a perspective, one the reader has to come to through a transformative movement. Nietzsche offers us a style for living. Simply put, pessimism leaves a bad taste in Nietzsche's mouth and a foul smell in the air. As a prescription for life it fails due to its sheer ugliness. But affirmation is much more florid. "To 'give style' to one's character—a great and rare art."[19]

Although Nietzsche doesn't offer us arguments in the traditional sense, he is attempting to persuade us. How successful he is depends on the receptivity of the reader. Some will find this approach flawed or perhaps even fraudulent. After all, aren't philosophers supposed to offer irrefutable arguments premised on absolute, objective truths? But Nietzsche chooses to venture into dangerous waters chartless and free to create novel answers and new approaches that are ready to be taken up by those who are ready for him. Such an adventurous and playful approach to life requires a strong and free spirit, one that is rare and must be cultivated. Nietzsche declares, *"I place this new tablet over you: become hard!"*[20] In this life a strong yet playful constitution is needed, and a nice big bat helps, too.

~

CHAPTER THREE

Gertrude McFuzz Should've Read Marx, or Sneetches of the World Unite

Jacob M. Held

Pairing Dr. Seuss and Karl Marx (1818–1883) is risky. Doing so associates Dr. Seuss, beloved children's author, with the specter of Marxism. This is problematic because some people might find such a combination infelicitous, not because Dr. Seuss and Marx are incompatible but because most people have a built in knee-jerk hostile reaction toward all things Marxist. Unfortunately, this reaction is not the result of being well informed on the topic; it's probably because of the exact opposite. But I am going to use Seuss to explain and illustrate Marx and Marxism. My motivation is that I both like irritating people and think that several themes in several of Seuss's works are illustrative of an important aspect of Marxism. I am going to focus on one paramount aspect of Marxism: alienation. My goal is modest. I plan simply to explain the humanism of Marxism by offering an account of alienation; what it is, its causes, and why it's bad. But alienation as a phenomenon needs to be put into context, and the context is the capitalist mode of production.

You Capitalist Old Once-ler Man You!

Even if you've never picked up a political philosophy textbook or read a sentence of Marx you know one thing already: Karl Marx didn't like capitalism. Why? Short answer: He was morally opposed to the capitalist way of distributing property since it seemed fundamentally inhumane. Long answer: Keep reading!

Capitalism is an economic system. It's a way to distribute property. As a distributive paradigm it's designed by people and implemented by states. Capitalism is not a law of nature or rule of the universe; it's one among many ways to distribute resources. Societies decide to be capitalist. They may do so because they think it's highly productive, efficient, or just. But they choose to be capitalist, and this choice is reflective of that society's values. So what is it they chose to be when they decide to be capitalists?

First, capitalism is a way of distributing property, specifically the "means of production"; that is, the factories and manufacturing sites where all goods are made. For example, the Once-ler owns the means of production of Thneeds. He owns the factory, equipment, land the factory sits on, the Truffula tufts, and even his relatives' labor. The Once-ler is a capitalist, and understanding his relation to his factory, employees, and society will help us understand capitalism.

The Once-ler owns his Thneed factory. He has invested his own time, money, labor, and ingenuity into building and biggering his factory until it's productive and profitable. The Once-ler opened a Thneed factory in order to make money. His original investment paid out, and the profits he made were reinvested in his factory to bigger it and increase production in order to make more money, and so on indefinitely, or so he'd hope. There is nothing controversial here, or seemingly problematic. People own their businesses and run them how they see fit in order to make money, which everyone needs. They produce goods and/or services, sell them, and collect the money. Likewise, in so doing they provide the consumer with everything they need or want, even if they don't know they need it or want it, like a fool Thneed. So where does that leave the rest of us? After all, we can't all own a factory.

Well, beyond Thneeds, our food, shelter, clothing, medicine, health care, and every luxury or leisure item are produced by private individuals or corporations who own the means of production and from whom we must buy them. And you need to buy some of these things, unless you're completely self-sufficient. But for those of us who aren't or can't be self-sufficient, we need to buy these things; we need them for survival, and we need money to do so. Where do we get money? Assuming we're not independently wealthy, don't own a factory, or have opulent and gracious parents or beneficiaries, we'll get a job.

Luckily, jobs are as bountiful as factories. So we can knock on the Once-ler's door and ask if he needs any more knitters, and hopefully he can look past his nepotism and hire an outsider. Or if you desire a more adventurous line of work, you could beg Morris McGurk to give you a role in his Circus McGurkus. I'm sure old Sneelock would welcome some help. Hopefully, someone is hiring. If they are and we're lucky enough to get a job, we know the arrangement. We'll sign a contract wherein we sell our labor power in the form of productive time to our employer, be it the Once-ler or McGurk. He will pay us a wage. Or maybe even a salary, which is just a wage without the possibility of overtime. We can then use this money to pay bills or buy whatever we needed or wanted the money for in the first place. So we'll all become wage laborers, members of the working class, the proletariat. We'll work for a paycheck, which means for the majority of our lives we'll do what someone else tells us to in order to earn enough money to keep ourselves alive and hopefully happy or at least distracted, so we can go back to work and do it all again, day after day, week after week, year after year. Even if we're thrilled to do the things demanded of us, say knitting Thneeds, we're compelled to do so because we need the Once-ler's money. And if we leave the factory we'll need to find a new employer since we will still need money. So we can't escape the fact that we will work for somebody else for the rest of our lives; capitalism is built on this relationship. You can't have capitalism without wage laborers.

To a modern reader this situation looks normal, and maybe even natural or inevitable. For Marx it wasn't so. Capitalism was a relatively new invention, and one that could and should be altered. According to Marx the economy and production itself should serve the interests of the people, not vice versa. At the root, it's about human well-being and flourishing; that is, living well. People need to produce so that their needs are met. People need things and can produce things well and efficiently in groups, but production should be geared toward usability. We should make what we need so that we can all have a good quality of life. But in capitalism we don't produce for need; we don't make things because they are useful. Think Thneeds! Instead, things are produced simply to be sold, so that producers can accumulate more money, bigger their businesses, sell more, and so on. We don't make things to satisfy real human needs—things are made to be sold, because wealth is what drives capitalism, not well-being. Production is dictated not by what people need but by what they can be sold.

Consider again the ridiculous Thneed. It is ridiculous; no one needs a fool Thneed. It's a thing that is made only to be sold. If there is no market for it, the Once-ler will manufacture one through ingenious marketing. He'll make sure you know you "need" a Thneed so he can sell you one. I'm sure he could find plenty of clever advertisers who could prey on some latent insecurity to motivate you to buy a couple. Imagine how much money you could make from selling pill-berries to Gertrude McFuzz and her friends or how much money Sylvester McMonkey McBean does make selling and removing stars.

If the Once-ler, or any capitalist, can convince someone they "need" their product, then they'll be able to sell it. He could, and we do, sell just about anything this way from new fashions to makeup to superfluous gadgets whose sole purpose seems to be distraction. Production is geared toward selling and meeting artificial demands, not the satisfaction of real human needs.

Pontoffel Pock, Who Are You?

To oversimplify, under capitalism workers are forced to sell their labor in order to buy necessities. And to add insult to injury, their work is often unfulfilling, dull, and mostly pointless. Take Pontoffel Pock, for example. In the animated story, "Pontoffel Pock and His Magic Piano,"[1] alternatively known as "Pontoffel Pock, Where Are You?," we're introduced to Pontoffel Pock, a bumbling doofus who just can't get things right and wishes to get away from it all. Ultimately, he gets his wish when a fairy, McGillicuddy, gives him a magic piano that takes him all over the world.

Pontoffel Pock's troubles begin at Gicklers Dill Pickle Works. Pontoffel Pock wants a job in works, and he gets hired. And the job seems simple enough. His training consists of a twenty-second song introducing him to his job, "Just pull on the pull'em and push on the push'em and the pickles go into the jars" (Pock). Now imagine you're Pontoffel Pock. Your job is dull, even if you like it. Pontoffel Pock wants this job and is very saddened when he loses it. But it is still undeniably dull. It dulls your mind and your senses. There's no room for development. And you are stuck here so long as you need a paycheck, insurance, or what have you. To leave the job is to leave behind your ability to make a living. Most people can't afford to do so, so they find themselves trapped in jobs that are unfulfilling, with no real possibility of escape. Like Pontoffel Pock they can wish, wish, wish to get away, but no McGillicuddy is going to award them a magic piano, so they'll continue working as long as they can or are allowed to. But why is this so bad? We all have to do it, and it is just the way the world is, right? We can make do and enjoy what we can, like vacations, flat screen TVs, video games, sports. . . . But is this what life should be? Should life consist of working undesirable jobs for other people and merely tolerating it through the consumption of a few luxury items? If you want to understand why Marx is morally opposed to capitalism, you have to begin at the pickle works and with an understanding of what it is to be a human being.

For Marx, the essence of humanity is activity, specifically free, conscious activity.[2] People are first and foremost producers; we can create and recreate our environment to suit our needs, and as an expression of ourselves. In this sense, Marx is indicating that the unique characteristic of humanity, its species difference, what distinguishes the human being from all other creatures, is that we can produce or create according to a freely chosen plan. In addition, our activity is inherently social. We produce in a community in order to not only secure our necessities but also to free ourselves up for leisure activities, and thus freer production. "[Man] only truly produces when free from physical need. . . ."[3] Until our necessities are net, our needs dictate how we will produce. Once our needs are met we can produce freely.

Marx's account of the role labor plays in human life is influenced heavily by the account of artistic expression given by G. W. F. Hegel (1770–1831). Hegel writes: "[M]an is realized for himself by *practical* activity, inasmuch as he has the impulse, in the medium which is directly given to him, and externally presented before him, to produce himself, and therein at the same time to recognize himself."[4] Through the productive act in general, the individual expresses herself in the material world. One's essence as productive is seen in the world of art perhaps more clearly than in the world of work, but both activities are productive, and thus both are, ultimately, expressions of oneself. Our labor expresses who we are, and through our products others recognize us. Marx states: "Suppose, we had produced in a human manner. Then each of us would have in his production doubly affirmed himself and the other. . . . Our products would be like so many mirrors, from which our essence shown."[5] If we all produced in a way that was expressive of our individuality, then our products would reflect who we are. Think about Dr. Seuss himself. In his artistic expression through his books you get a sense of who he was as an individual. His works are expressive of the man, Theodore Geisel. But for how many of us is this really the case? Not of Pontoffel Pock to be sure. How can one see oneself in or feel fulfilled if his life is devoted to filling pickle jars? And we don't have time to begin to get into the demeaning, degrading, and objectifying job of Pontoffel Pock's girlfriend Neepha Pheepha, the eyeball dancer for the king.

So Marx's ethical critique of capital is grounded in his belief that one's essence ought to equal one's existence; that is, how one lives her life should be consistent with her essence as a free, productive being. Her labor, her productive activity, should be a free expression of her own consciously chosen life. Consider his example of the river fish from *The German Ideology*. "The 'essence' of the river fish is the water of the river. But this ceases to be its 'essence' and becomes a medium of existence no longer suitable for the fish, as soon as it is polluted with dyes and other wastes. . . ."[6] The water is the essence of the fish, and when it becomes glumped up with Gluppity-Glupp and Schloppity-Schlopp it ceases to be the fish's essence and becomes simply a medium of existence, one detrimental to the fish. Humming fish can't hum with their gills all gummed, and so people can't freely and consciously produce—that is, express their essence—if their work is coerced, chosen for them, and unhealthy. In a polluted river or pond there is a disparity between what the fish is and what the fish ought to be—between a fish being and a fish flourishing. Under capitalist production there is a disparity between the human being's essence, free-conscious activity, and her existence as a wage laborer. One's essential life activity becomes simply a means for life, a way of earning money so one can buy the necessities and maybe a few toys, not an expression of one's individuality. Since capitalism does not allow for the free-conscious activity of the majority of human beings, it is a perversion of life, an unhealthy social structure. The result of living in such a "polluted" social environment is alienation, a constant state of dissatisfaction and discomfort, and the development of various coping mechanisms that attempt to make alienated life bearable.

He'll Be Simply Delighted?

Workers who don't control their work environment, who have no control over what they do day in and day out, tend to develop a kind of psychology wherein they dissociate themselves from their job; that is, they become alienated. In the *Economic and Philosophical Manuscripts of 1844*, Marx provides his most detailed account of alienation. But we only need a general overview.

When a worker sells his labor time, he alienates himself from his labor; it's no longer his. His labor becomes foreign to him, something he does, but not what he is. Therefore, he no longer finds himself in the activity he performs, the activity that will occupy the majority of his life. When Pontoffel Pock sells his labor to Gil Gicklers at the dill pickle works, he dissociates his labor from himself. Pickle jar filling is just something he does, it's not who he is. Yet he spends every day doing this one thing. Laborers exercise no, or very limited, control over the process of production. Labor is not expressive; it's necessary and often undesirable. Really, how many people like to go to work? How many people, if they had their druthers, would continue doing their current job? For many, work is a necessary evil because work is not where they find satisfaction. And since many can't find satisfaction in their jobs, they begin to identify with those functions over which they do have control. If one spends one's life filling pickle jars, then off time is where he will find his true self. Marx believes that the worker will identify with those things he does have control over; satisfaction of basic animal urges such as eating, sleeping, or sex; his consumption patterns; and what he buys. "The result we come to is that the human being (the worker) feels freely active only in his animal functions, eating, drinking, procreating at most also in lodging, attire, etc., and in his human functions he feels like an animal. The bestial becomes human and the human becomes bestial."[7] Of course, Marx is not saying that these activities have no place in a full human life. Clearly, eating, drinking, and procreating have their place. Who doesn't enjoy a round at the bar? But Marx's point is that when these functions take on a character of being the sole focus, end, or purpose of one's life, then we're attempting to satisfy our need to be producers with ultimately unfulfilling activities or the mere acquisition of goods. You can't buy happiness when happiness is only found in expressive activity, yet this is proletarian life. One copes with alienation through distraction; that is, through conspicuous consumption or filling one's life with one idle entertainment after another. The individual becomes a consumer, not a producer, and so our existence fails to live up to our essence. This may work, for a while. We may be momentarily happy on the surface, but this is only so long as we can distract ourselves from the realization that our lives are not expressive of what we at root are. When this realization hits, it hits like a ton of bricks, and we cope the best we can with what is within our control, and red sports car salesman and plastic surgeons like Sylvester McMonkey McBean make out like bandits.

Just Pay Me Your Money and Hop Right Aboard

Consider the plight of both the Sneetches and Gertrude McFuzz. Dissatisfied with their respective lots in life they attempt to consume their way out of their misery. The Sneetches, originally the ones without stars but later all of them, believe that they must occupy a certain social position. The Sneetches without stars seek recognition; they want to be seen as equals to those with stars. But there is nothing they can do about this. They can't make stars, they can't take stars, it's their lot in life to be "less than." Thankfully, Sylvester McMonkey McBean offers them the opportunity to elevate their social status. For a nominal fee they can buy stars. Since they can't actually do anything to make life bearable, to earn status as equals, they will buy it. Gertrude McFuzz is in a similar position. She wants to be accepted; she wants to be pretty and presumably liked by the other birds. But she only has one droopy-droop feather. She needs two, just like that fancy birdie, Lolla-Lee-Lou. Then she'll be happy. Again we have a disaffected person who seeks acceptance, recognition, and affirmation. At first it appears that she is powerless. Then after she pleads with him, Uncle Doctor Dake reluctantly informs her about a pill-berry bush that will give her what she needs, more feathers. But he knows it's a fool's errand. "Such talk! How absurd! Your tail is just right for your kind of bird" (McFuzz). This is good advice against vanity and for self-esteem and a realistic and healthy body image. But Gertrude is having none of it. She knows what she needs.

With both the Sneetches and Gertrude McFuzz we see similar themes. People seek to be accepted as part of the group; we all want to belong. Often, unfortunately, being a part of the group means conforming to an artificial ideal, possessing the right things and being the right kind of consumer. Do you own the right star or number of feathers? So both involved parties consume in order to belong and eventually come to realize—because Gertrude becomes wiser, and contrary to common wisdom, you can teach a Sneetch—that consumption is not the answer. Consumption may seem to be the answer to the alienated mind that can't find satisfaction or belonging in their work or endeavors, but nothing could be further from the truth.

One Marxist scholar, Erich Fromm (1900–1980), formulates the problem in terms of what he calls "normative humanism." Fromm believes it's the task of psychology to find the "inherent mechanisms and laws" of humanity. Although human essence is malleable insofar as it can be expressed in many ways, it is not infinitely so; there are limits. Fromm's analysis of capitalism is based on how well it allows our essence to be manifested; that is, how well it allows us to express ourselves. Human beings all have the same needs, some of which are common among all animals and others that are specifically human. Among the former are hunger, thirst, sexual gratification, and sleep. However, there are other needs that are exclusive to human beings. Fromm lists these needs as the need for relatedness, transcendence, rootedness, a sense of identity, and a frame of orientation and devotion.[8] All of these specifically human needs are satisfied through one's relation to others and the world. We do need other people in order to truly be human, so it's not irrational for the Sneetches or Gertrude McFuzz to seek acceptance or their place in the world, but it is unfortunate that they try to achieve this through consumerism. If only society had been organized in a way that allowed them to fully express themselves through productive activity instead of merely through consumptive habits. Consider each of the needs Fromm enumerates.

Relatedness is an object relation that distinguishes between the self and other. Rootedness is equated to "brotherliness" and provides a foundation to the self similar to that found in traditional family ties. Sense of identity is opposed to conformity and, thus, is a perspective of uniqueness. The need for orientation and devotion is about grasping the world as a totality and locating one's place within it. Finally, the fact that humanity is endowed with reason means that humanity demands transcendence. Human beings are not content with a passive existence; they need to be active, to become more than they currently are. Humanity's demand for transcendence defines it as a creator, not solely a consumer.[9] This account grounds Fromm's distinction between the "having" and "being" modes of existence and sets the framework for explaining why buying things will never satisfy the inescapable human need to become part of the community as a unique, active, productive member. This is the hard-learned lesson of the Sneetches and Gertrude McFuzz. It takes them a whole book to learn that it's not about what you have but what you are.

Fromm's major point with respect to the "having" mode is that it destroys one's communion with one's fellow human beings through the dissolution of social bonds. The Sneetches seek to be recognized by their fellows. They need to be accepted as a part of the group, yet all the Star-Belly Sneetches recognize are stars, not the Sneetch beneath. So the Sneetches without must buy their way in. Their comrades only recognize their status as a possessor of things. Instead of relating to other Sneetches as people with merit and worth, they relate to things; namely, stars. Since the Sneetches without want to be recognized as valuable, they seek to buy that which is valued. Like Sneetches, the average worker tries to own their way to respectability and acceptance because it's not about what or who you are, it's about what or who you own. Is your car, phone, or TV the newest model? Is your wife, girlfriend, or significant other the prettiest or most desirable? Are you? What could you buy to be so?

But when all relations become relations between commodities or things, consumption becomes the primary mode of meeting the demand for social recognition. Individuals unable to form human bonds sate their desire for belonging through conformity by means of conspicuous consumption. One can best describe the culture of consumerism as the unbridled consumption of commodities for the satisfaction of psychological needs that cannot be satisfied through the practice of consumption. Advertisers know this. That's why commercials are premised around the idea that you are unacceptable as you are, but you may be able to remedy the situation through just one more purchase. Consumption becomes the way in which we orient ourselves to the world and others.

Human beings also have the uniquely human need for a sense of identity and self-worth. However, in a consumer culture this can only be expressed through one's market value. Since all things become commodified, one is only worth what she can sell herself for on the market and what she owns. She views herself as an object that possesses exchange value but not value in itself. She can thus add value to herself through the addition of possessions, skills, degrees, etc. She can add value by becoming the idealized product—the prettiest, most stylish product around. Consumption is thus not only the means by which one conforms in order to belong but also the means to acquiring value and, thus, satisfying the need for identity and self-worth. One is infused with the value of one's possessions.[10] This desire for acquisition is maintained in perpetuity since comparative worth fluctuates as quickly as new innovations hit the market. If one is only as valuable as one's possessions, and the value of possessions is relative to their relation to other commodities, then as new and improved products hit the market one must acquire these in order to maintain their relative level of value. And so we go round and round. "Off again! On again! In again! Out again!" through the machines, round and about again, star on and star off, until we are dizzy and broke (Sneetches). There is always something newer, better, prettier, and Fix-It-Up Chappies will always make sure you know you "need" it. So long as they can convince you that you aren't acceptable the way you are, then they can prey on your need to be so by selling the snake oil of superfluous consumer goods and the image attached to them. Anyone with daughters knows exactly what I mean. Fashion and makeup are premised on exploiting a need to belong by promoting an ever-changing and unreachable ideal of beauty and style. The only way to win this game is to refuse to play and find value in yourself, although the social consequences of integrity can be difficult to bear. So in the end, our need to be related to others is so powerful that often our fear of isolation promotes conformity.

With regard to conformity, another notable Marxist scholar, Max Horkheimer (1895–1973), states: "From the day of his birth, the individual is made to feel that there is only one way of getting along in this world—that of giving up his hope of ultimate self-realization. This he can only achieve by imitation."[11] One gives up hope of self-realization since one knows his life will be defined by the job he must take. His life won't be his own. The best he can hope for is survival, not self-determination. One molds oneself to meet social expectations and accepts these as acceptable criteria on which to base one's sense of identity and self-worth. One becomes what society expects one to be, at whatever cost. So we see the Sneetches driven to madness in an attempt to become what they expect others want them to be, owners of stars. They will not be satisfied until they own the right thing and are thus the right kind of Sneetch, but they'll never own the right thing since the process demands that there never be an end to the process. McBean will see to this. His business is built on Sneetch insecurity and his ability to exploit it. McBean's a good executive—he knows how to make profits, and he doesn't worry himself over the needs of his customers or the effect he is having on them and their society. He knows he is making money, and that's enough.

The problems with consumerism are expressed well through Horkheimer and Theodor Adorno's (1903–1969) discussions of what they call the culture industry. Horkheimer and Adorno state: "The power of the culture industry resides in its identification with a manufactured need . . ."[12] Manufactured needs like Thneeds, stars, or multiple feathers are the commodities capitalism trades in and can trade in since we as workers/consumers are willing to try to buy our way to satisfaction so long as we remain essentially dissatisfied. But we will remain perpetually dissatisfied until our lives are free expressions of our essential selves, which is impossible under a capitalist mode of production.

Since many people don't or can't express themselves through their work, they get no satisfaction from their lives. Instead, they spend the majority of their lives attempting to develop a sense of self and belonging through the consumption of manufactured needs or doping themselves into acceptance by popping not berries, but pills.[13] Adorno explains: "In a supposedly chaotic world it [the culture industry] provides human beings with something like standards of orientation, and that alone seems worthy of approval."[14] Our genuine human needs become the condition for the possibility of our submission to a manufactured consumer culture and massive drug industry peddling "cures" to the problem of capitalism. The problem with Gertrude McFuzz and the Sneetches isn't that there is anything wrong with either of them—every child sees this. The problem is that insofar as they are "human" they have needs that can only be satisfied through proper interpersonal relationships. But their culture has been set up so as to deny them this. Instead all they are offered is false cures. They buy stars or take pills and foolishly believe their dissatisfaction will go away. But the problem was never with them, it was with how their societies were organized. And no amount of stars or self-medication, no amount of adornments or medicines is going to fix Gertrude or the Sneetches, because they aren't broken—their culture is; it is not a home for them.

You Can Teach a Sneetch

Human beings, like birds and Sneetches, are psychologically vulnerable as a result of specific needs that can only be satisfied through social interaction. These needs, when unfulfilled, make one more vulnerable to manipulation. In fact, consumerism capitalizes on human vulnerability and exploits it. What Fromm and company argue is that a fundamental human need is to belong; that belonging, connectedness, and rootedness are necessary for a sense of identity and worth; that human beings are essentially social in virtue of these needs; and when denied the possibility to realize themselves as social producers, they compensate. But the answer to this problem is not newer gadgets or better drugs but to organize society in such a way that each person is capable of expressing themselves through their labor, through their productive activity—a society wherein one's work is freely chosen and meaningful. The answer to these problems is not to dope the Sneetches or Gertrude McFuzz into complacently, not to tell them to deal and get along as best they can, but to reform society.

Is this idea of making society a home to all of its members utopian or idealistic? Yes. But what's wrong with being idealistic? Isn't that why we read Seuss to children, to teach them life lessons and ideals that we hope they'll have the courage to exemplify as they grow older? The Sneetches learned their lesson. Luckily, they caught on that what matters is being a certain kind of Sneetch, not a certain brand of Sneetch. Gertrude McFuzz learned her lesson as well. "That one little feather she had as a starter . . . now that's enough, because now she is smarter" (McFuzz). Gertrude learns that the ideal of beauty, of feather possession, is artificial, constructed, and meaningless and buying into that image leads to dissatisfaction, low self-esteem, and eating disorders. Better to be Gertrude McFuzz droopy-droop feather and all than a shallow copy of a corporate, mass-marketed "ideal."

Marx objected to capitalism because of what it does to people. It harms their relations to themselves and others by denying them the capacity for self-expression through free, conscious activity. People need to be recognized for what and who they are, and wage labor doesn't provide that. But the need doesn't go away just because it is unfulfilled, it manifests itself in other behaviors. When our work is unsatisfying we compensate with other ways of being recognized and belonging, ways that ultimately culminate in a culture industry selling worthless goods that are poor substitutes for true self-realization and meaningful relationships. Marx may be an easy target when it comes to everyday conversations. He's demonized most often by those who know nothing about him. So stick to Seuss if you must. The Once-ler and McBean are notorious characters, and we're surrounded by them. We read our children Seuss and tell them to be individuals, to be themselves, but then we send them off to school where we tell them to "play the game." They continue on to college where we pay thousands upon thousands of dollars to buy them MBAs hoping they'll become the next Once-ler. We do this while lamenting our jobs, the result of doing the same thing we now ask them to do, only hoping maybe they'll make a little more money so they can have a little more stuff. Should we? Criticism serves the purpose of making the status quo justify itself by measuring it against what could or ought to be. Doing so helpfully makes us a little bit wiser. And if you can teach a Sneetch, we can't be far behind.

CHAPTER FOUR

~

Socratic Seuss: Intellectual Integrity and Truth-Orientation

Matthew F. Pierlott

Never separate the life you live from the words you speak.

—U.S. Senator Paul Wellstone (D-MN, 1991–2002)[1]

If philosophy is concerned with anything, it is concerned with developing and maintaining intellectual integrity in ourselves and others. Philosophy doesn't aim only to further knowledge and to assess knowledge claims. It also aims to orient individual characters toward the truth and promotes self-reflection on philosophical practice itself in order to best guard against the disintegration of its methodology. It does so because it understands being oriented toward the truth as a component to living well. Why is the truth valued? First, it seems by nature we generally desire the truth for its own sake, even though at times we might fear the pain associated with knowing a particular truth. We are curious, and oh, the places we'll go to satisfy that curiosity. Second, we certainly desire the truth for its instrumental value. Knowledge helps us navigate the world so that we can live as we wish. Think of Gertrude McFuzz being happy with one feather once she comes to understand the implication of having too many. So the philosophers within us want the truth, and intellectual integrity is an essential component of the properly philosophical character.

What is intellectual integrity? However one eventually defines it after philosophical debate and reflection, it will probably involve all of the following

41

aspects: (1) being open to different ideas; (2) carefully considering the strength of the support for those ideas; (3) drawing out the implications of those ideas, including their coherence with other plausible ideas; (4) reflecting on the limits of one's ability and methods to carry out the previous two tasks; and (5) honestly representing the results of the previous three tasks both to others and oneself. While there may be more to include and philosophers have and will explore complications even with these components, these aspects serve as a basis for beginning to think about intellectual integrity. What ties them all together is how they promote truth-oriented activity. If I care for the truth (which I should, of course), I will try to develop my capacities and habits with regard to these tasks.

One threat to intellectual integrity in our own person and in others is sophistry, the use of seemingly plausible and persuasive rhetoric for ulterior motives (e.g., either to deceive others or to impress them for personal gain). The traditional story about the Sophists of ancient Greece has Socrates opposing them in principle and practice. They charged a fee, while he did not. They claimed to be experts, while Socrates humbly admitted his limits. They taught how to be clever in one's words in order to make weak arguments appear stronger, while Socrates modeled clarity in thought to expose arguments for how strong they really were. They promoted persuading others to further your own agenda, while Socrates emphasized self-examination for the sake of the truth. In short, Socrates attended to his own intellectual integrity and promoted it in others, while the Sophists did not. So, Socrates is praised for striving for wisdom, not just its appearance, and becomes the model for genuine philosophical inquiry.

If we accept that my list above is fair, then we should expect Socrates to embody those aspects fairly consistently. It's not clear to me that he always does. In Plato's *Apology*, in particular, Socrates appears to engage in sophistry. For example, he gets his accuser Meletus to specify the charge of impiety toward the gods as an accusation of atheism.[2] Then he argues that Meletus accuses him of teaching new spiritual ideas, and since Athenians traditionally believe spirits are gods or their children, Meletus must think that Socrates believes in gods.[3] Of course, what Athenians conventionally believe and what Meletus accuses Socrates of are both beside the point. Does Socrates believe in the traditional gods, or not? Socrates cleverly diverts our attention from the question at hand, obscuring the truth in the process. Nevertheless, the character of Socrates does spur reflection on the nature of intellectual integrity and its value, as well as threats to it. Thus, the stereotype of the Sophist can regulate our own tendencies if we are mindful not to imitate it. Furthermore, our resources are not limited to Plato and Socrates. After all, we have Dr. Seuss.

Next, I will explore how Seuss helps us stay alert to the potential dangers of becoming distracted by interests other than the truth in our interactions with others and with respect to our own endeavors. Seuss helps us by giving illustrations both of the drives and desires that engender dishonesty and those that if left unchecked can also end up misaligning us. Like Plato's Socrates, Seuss acts as the gadfly, biting us awake whenever we're weary of attending to our intellectual integrity.

Green Eggs and Bull

If Sam-I-Am asked you if you liked green eggs and ham, what would you say? I once tried to make this Seussian treat for my young children, using green food coloring in scrambled eggs. My daughter took a look at my masterpiece and scrunched her nose. "I don't like it," she reported. Whether you blame her or not for her response, one thing is sure: like the protagonist in Seuss's famous piece, she had not tried them. So, what are we to make of her definitive claim that she does not like them?

Obviously, her claim is meant to ensure that she doesn't have to try the odd-looking food. But the claim is not one she can really verify, since her experience of the green eggs was limited to its looks. One extreme possibility is that her claim is a lie. She is stating as a fact something that she does not know as a fact and is therefore engaging in a deceptive activity, trying to avoid an unusual cuisine. Of course, interpreting a four-year-old's simple response as a conscious effort to mislead is rather presumptuous. Perhaps it is better to just say that she, like Sam-I-Am's friend, is spewing "bullshit."

While it may seem surprising, "bullshit" has become something of a technical term in philosophy. Ever since Princeton's professor emeritus of philosophy, Harry G. Frankfurt, reprinted his essay "On Bullshit" in 2005, philosophers have started to explore the concept in greater depth with renewed intensity.[4] According to Frankfurt, a liar retains an implicit respect for the truth, while a bullshitter does not. Frankfurt states, "One who is concerned to report or to conceal the facts assumes that there are indeed facts that are in some way both determinate and knowable."[5] In the act of lying, a liar assumes that there is a truth to lie about, wishes to hide that truth from her victim for some reason, and intentionally speaks falsely or at least misleadingly.[6] In other words, a liar is still truth-oriented, just like a truth-teller.[7]

So is Sam-I-Am's friend trying to deceive Sam-I-Am? We should note that actually deceiving someone is an insufficient and unnecessary condition of intending to deceive someone. I can try to deceive and fail, and I could accidentally deceive someone without meaning to do so. In order to claim lying in this case, Sam-I-Am's friend would need to know, or at least believe, that he in fact does like green eggs and ham, as he repeatedly insists that he does not. But we know that he learns something new when he finally tries the dish, i.e., that he would eat it and would even do so with a fox, unless he is just pretending to love green eggs and ham at the end of the book to get Sam-I-Am off his back! In that case, he is outright lying, but we don't have much of a reason to think this was Seuss's intention.

So Sam-I-Am's friend is probably not lying. Considering that he freely admits that he does not like "that Sam-I-Am" at the start, it is more likely that he is bullshitting. The bullshitter uses propositions, or claims, without regard for their status as true or false and is not directly concerned with the recipient's belief of those propositions. A bullshitter is using those propositions simply to promote her agenda, without a care of whether they are true or false. Sam-I-Am's friend just wants to be left alone and so is making a claim about not liking green eggs simply to shut Sam-I-Am up. Indeed, Sam-I-Am's persistence, acting like the Socratic gadfly, brings this driving desire to the forefront since the friend is finally willing to try the eggs just to be finished with the nagging. Similarly, my daughter wasn't concerned much with the truth status of her claim; she just didn't want to stick those green eggs in her mouth.

If bullshitting is understood as using claims for some purpose other than representing or misrepresenting the truth, of conveying information or misinformation, we can fairly quickly recognize that we are often engaged in bullshit as both generators and recipients. This occurs any time we have desires that drive us to use propositions without a concern for their veracity. As such, engaging in bullshit is a constant threat to our intellectual integrity, which we can see by considering its effect on the five aspects I listed previously. First, it can reinforce already accepted ideas without warrant, undermining aspect (1). Second, bullshitting skews considerations of the genuine support for those ideas being true, undermining aspect (2), and clutters our minds and conversations with too many conflicting ideas, making it more difficult to attend to aspect (3). Most importantly, it devalues the honesty required within intellectual integrity, highlighted in aspect (4). Completely refraining from bullshit may be practically impossible, but complacency with regard to it completely deteriorates our sense of intellectual integrity. Philosophy provides the tools of rigorous critical thinking and the concern for the truth to purify our minds of such fecal matter.

Delusion Ain't Just a Sport in D'Olympics

Just as we can lie to ourselves as we lie to others, we can also fall victim to our own lines of bullshit. Sometimes we say things without caring about its truth because we are really just managing other people's reactions; sometimes we care a lot that what we say is true, but we do so in a way that is not itself truth-oriented. Rather than wanting to say only those things we think we have good reason to believe are true, we believe as true those things that we really want to be true. This is when we delude ourselves.[8]

The most straightforward example that Seuss provides is in "The Big Brag." The poem starts with a rabbit, feeling self-important, exclaiming aloud that he is the best of all animals. An offended eavesdropping bear calls the rabbit ridiculous and claims the title as his own. Attempting to prove his superiority, the rabbit has the bear witness him use his long ears to hear the cough of a fly on a mountain ninety miles away. The bear in response smells a smell six hundred miles beyond the mountains. In a nest in a tree on a farm by a pond are two hummingbird eggs, and the one on the left smells a little bit stale. So which is the best of all animals?

Well, each has an ability that surpasses the same capacity in the other, and both capacities seem important. So it is difficult to judge, even if we take the issue as seriously as they do. We can immediately recognize, however, that the question itself is a bit silly and that we should question the framing of their inquiry, as Socrates would. First, it is vague. Something is always only "good" in some respect and so can only be "the best" in some respect, and that respect is not specified here. Or, if we take it that it is specified, then "being the best animal" would mean "being the best at being what an animal is." Since neither smelling nor hearing are necessary to being an animal, both rabbit and bear are barking up the wrong tree (if you can forgive mixing in the canine imagery). Second, neither rabbit nor bear is in a position to verify the claims of the other. Bear can't hear the cough, and rabbit can't smell the egg. If we assume they are being truthful, Mr. Bear should be able to smell the fly, which would corroborate the rabbit's claim; Mr. Rabbit, on the other hand, has no easy means to check the bear's claim (unless he seriously underplayed his hand . . . or ears, as the case may be).

Third, and perhaps most importantly, establishing the claim of who's the best animal doesn't seem to serve a purpose, except to inflate the egos of our braggarts. Show-offs will say whatever it takes to reach the conclusion they desire and are not really open to the possible validity of their opponent's replies. It's their self-importance that motivates them. Socrates often took the opportunity to humble those who professed great knowledge simply to promote their own importance. In the *Euthyphro*, for example, we find Socrates suckering a bold and self-righteous, self-proclaimed religious authority into a line of inquiry that ultimately reveals his ignorance with regard to the nature of piety, a topic of which he considers himself an expert. Both Seuss and Socrates are inviting us to examine how often we spout off because our ego is on the line.

It's the little worm who pops up and plays the role of Socratic gadfly in order to settle the debate and set the two braggarts straight. The worm says that he can see farther than either of the two can smell or hear. He looks straight ahead and all the way around the world right back to where the three are gathered to see "the two biggest fools . . . who seem to have nothing else better to do / Than sit here and argue who's better than who!" (Brag). With that, the worm dived back to his hole to get back to something better to do. The rabbit and bear are taken off guard by the worm, and the worm leaves them with surprise in their eyes. He has no reason to stay longer, since what happens next is not up to him. We don't see what happens next, but the two braggarts have a choice: they can recognize that their present endeavor to prove superiority is intellectually bankrupt and driven by insecurity, or they can ignore the worm's critique, remaining oriented on their egos instead of truth.

The worm's critique of the braggarts is reminiscent of Socrates' own critique of the alleged experts in Athens. He does not despise the speculation of natural philosophers but prefers to ask the questions of ethics and politics, which are more vital to living well. Natural philosophy, at least in Socrates' time, seemed as unverifiable as Mr. Bear's claim to smell that stale egg. And it was at least less important than issues about the good life. And of those Sophists who profess knowledge about living well, Socrates finds them fuller of themselves than full of knowledge. Like the practical worm, he exposes them for their lack of intellectual integrity and shows them to be braggarts wasting the time (and money) of their students.

The braggarts lack intellectual integrity because they embrace beliefs that are vague, unverifiable, and unimportant. They each want it to be true that they are the superior animal, and so they believe it to be true. Further, they won't be content until their superiority is accepted. But Seuss recognizes that this temptation doesn't simply catch those poor ignoble characters of whom we expect no better. Even noble desires for certain states of affairs can seduce us. Seuss invites us to indulge in just such a fantasy in *Horton Hatches the Egg*.

Mayzie, a lazy new mother bird, wishes to get a break from sitting on her egg. She begs Horton to take over and promises to return shortly, but she soon decides not to return, preferring her stay in Palm Beach to the burdens of motherhood. Good-hearted Horton sits through storms and seasons, through ridicule and even the threat of death. His resolve to stay sitting has him being hauled over mountains and across the ocean and then around the country in a circus until he reaches Palm Beach. Mayzie, breaking from her sunbathing, swoops in to see the circus that has come to town, only to find Horton still on her egg. At just that moment, the egg begins to hatch. Wretched Mayzie screams that she wants her egg back, accusing Horton of stealing it, and Horton brokenheartedly withdraws. But when the eggshell breaks open a winged little elephant flies over to Horton. Seuss ends the poem with an emphatic "IT'S AN ELEPHANT-BIRD!! And it should be, it *should* be, it SHOULD be like that! Because Horton was faithful! He sat and he sat!" (Hatches). Horton, unlike Mayzie, upheld his word, and the humans deliver Horton back home with his new child.

Here Seuss is moved by the moral worthiness of Horton compared to the undeserving, lazy bird mother, Mayzie. Adult readers recognize that Seuss's repeated insistence, based on moral appropriateness (i.e., "it should be, it *should* be, it SHOULD be . . ."), implicitly acknowledges that outside the world of the poem such an egg could not really house an elephant-bird. We want it to be so, though. And it seems implausible that the same humans who would hunt an elephant to kill it, then decide to capture it to exploit it as a circus act, would suddenly opt to release it. An elephant with a winged offspring would fetch more attention than an elephant sitting on an egg, after all. Yet we would like things to end well for Horton, wouldn't we? We want it to be the case that virtue is rewarded in the end, and vice punished. This is a noble desire to have, but it may lead us to deny the sometimes harsh realities of our lives and leave us unprepared to deal with them when they inevitably strike. Beyond self-esteem, insecurity, or even a desire for meaning and purpose, there may also be aesthetic reasons for deluding ourselves, as Marco clearly illustrates.

In *And to Think That I Saw It on Mulberry Street*, we find Marco, a young boy who would prefer that he have an interesting story to tell about what he sees on his walk home from school to the drudgery of what he actually encounters. He knows his father instructed him not to tell outlandish tales and not to exaggerate the truth, but his creativity and urge to embellish the facts of the matter have his mind overflowing with possibilities. He continuously revises the plain horse and wagon he saw into more and more fanciful visions, until he has dreamt up a parade, complete with a Rajah on an elephant, a six-piece brass band, an airplane dropping confetti, a police escort, and the mayor.

In our desire to make things more interesting, we can fabricate and exaggerate the truth. How often do we massage the truth to make the story more entertaining? To make ourselves appear more articulate, reasonable, or innocent? To make others appear in our retelling of events more obviously how we interpreted them to be? More importantly, how easily do we begin to believe the retelling we've fashioned? In the beginning of *Mulberry Street*, the boy informs us that he only tells his father what he thinks he has seen, suggesting that the boy lets his imagination get the better of him. At the end of the book, the boy reports to his father only the plain horse and wagon he actually saw.

The father serves as an external check on the boy's tendency to abandon the truth, just as the worm did for the bear and rabbit, and Socrates may for us. The more familiar we become with the character of Socrates, the more comfortable we will become playing the role of gadfly to ourselves. Let's return to *Euthyphro* for an illustration. If we settle for a rather unexamined view of some matter, as Euthyphro does with respect to his definition of piety, Socrates will help us test our definition. Being pious is doing what is dear to the gods? If the gods disagree, then this definition generates an inconsistency, since the action is both dear and hated by some god or other. Further, such a definition leaves unresolved a fundamental issue: why are some things dear to the gods, and so some actions pious to perform? If there is some reason, then that reason is what really makes some action pious. If there is none, then the virtue of piety rests on the fickleness of the gods, and it is unclear why one should strive to be pious except to appease the mighty.

It is important to recognize what we want to be true, since this is a reflection of our values. Only once we register these desires can we determine which desires reflect misplaced values and which reflect noble ideals. The bear and rabbit can begin reforming their conceited characters, all of us can reaffirm our appreciation of virtues like Horton's, and the boy can find a nondeceitful venue for his creative fabrications (say, in truth-oriented children's illustrated poetry). Equally, it is important for us to recognize the extent to which our desires for certain claims to be true might interfere with our own intellectual integrity. How can we say that we are oriented toward the truth when we only care to define the truth as we see fit? If bullshit is indifference toward the truth, self-delusion is valuing the *status* of truth but not the *reality* of it.

Walking in Another Man's Pants

We have seen how an agenda or a deep-seated desire might make us less careful about how we represent the way things are, leading us to make and accept assertions even without evidence simply because they are efficacious or comforting. Sometimes our drives and desires get us to gather evidence but interpret it in a biased way. Examining emotions like fear can easily illustrate how this can happen, and Seuss gives us an example in "What Was I Scared Of?"

The narrator, who is self-reportedly not prone to fear, finds himself in a deep, dark wood one night when he encounters a pair of pale green pants with nobody inside them. He stands curiously, not scared, until the pants move. Then he runs, heart thumping. Again he tells us he wasn't scared; he just didn't care for pants that move by themselves. Later those pants race around a corner, almost knocking him down, and still later they row out toward him on the river while he was fishing. He runs and hides for a couple of nights, until he has to do an errand. At least now he admits that he is scared: "I said, 'I do not fear those pants with nobody inside them.' I said, and said, and said those words. I said them. But I lied them" (Scared). His fear ironically forces him to recognize he deluded himself earlier by believing he was fairly fearless. But it also made him misinterpret what he was seeing.

As he reaches into a Snide bush to pick a peck of Snide, he touches the pale green pair of pants. Face to face, they both react with extreme fear. It is only by seeing how afraid the pants are that the narrator understands his mistake: he was "just as strange to them / As they were strange to" him (Scared). The pants weren't racing by on a bike to knock him down. The pants came down the wooded path and later came out on the river not even knowing he was there. The narrator interpreted the actions and motives of the pants according to his own construction of the pants as a spooky, ill-willed stalker. What he needed to do to align himself to the truth of things was to imagine the range of possibilities that might explain what he saw, to explore the potential motives and perspectives of another person by stepping into his shoes (or pants) for a while.

In this case, there was evidence supporting the belief that the pants were out to get him, but the evidence was interpreted through a lens of prejudice, created and perpetuated by fear. Emotions like fear pressure us to accept a view since we run the apparent risk of making the object of our fear a reality by ignoring fear. If I don't listen to my fears about that approaching lion, I might just become its dinner, as I was afraid might happen. Although the fear is sometimes warranted, fear always places a high burden on our external reality to prove to us that there is no risk, even when there was none to begin with. This can close us off to the possibility that the view being promoted by our fear is in fact incorrect. Consider our narrator: He was so disturbed by the sight of the unfamiliar that he could not recognize the humanity of those pale green pants. The pants were only doing things that the narrator himself was doing: taking a walk in the woods, strolling through town, rowing out on the lake, and picking Snide.

The narrator allowed fear to dominate his perspective of the pale green pants, even though he originally boasted to be a brave sort of fellow. Fear is a strong poison to truth-orientation. That's why we see so much fear-mongering in politics. Fear reinforces our ideologies and assumptions. It also can explain why someone might accept Euthyphro's definition of piety, as mentioned previously. I might simply accept out of fear of punishment that some action is pious when I am told that some deity desires it. Trying to understand why such a thing should be desired, so that I can actually test the claim that the action belongs to the category . . . well, that is beside the point. When I am afraid of a bad fate at the hands of the gods, why should I bother challenging the legitimacy of the claim? My fear has distracted me from a concern for the truth.

Remember the aspects of intellectual integrity I offered at the beginning of this chapter. Since I am now not open to alternate views, as in aspect (1), I am unable to genuinely take up the tasks that require such openness for success. I cannot carefully consider the strength of the support for those differing ideas (2), since my fear has defined only one alternative as possible and significant. I cannot genuinely draw out the implications of those ideas, including their coherence with other plausible ideas (3), again because of my narrowed perspective. Finally, I cannot reflect on the limits of my ability and methods to carry out the previous two tasks (4), at least until I begin to master my fear. Insofar as I am merely reacting to my fear rather than recognizing it so as to gain perspective on it, my fear is going to govern me and destroy my intellectual integrity and my chances at living a successful, examined life.

In Seuss We Truth

Seuss has provided us with some tips for maintaining our own intellectual integrity.

Many of our emotions and desires certainly can skew our perspective. We see this easily in others and can note how effortlessly one can fall into the trap. Knowing this, we should be on guard with respect to our own intellectual commitments. First, when we feel strong emotions with regard to something, we should try our best to take a step back and see if we might be allowing the emotions to steer our understanding. Second, when we discover that we are easily accepting certain things as true, we should examine whether we have a preference for these things to be true. If so, we should begin to examine the strength of our evidence for them, if there is any. Finally, we should always be mindful of the tendency to disregard the truth. Throughout the day, we will deal in marketing rhetoric, ideological propaganda, flattery, and small talk; we're mired hip deep in bullshit. No doubt we will produce some ourselves. We should do our best to curb both our intake and output of such nonsense.

It's up to us to maintain our own intellectual integrity. Since we know we will fail from time to time, we should surround ourselves with reliable friends who help keep us straight. For that we have the likes of Socrates and Seuss, as well as all of our fellow collaborators on the quest for truth and wisdom. Following up on "On Bullshit," Harry Frankfurt says at the end of his 2006 essay, "On Truth":

> To the extent that we learn in greater detail how we are limited, and what the limits of our limitation are, we come thereby to delineate our own boundaries and thus discern our own shape. . . . Thus, our recognition and understanding of our own identity arises out of, and depends integrally on, our appreciation of a reality that is definitively independent of ourselves. . . . How, then, can we fail to take the importance of factuality and of reality seriously? How can we fail to care about truth? We cannot.[9]

So when it comes to your own intellectual integrity, whether you have a desire to be famous as famous can be or to escape a dull Waiting Place or you have a fear of some scary thing down the road between hither and yon that scares you so much you don't want to go on, step with care and great tact! And explore the world of ideas with an open mind. After all, "it's opener there in the wide open air" (Places).

~

CHAPTER FIVE

Neither Here, nor There, nor Anywhere?

Randall E. Auxier

Say It Isn't So!

A "contrarian" is a person who just likes to disagree with everything you say. Most of us have a contrarian in our lives. You've probably had an uncle or a brother like that, or a boss or a friend—or if you're saying "no, I haven't," you're probably the contrarian in your own life . . . and, if now you're saying "I am not!," well, I rest my case.

Contrarians can be plenty annoying, but it's actually good to have one around if you really want to *learn* something. One of the easiest ways to go wrong is to get all excited about something you *think* you've learned but in reality you haven't fully understood it, and you haven't yet discovered the gravity of your own . . . well, let's call it "innocence." ("Ignorance" is such an ugly word.) For example, I don't know about you, but some of the best teachers I ever had were ones I didn't like right off, and some of them I even dreaded after the first class or two. But by sticking with them for a while I began to recognize qualities that weren't obvious at first. Maybe I needed a contrarian around to say, "Well, you think you don't like Mrs. Jones, but you might be wrong." Of course, sometimes I was right, and I didn't need a contrarian at all. But how could I have known? And once in a while I meet someone and I'm so sure we will be good friends and I'm stoked about that, but after a while we may realize we don't have much in common. A good contrarian would say, "You just wait, you'll see otherwise in a few weeks . . ." You know the type.

Even if contrarians are a bother, they have their uses. That's because learning is often a process of negating in your imagination what you believed at first, paring down your first impressions and eliminating gratuitous judgments and wild guesses until only the really stable and lasting ideas remain. And learning even more than *that* may require that *you* be a stick-in-the-mud, a wet blanket, a killjoy, a party pooper, in short, a contrarian.

A Little Bit Creepy

Sam-I-Am has one of these contrarians for a friend—well, *are* they friends? Sam is very much concerned to improve the life and outlook (maybe even the health?) of our unnamed contrarian (I'm going to call him "C"), but C does not like that Sam-I-Am, and he says as much. Can friends not like each other? I actually have a couple of friends who don't like me, I think. It's just the first of many educational puzzles in *Green Eggs and Ham*. Some people sort of like being not altogether likable. But Sam is, I think, an earnest fellow, even if he is annoying, and I see no reason to doubt his motives. He apparently wants nothing beyond the practical happiness of everyone, and for him that apparently involves getting shed of at least one meal at nearly any expense of effort.

We all know that there is something cool about this book. Even among the many works of genius created by Dr. Seuss, this one stands out. But the book is just silly, isn't it? It was written on a bet, that Seuss couldn't write a whole book using only fifty different words. And it has such a simple message, "You don't know whether you like something until you try it." Or maybe it's "don't be a contrarian." Or perhaps it's about the value of perseverance in helping others out of their narrow habits. Surely parents have appreciated these clear and convincing messages as they watch their children not only learn to read from this book but also *memorize* the book and even get excited as C finally agrees to try what he has been swearing he'd never like. It helps parents with their weekly broccoli argument, I'm sure.

But apart from what is obviously wholesome and good for the moral development of kids, there is in this book, as in many Dr. Seuss books, an element of mischief, something a little outside the rules, edgy, even dangerous. Part of the reason these books capture the imaginations of children has to do with just that mischievous element, and that is also part of what keeps adults reading them too—come on, don't try to pretend you don't still read them. There is just something sort of creepy about the Cat in the Hat, something deeply disturbing about the Fix-It-Up Chappie who sells stars to the silly Sneetches, and while we're on the topic, who, by the way, *is* this Sam-I-Am, and why should he care whether C tries this meal that looks like it has gone over? *Green* eggs? *Green* ham? Those things ought not be green, as everyone knows. Has Sam taken out an insurance policy on C? Double indemnity for death by food poisoning? It's a little creepy, a tad bit gross, and that's part of the reason kids love it.

You Got a Problem with That?

Let's slow down. *Green Eggs and Ham* is really quite rich with undertones, suggestions, and moral worries, and so the questions crowd in on every single page, if you're of a philosophical temper or if you're just plain contrary. But *this* chapter isn't about your moral worries, it's about three of the toughest branches of philosophy: metaphysics, epistemology, and logic, and how they come together to "settle belief." Some philosophers who call themselves pragmatists say that when we are hindered by our doubts, we try to solve our problems with "inquiry," and that means that we take on three really tough things at the same time—we want to know *what is and is not* a part of our problem (metaphysics), and how we should *think* about the problem (logic), and we want to know *what we know* when we know the answers to the first two parts so that we know why we solved or didn't solve the problem (episte-mology). Together these three branches are sometimes called the "theoreti-cal" branches on the philosophy tree, as opposed to the "practical" branches: ethics, politics, and aesthetics.

Some philosophers like to separate theory from practice, and pragmatists have nasty names for philosophers like that, names such as "intellectualists" and "abstractionists" and some names even longer than those. The ones who want to keep theory and practice together are those "pragmatists." You've probably heard that label before, in epithets like "Oh, he doesn't worry much about principles and scruples, he's a *pragmatist*." On the high side, it's a word for people who get things done no matter what obstacles they face, but on the low side, it's a word for people who will stop at nothing to solve their problems, no matter how nefarious may be the means. In philosophy, though, the word doesn't stand for opportunists and bullies. It's reserved for people who think that theory is really practical and that practical activities are the best source of theoretical ideas. They think, "Hey, when you have a problem, you have a problem, and whether it's a math problem or what to get your mom for her birthday or the meaning of life it's important to be able to think it through."

To get us going then, pragmatists always want to ask *what* the problem is. In *Green Eggs and Ham*, then, what's the problem, and how can we think about it? Is it one problem or several? Anyone can see that C has at least one problem, which is Sam-I-Am won't leave him in peace. But maybe C's real problem is that he doesn't get out enough, try new things, and without some prodding he'll miss what needs doing in the world. Sam has a problem, too, and his really is mysterious: C won't eat the foodstuffs. But we all vaguely sense that Sam has made this his own problem, has chosen the problem, perhaps even invented the problem. And we have to wonder whether it is a real problem at all.

That brings us to our first lesson in pragmatism. There was a curmudgeon of an old philosopher named Charles Sanders Peirce (it's pronounced "purse") who lived from 1839 until 1914. He actually invented the philosophy of pragmatism, and everyone pretty much agrees that if there was ever a contrarian in the world, it was Peirce. And in fact, he actually looked a little bit like C in *Green Eggs and Ham*. Peirce noticed that when we have a problem, we become aware of it when it paralyzes the flow of our action and causes us to think, whether we want to or not. In the case of C, he has a problem with Sam because Sam interrupts his reading. C never would have formed an opinion about Sam otherwise. It's like that with all problems. I suppose Sam doesn't feel he can get on with his life until C eats the meal—although *why* that is so is exactly what *we* need to figure out. So, by listening to Peirce, we just figured out that *we* have a problem, too, which is: why is Sam so very serious about disposing of *this* meal in *this* way? I have a feeling that we won't get to the end of this chapter until we have worked that one out.

So that's our problem. We want to know Sam's motives, *why* it's a problem for him not only that this meal is uneaten but also that C must eat it. I assume that when he solves his problem, he'll go back to whatever he does when he isn't pushing ova and pork. I mean, where did he get his supplies? He clearly has lots of friends and a large menagerie of friendly beasts. So let us at least venture a hypothesis, because without that, we have no direction. What do *you* think Sam would be doing if not for this problem? Go on, think about it while I fill in a little more about pragmatism.

The Shadow of a Doubt

You already have lesson number one about pragmatism, which is that you would never think at all unless you had a problem, and a problem is nothing apart from the interruption of your usual activity. We can go a little further. Thinking is an activity that is a substitute for bodily activity. What we do when we think is we sort of pretend to act without really doing it—we see how this action or that action will probably come out, and then decide to try it out for real, or we think about a different action and imagine how that one will come out. It may not ever have occurred to you before, but thinking is just acting out in your mind what you might do and then saying either *yes* or *no* to *really* doing it. (Most of the time it's *no*, thank heavens.) If the answer is no, you're still thinking. If it's yes, you're through thinking and now you're acting something out. This can happen very fast or very slowly. But that is *all* thinking really is, as far as we know: thinking is considering what to do. That's why you don't think when you don't have a problem.

With the problems in *Green Eggs and Ham*, though, we come to a sort of moment of truth. Not all problems are equally important, and we can actually be mistaken about whether we really *have* a problem and about *what* the problem is, as well as about *how* we should think about it and *what* we should do to solve it. Some problems aren't *really* problems at all, Peirce said. You can get so used to thinking about this, that, and the other that your habit of thinking can just take off on its own and *invent* problems for you to think about: stuff that isn't really hindering your regular actions. I know you know what I'm talking about here. Chances are pretty good that you're obsessing over something right now that doesn't amount to a hill of beans. These are pseudoproblems, and a lot of problems in philosophy are like that.

For example, you may be convinced that your dog is embezzling from your bank account, and you may even be able to find suspicious bits of evidence that seem to confirm it. People have believed crazier things, after all. And in that case, you certainly *do* have a problem, but your problem is not that your dog is embezzling from you, it's that your thinking processes and your habitual actions have come into an unhealthy relationship. And in fact that is what happens *whenever* we believe something that is false—we have a belief we cannot hope consistently to act upon without eventually coming to grief. So: Does C *really* dislike green eggs and ham? Obviously not. So why does he *think* he dislikes them? Now that is a grand puzzle.

To keep our thinking and our actions in a good, healthy relationship, Peirce suggests that we seek to discover whether any problem before us inspires "real or living doubt" or "genuine doubt." *Genuine doubt* is an "uneasy or dissatisfied state from which we struggle to free ourselves and pass into a state of belief," while *belief* "is a calm and satisfactory state we do not wish to avoid."[1] And that is really the key—if you *don't really* feel dissatisfied, you *aren't* in doubt. You are in belief. Now this sounds so simple, but when you take it to heart, it changes everything. A lot of people want to lead you into *belief* about lots of things, but not many people really want to lead you into *doubt*. In a condition of belief, you will *act on* what you believe. In a condition of genuine doubt, you won't do what anybody says until you are satisfied that you *do* believe something. So, with you and your dog, your problem is not *doubt*, it's a silly belief you've settled into. If your mind is still dissatisfied and uneasy, it's because you doubt the soundness of your belief, not your dog's character. If you really had *no* doubt, you would get rid of the dog, and without regret—try explaining that one to people.

People really get quite upset when you try to inspire doubt in them, which is why so few people set out to do it. One of the glories of Dr. Seuss is that he actually found ways to bring people into doubt without getting them angry, but it is good to remember that he was criticized by a lot of people—some called him a communist, some called him a fascist, some said he hated this or that or some other group, and some people said his books should be banned. They accused him of subverting the minds of children. This is sure evidence that he was inspiring genuine doubt in people, bringing their minds into a constructive and creative state of dissatisfaction. Be warned though: do what Seuss did and you *will* be attacked for it, even if you are loved by many who come to recognize that the uneasiness you brought to them was beneficial.

Sam-I-Am?

Do you have an idea yet about Sam-I-Am? I think that when we know what Sam does the rest of the time, we'll know why it is a problem for him that C won't try the green eggs and ham. So let's brainstorm about Sam. What is he about, and what's with the ova and shoulder routine? Does he do market research for the Associated Egg Producers? For the Pork Industry? Maybe Sam works for the U.S. Department of Agriculture? Maybe he gets a commission? I mean, he must have an angle, right? Is he trying to get C addicted, and the next batch will cost him but the first batch is free? Maybe Sam wants a favor and is softening C up for a request that won't come until later. Maybe it's a bet Sam made with the Grinch. If none of these suggestions has any purchase with you, then you tell me, what's up with Sam? He's just a silly character, you say? Part of the whole reason he is a comic is because no one would go to such lengths to bring a person into doubt about something so silly. The aim is to make us laugh. So maybe you'll say that Sam is not real and his problem is not real.

But I don't believe that, which is to say, I'm experiencing genuine doubt. And here is the reason. If you were right about this, that this character of Sam is just a puff of air, then why do I admire him? Why do I empathize with his struggle to achieve his goal? In short, why do I care about this story? I do care about it, and you do too, if you'll be honest.

Oh, but that gives me an idea, because I remember reading about someone who was a lot like Sam-I-Am. Her name was Saint Monica, and her son became one of the greatest philosophers in Western history. He was called Augustine—Saint Augustine, Bishop of Hippo (354–430)—and he was a handful. He liked the loose life of wine and women and song, and all along Saint Monica stayed as near him as she could trying every day to tell him that he had serious and important work to do in the world and that he should become devout (that's the ham) and pious (that's one green egg) and serious (that's the other green egg). In return, he was mean to her and ignored her and avoided her—in short, he was a contrarian, and worse. But she kept at it, and eventually he found himself in the midst of some genuine doubts. The answers to his problems were the ones she had suggested for decades, and the boy made good. That was over 1,600 years ago and people still read his books, and they even named a city in Florida after him (and one in California after her).

My point is that people sometimes do things as extreme as Sam does, if we don't take the green eggs and ham too literally. What the story teaches is not just trite sayings about perseverance, but rather it shows us something about the structure of learning and knowing about the world. C's problem is precisely that he is too numb and too comfortable. He lacks doubt where it ought to exist, and Sam isn't going to let that situation deteriorate any further. I might also add that C's sitting and reading his newspaper while Sam whizzes by astride a variety of animals taps a psychology every child knows. My father and probably yours too would rather have read his paper than be drawn into a world filled with the nonsense of my imagination, my green eggs and ham. I admire Sam because he finally succeeds in drawing the contrarian out of the world of belief and into the world of doubt, which is the world every child is obliged to inhabit until the habits we acquire render our doubts inert. Thus, I suggest, Sam is your inner child, or at least the shadow of your doubts (if you have a Freudian bent).

Just Don't Make a Habit of It

That brings us to the crux of the matter, which is getting rid of an uneasy mind, irritated by genuine doubts. The struggle is very real and never to be taken lightly. You will never come to a place where you are truly comfortable with *genuine* doubt. What happens instead is that we find ways of avoiding doubt so that we can feel satisfied. The magic of habit is what makes this possible. By doing something over and over, you can ease your doubts. But some habits arise because they help us solve problems, while we acquire others precisely because we can't find solutions and we want substitutes for thinking. I said earlier that thinking is a substitute for action, but it's really a two-way street, because action, especially habitual action, can also be a substitute for thinking. (Remember whatever you may be addicted to when you ponder this, even if it's just crossword puzzles.)

Peirce said: "And what, then, is belief? We have seen that it has just three properties: First, it is something that we are aware of; Second, it appeases the irritation of doubt; and, third, it involves the establishment in our nature of a rule of action, or, say for short, a *habit*."[2] What the curmudgeon is saying is that every belief you have is really a habit of your thinking—remember that thinking is a kind of action. The reason you have the habit is that it eased some doubt in the past. Now that's pretty amazing when you consider it. I believe lots of stuff, personally, and so do you. Every single one of those beliefs is a habit of thinking I acquired because of a doubt I had. Some of those doubts would be pretty hard to discover now, I'll bet.

For example, I believe baseball is better than football. I like both, but I can't ever remember thinking otherwise. I can now guess that maybe somebody once asked me which I liked better, and to solve the problem of the question, I simply chose, and for the sake of consistency I adopted it as a rule. But no, it's deeper than that, which is to say, I *really* believe baseball is better than football and I can give you a hundred reasons. We become more interesting to ourselves when we begin looking at our beliefs as the solutions to our past problems, and it also tends to help us recognize that if not for our past experiences, our firmly held beliefs might be other than they are. We do not, according to pragmatists, develop habits of thinking or action that we don't need at all.

So there you sit, a bundle of beliefs. And the whole story of your life, all the problems you've faced, are embedded right there in your habits of thinking and acting. And there sits C, and he's more than just a little bit unwilling to try the green eggs and ham, isn't he? Stepping away from our admiration for Sam's persistence and the lengths to which he will go to solve the problem he has taken on, we now are free to wonder, why on earth does C *drive* Sam to such lengths just to maintain his self-imposed rule of action—and here we are finally making some serious progress. We know, we all *just know*, that C has never tried green eggs and ham and that he has no good reason to adopt as his rule that he doesn't like them. That is not the real reason he won't eat the free breakfast. So what *is* the real reason? The only clue we have is that he did not wish to be disturbed from his reading and decided to meet the disturbance with noncooperation. His rule of action ("I will not eat them because I do not like them") is arbitrary, momentary, and simply contrarian. It starts as a whim and then becomes a habit as he digs his heels in. Sometimes we say things without thinking and our answers are neither stable nor exactly true, but we become invested in them and cannot easily let them go. To do so brings back not only the original doubt but now also *self*-doubt, as we try to understand *why* we behaved as badly as we did. C is just plain avoiding all that complexity.

Fixing a Belief

Peirce says there are exactly four ways we can arrive at our beliefs—our habits of thinking and acting that ease doubt. Each one has a name. There is the Method of Authority, which is to say that when I am confronted with a doubt, I can do whatever I am *told* to do by those in authority and then I don't have to think it through for myself, and if the problem isn't solved, then it isn't my fault and I can at least avoid self-doubt. You probably have a lot of beliefs that are like this. I know I do. Sometimes if I do what I am told, the problem goes away, but I have to admit that genuine doubt remains, for me at least. A good example is computers, which I don't fully understand. Something goes haywire and the blasted thing won't work, and then the tech support people say "do this, then this, then that," and I do, and it works, but the only rule of action I really learned is "do whatever tech support says." I don't know why the solution worked and I don't know how to vary the solution when the problem comes up again, and this causes me doubt of a very genuine sort. What if, next time, there is no tech support? It's similar in all sorts of situations in life. We can't have all the beliefs we need, and we will always have some based on the Method of Authority, but the trick is not to fall into the habit of believing this is a stable method for addressing doubt. It is a stopgap until you can learn for yourself what needs to be learned.

Sam and C do not have an issue like this. Whatever is going on with C, he isn't saying to Sam "I read somewhere that green eggs and ham are bad for your stomach," or "the king says we shall not eat these." Maybe somewhere in C's childhood there was a traumatic encounter with chickens and pigs and his mother said he must avoid such beasts, and his rule is "always obey your mother," but I seriously doubt this. C seems not to be handicapped in his habits of thinking by an unhealthy use of authority.

The second method of settling our doubts is called the A Priori Method, and it is less common than the Method of Authority. What it means is that we invent abstract reasons for our beliefs that have no clear relationship to our actual experience, and we connect those reasons together to form justifications and arguments for why the thing that has placed us in doubt *must* be thought about one way rather than others. My favorite example of this is the reasoning used by the Monty Python troop to prove that a certain woman is a witch. You may remember it: some peasants and their lord are in dialogue. What do you do with witches? Burn them. And why do they burn? Because they are made of wood. And how can we tell if she is made of wood? If she weighs the same as a duck, because both float in water. And they weigh her with a duck, and she *does* weigh the same, and interestingly, she is in fact a witch. So even though every principle is absurd, every inference silly, they solve the problem. They aren't even wrong in their final conclusion (not to endorse witch burning by any means), but the point is that they used a priori (that just means "prior to experience") reasoning to do it. You can settle your beliefs that way if you like, but the chances of wise rules of action coming from such a process are small. And you won't be able to discover your own mistakes, either. And as with the last method, if you do get it right, you won't know why, and so you really just got lucky.

C's problem with Sam is not due to a priori reasoning. He surely has some kind of bad habit settling his beliefs, but this isn't it. He gives us no reasons at all for his refusal to try what is offered. He doesn't say "Well, if it weighs the same as a duck . . . then, I'll try it." But most people do have some beliefs based on a priori reasoning, and I'm sure C is no exception. It may be that he believes that it is better to be consistent in what you say than to be flexible or adventurous or even cooperative. Being consistent requires that he give the same answer to the same (or similar) questions, and no amount of variation in what Sam offers is important enough to supersede the rule of consistency. That would be the A Priori Method. But it doesn't seem to me that this is how C thinks about the matter.

Yet, before I move on to the next method of settling our beliefs, I can't resist pointing out something about *Green Eggs and Ham* that only philosophers would really love—and many philosophers do love Dr. Seuss, and many want to count him as a philosopher. One thing Sam does in the course of trying C's resolve is to use what philosophers call "modal" arguments. Sam does not say "*do* you" or "*will* you" in the book, but "*would* you" and "*could* you" all the way through—even though C switches back and forth between saying he does not *actually* like them (indicative mood) and saying that he *would* not or *could* not (subjunctive) like them under various circumstances (none of which has very much to do with whether we might like the taste of something, although I admit that eating with a goat could *curb* my appetite).

The reason this little difference in the use of subjunctive mood appeals to philosophers is that the standards of good reasoning are very different when we are discussing what is *possible* as distinct from what is *actually* true. It is very difficult to prove that something is impossible, but proving that something is not actually true is fairly easy. Peirce says that scientific knowledge grows by showing what is actually false. But showing what isn't even possible requires almost godlike knowledge. It is better, pragmatists say, to keep an open mind about what is possible, since plenty of things that were called impossible at some time actually came to pass later. For a pragmatist, none of what C is saying is very convincing because he is making all kinds of pronouncements about what isn't even possible, and the things he says are *not* possible are really *quite* possible. So in a way, C does use the A Priori Method of settling his beliefs about what is possible, and maybe Sam is a pragmatist and really knows he can't lose this argument because C is overcommitted, logically speaking, having claimed far more than he can ever prove.

The third method for settling beliefs is what Peirce calls the Method of Tenacity. Here what we do is simply repeat the same formulas and rules of action no matter what variations we are met with. As with the first two methods, this one works pretty well, as long as your aim is to remove doubt. Many, many people live most of their lives relying on the Method of Tenacity to relieve them of their doubts. But it is unwise. The doubt may go away, but it doesn't have to. It can persist and recur, and every time it does, we have made no progress in solving it because we haven't really even thought through the problem in its own right. Tenaciously clinging to whatever we happen to believe already, especially in the presence of important variations in our circumstances, will lead us to grief sooner or later.

Obviously this is C's main problem. He has no idea whether he likes green eggs and ham, and neither does Sam, and frankly, neither do you. Or I. Or anyone else. C is repeating a formula and just negating every qualification and variation so that his formula stands out. Negating all the variations is what makes him a contrarian, but the reason he will never learn anything this way is because his negations are not motivated by genuine doubt, they are only a means of avoiding the onset of any and all doubt. And that is what the Method of Tenacity does. It preempts genuine doubt by pretending to furnish a satisfied mind in advance of the actual problem. Dr. Seuss and you and I have all encountered people like this, and we have struggled with the same tendency in ourselves. By the time you reach thirty-five or forty, it begins to get difficult not to give in to tenacity. There is a difference between holding on to what you really learned in your life and being tenacious about it, and the difference is whether a person is open to genuine doubt.

And that raises an interesting question. Do you think C *ought* to doubt whether he will like green eggs and ham? I mean, is it important enough to warrant serious consideration? Maybe he has had yellow eggs and pink ham before, didn't like them, and is generalizing appropriately. He doesn't say so, of course, and so he appears to be just a tenacious type, but life is short and there isn't any reason to try every little thing. For example, I am not going skydiving. I don't have a very good reason, I admit. It just doesn't interest me. On the other hand, I won't say "I do not like it," or, even more broadly, "I would not like it if . . . what, with a fox?" And that is where C makes his mistake. If he wants to avoid the Method of Tenacity, the right answer to Sam is, "Look, I haven't tried them, maybe I'd like them, maybe not, but I am not interested either way in finding out." Here one admits to being incurious, but that is probably better than being discovered to be tenacious.

I Stand Corrected

By now you might well wonder whether we can ever develop healthy habits of thinking about the doubts that rob us of our ease of mind. Peirce and the pragmatists say we can always do better than we've done so far, but there is a trick to staying on the right road—Peirce calls it the "road of inquiry." The bottom line is this. To stay on a healthy road you need to be in a position to discover your own mistakes and to correct them when you find them. The trouble with the first three methods is that even though they often succeed in solving certain kinds of problems, the main thing we know is that our doubts disappear. We don't know why, and we don't necessarily know what to do when new problems occur. We cross our fingers and try what worked before.

But the last method is different. Peirce calls it the Method of Science, and by that he means that we formulate the problem carefully in light of the way it has actually inspired doubt in us. This requires very careful thinking about the problems and critical examination of the difference between what is and what is not really in doubt. The Method of Science requires that our hypotheses answer closely to what is genuinely in doubt, and an hypothesis should propose a course of action that will settle belief, but even if successful, it will not be regarded as knowledge. Genuine scientific knowledge is about what was carefully and experimentally tried but which failed to settle belief. How contrarian is that?

The bad news is that if Peirce is right, C still doesn't really know if he likes green eggs and ham, he only knows that eating them settled the doubts in the one context he encountered. Wouldn't it have been funny if, after all that, he tried them and *didn't* like them? In that case, he would actually know more, since the hypothesis offered by Sam, that C would like them, would now be one we could safely treat as having been tried and found insufficient in at least one case. This we could file away for future purposes, and both Sam and C could agree that C doesn't yet like green eggs and ham, but future trials may need to be undertaken to confirm the result. After all, they haven't yet been tried on a plane to Spain.

CHAPTER SIX

~

McElligot's Pool:
Epistemology (with Fish!)

Ron Novy

If I wait long enough, if I'm patient and cool,
Who knows what I'll catch in McElligot's Pool. (Pool)

People believe all sorts of things: that dogfish chase catfish, that coffee tastes better than beer, that over one million people live in Chicago, that no more than nine angels can balance on the head of a pin, that . . . you get the idea. There are really no rules governing what we can believe. However, some of our beliefs are not merely things we believe but are also things we know. What is it that must be added to a belief for it to be knowledge? For example, I could believe that catfish are chased by dogfish, but I cannot know this if for no other reason than that such bewhiskered and floppy-eared creatures don't exist![1] On the other hand, I can know that there are over one million Chicagoans; there is, for instance, a reliable census upon which to base my belief. Figuring out what justifies beliefs—and how it is done—underlies much of our investigation into the nature of knowledge.

So, here's the story: a farmer comes across a boy named Marco fishing in McElligot's Pool and tells him: "You're sort of a fool! / You'll *never* catch fish / In McElligot's Pool!" (Pool). Worse still, the boy is told that the pool is far too small to catch fish and that the locals use it as a trash receptacle. Ever the optimist, Marco replies: "*Cause you never can tell / What goes on down below! / This pool might be bigger / Than you or I know!*" (Pool).

Marco considers the possibility that his little pond is connected to the sea by a great underground river that flows under the highway and under the town. Then, in Seussian rhyme, he begins to list all the sorts of extraordinary fish (plus one gristly lobster and fifty spouting whales) that he might catch in McElligot's Pool: "I might catch a thin fish, / I might catch a stout fish. / I might catch a short / Or a long, long drawn-out fish!" (Pool). But why should Marco believe what the farmer calls "foolishness"? And should we even care, since Marco's belief that there are fish in the pool doesn't seem to harm anyone?

Marco doesn't merely believe there may be fish to be caught, he acts on that belief. As a carefree youth, little more than a sunburn and boredom is riding on the truth or falsity of his belief. But, we can certainly imagine things differently. Say that Marco hopes to catch his dinner in McElligot's Pool. Now, it matters if his belief that the pool is inhabited is true, for without good reason to expect to find catchable fish there, he'd be wasting his time and going to bed hungry.

Given that many of our decisions impact the lives of others, it seems important to not merely have correct answers to any particular question but to have good reasons for them. Doctors Galen, Zira, and Zaius may each diagnose that the farmer is suffering from a migraine, but to determine that the headache is due to dehydration—rather than to a brain tumor or demonic possession—leads to a very different treatment and different quality of life for the sufferer. As a practical matter, this difference requires that beliefs be investigated and justified as our chances of performing right actions (in this case, treating the actual cause of the migraine) increases as mere belief is replaced with knowledge.

Epistemology is the philosophical effort to understand the nature, limits, and sources of human knowledge. An epistemologist asks questions like "What is knowledge?" "Is it possible to have knowledge?" "How do we get knowledge?" and "Of what can we be certain?" While it isn't obvious which of these questions comes first, philosophers have generally focused on sorting out the appropriate link between beliefs and the actual state of the world. In Plato's phrase, "Knowledge is true judgment with an account."[2] Consider Marco's claim that the pool may be well stocked with catchable fish of "Any kind! Any shape! Any color or size!" To say he knows—i.e., to change his "might catch" into "will catch"—requires that it's in fact true that he'll catch such fish and that he has good reason to believe he will. Plato's definition of knowledge, usually restated as "justified true belief," is still with us today. Knowledge requires that what we believe is true and that we can justify our belief that it is true. In this way, the pursuit of knowledge resembles the work of police detectives: it's not enough to get the right man, you also must have the evidence.[3]

Tossing Junk into a Small Pool

If you would be a real seeker after truth, it is necessary that at
least once in your life you doubt, as far as possible, all things.

—René Descartes

Seventeenth-century philosopher René Descartes (1596–1650) asked just
what can be known beyond a shadow of a doubt. He imagined a powerful,
evil genius that has dedicated his considerable power to deceiving him. As
Descartes put it,

> I shall then suppose . . . some evil genius not less powerful than deceitful, has
> employed his whole energies in deceiving me; I shall consider that the heav-
> ens, the earth, colors, figures, sound, and all other external things are naught
> but the illusions and dreams of which this genius has availed himself in order
> to lay traps for my credulity.[4]

Such an evil genius could easily mislead us to believe five is larger than four
(or vice versa); that day-old halibut smells pleasing rather than horribly (or
horribly rather than pleasingly); or that halibut do (or do not) exist at all.
How could anyone have much chance of sorting out the actual from the illu-
sory when every thought we have may well be part of the evil genius's deceit?
The problem isn't merely with figuring out what is (or is not) an illusion but
with figuring out what would count as good reason to accept (or reject) the
"evil genius hypothesis" itself.

Skepticism is the notion that no adequate justification for holding this
or that belief exists (and so concluding that knowledge is not possible). A
"global skeptic" holds that no knowledge on any subject of any sort is possible.[5] To take Descartes's example, since we can never escape the possibility
that the evil genius's mischief stands between our beliefs and the world, we
can never know what is actually the case. On the other hand, "local skeptics"
hold that particular methods of justification fail to properly link our beliefs
to truth. Most of us are skeptics regarding reading tarot cards, tea leaves, or
the lines on the palms of the hand and would rightly dismiss Marco's claims
regarding the fish-bearing capacity of McElligot's Pool. But he tells the
farmer that

> This MIGHT be a pool, like I've read of in books,
> Connected to one of those underground brooks!
> An underground river that starts here and flows
> Right under the pasture! And then . . . well, *who knows*. (Pool)

So Marco's justification for his claiming that there might be fish in McElligott's Pool is that he has read about underground streams that connect seemingly isolated pools to other bodies of water presumably well stocked with exotic fish.

Even if we grant that Marco's book wasn't written by a crank, we know that even the most authoritative volumes sometimes contain errors. This is where the local skeptic risks slipping into the global skepticism camp—since even reference texts sometimes get the facts wrong—and getting the facts wrong was good enough reason to dismiss the powers of aura readers and astrologers as sources of justification. It would seem that we are not justified in trusting any source. Unless some good reason is offered for treating information gained via astrology differently from that gained via textbooks, we risk our local skepticism turning into global skepticism.

Even if Marco's belief regarding the possibility that there are catchable fish in McElligot's Pool was merely wishful thinking, it is testable. That is, we could seek and likely find support for or against Marco's claim: we might simply sit down and wait to see if Marco actually does pull a fish from the water, or we could dive in to look around, or we might drain the pool completely and see what is left behind. Such measures might satisfy us, but not Marco—he is already satisfied that there may be fish in the pool; after all, by the time the farmer arrives on the scene, Marco already has his line in the water. Assuming that Marco has no desire to waste his time and energy, he must have good reason for—that is, be able to give an account of—why he believes that there might be fish in McElligot's Pool.

What You See Is What You Get

Oh, the sea is so full of a number of fish,
If a fellow is patient, he *might* get his wish! (Pool)

Empiricism is arguably the most "commonsensical" of our theories of knowledge; its strength coming from the seeming match between our sense impressions and our ability to get on in the world. Basic empirical beliefs do seem to be reliable in a way that many of our other sorts of beliefs are not; what I know about the open tin of sardines before me—the smell, the glistening dark color, the can's cool, smooth surface—is immediate in a way that my knowledge of the migratory patterns of Pacific albacore or the primary cause of the extinction of the Caribbean monk seal is not. Light waves bounce off the sardines, which in turn trigger my retinas to transmit information through the optic nerve into my brain. In the brain this information is processed, producing information about—and eventual action toward—the tin of sardines. Successful interaction with the world based upon this information justifies the idea that there is in fact a tin of sardines before me. The question for Marco then is, "Does he have good enough reason to justify his inference that there might be fish in McElligot's Pool?"

Empiricism holds that knowledge is acquired through our sensory experience of the world or upon introspection of those experiences. An empirical belief is one that at base is the result of direct experience of the world. So when Marco sees his fishing line bobbing in the water, he is caused to believe that his fishing line is bobbing in the water. Further beliefs not directly experienced are then inferred, such as that there is something below the water's surface pulling at his hook. While Marco infers the possibility of fish in McElligot's Pool from his experience with the book and (presumably) his past experience with fishing, the farmer infers that no fish are to be found because, as he says, "The pool is too small. / And, you might as well know it, / When people have junk / Here's the place that they throw it" (Pool).

But inference is a funny thing—it can't guarantee that the thing inferred is in fact true. Instead, an inference gains and loses strength depending upon those things from which it is inferred. It's possible that that garbage-filled pools *might* be the ideal breeding ground for some fish species—a possibility that shrinks as the farmer encounters similar fishless, junk-filled small pools throughout the area. And it's possible that Marco's book is mistaken; a possibility that would decrease were he to find more references to underground brooks in other well-researched books. And the pool—like Marco imagines—might not be so small after all. Maybe.

As commonsensical as it is, the empiricist approach to epistemology is not without its drawbacks. At least some of these revolve around the difficulty of just how our perception generates and justifies our empirical beliefs. The empiricist holds that when we perceive a fish with a black-and-red "checkerboard belly" we are justified to believe that there in fact is a black-and-red checkerboard-bellied fish before us. This idea that our perceiving a thing to have some property justifies our belief that it does have that property is called "perceptual realism." The problem for the empiricist is to explain just how the latter follows from the former.

"Direct realism" is the idea that the world is more or less just as we perceive it to be—any property perceived to be of a thing is a property of that thing: the fish does have a checkerboard-patterned stomach and that this square is red while the square next to it is black. Were direct realism the case, perceptual realism—and with it empiricism—would be hard to reject as a theory of knowledge. Unfortunately, there is at least one serious problem: how to explain our perceptual errors; say, "seeing" a mirage in the distance on a hot day. Similarly, we watch top-hatted magicians saw their lovely assistants in half and people sometimes hallucinate when extremely tired, starving, or following the ingestion of certain drugs. If the world really is how it appears to be as the direct realist claims, the world would simultaneously have and not have a pool at that distant spot on the road, magicians' assistants would return from the dead, and pink elephants would need to be able to materialize in front of the drunk (then dematerialize before he wakes with a hangover the next day). The senses are not entirely trustworthy, so an account of knowledge based only upon sensory experience needs a way to discern between legitimate experience and hallucination and to connect veridical experiences to the things experienced.

Philosopher John Locke (1632–1704) proposed that objects have two kinds of properties: primary properties that are perceived and are actually in the object (à la direct realism) and secondary properties that also are perceived but are not in the object. These secondary properties instead have the "powers to produce various sensations in us."[6] This "two-properties" approach is known as "indirect realism." Imagine again an open tin of sardines sitting on the table in front of you. It has a variety of grayish colors: here a pinkish blush, there almost a creamy white, and just a little over from that it seems a luminous gray. So what color are the fish in the tin? If Locke is correct, color is all in our perceiving; the delicacy before you has no color. Color, like scent and taste, are "secondary properties," meaning that they are not inherent to the object but are brought to it by the perceiver—no nose, no scent; no eye, no color. On the other hand, some qualities of the tin of sardines really are "in" the object and so are considered "primary properties." These properties, such as size and shape, would be the case even if no one ever perceived it. According to Locke, the tin appears to be a three-dimensional, more-or-less rectangular object about one inch tall because it really is that size.

Unfortunately for the indirect realist, if Locke's correct, the way we perceive the world to be is not how the world really is. The tinned sardines appear to our senses with both primary and secondary properties, and so only some of what we perceive of them can be accurate. Similarly, since we don't seem to be able to perceive the world without secondary qualities like color and taste, we can never directly perceive the world the way it really is—our tools for perception are simply not built that way. So, how do we determine which of an object's properties are primary—that is, not mind dependent? If no properties turn out to be independent of the viewer, we cease to be realists about the world and become epistemological idealists.

What Marco Saw on Mulberry Street[7]

Esse est Percipi ("To be is to be perceived").

—George Berkeley

Bishop George Berkeley (1685–1753) gave us epistemological "idealism," the idea that the physical stuff of the world from whales to farmers, rusty teapots to Sneeden's Hotel is wholly a matter of perception. Imagine gazing deeply into McElligot's Pool and through the crystal-clear water, seeing: "A long twisting eel / With a lot of strange bends / And, oddly enough, / With a head on both ends!" (Pool).

Now close your eyes. There in your mind is the eel—long, striped, two-headed—just as it appeared in the depths of the pool. But wait. Isn't the object of your experience the eel in your head, not the one in the pool? Isn't any knowledge about the eel really knowledge derived from that image, reliant on your senses and a product of your brain? In fact, isn't the eel in the pool unnecessary for any of your knowledge since you're working from that mental image when you describe it as having a head on both ends? When pressed, we might even conclude that we can have no knowledge of the external world but only of our mental representations of it: in other words, our knowledge is about our "ideas." As Berkeley puts it,

> As for our senses, by them we have the knowledge only of our sensations, ideas, or those things that are immediately perceived by sense . . . but they do not inform us that things exist without the mind, . . . if we have any knowledge at all of external things, it must be by reason, inferring their existence from what is immediately perceived by sense.[8]

That our knowledge is not about things of the world but about our perceptions fits well with our understanding of experience: our brain doesn't respond to something in the external world, but rather to stimuli supplied by our sense organs. And yet, most of us would likely not give up on the notion that there is in fact an external world and that we can have knowledge of it.

If with Berkeley, we take all experience to be experience of mental images, there is no right to infer a corresponding external reality. So, how is it that an idealist would explain that each time I look at the first page of *McElligot's Pool*, there is always the same picture of a mustachioed farmer with suspenders and a pitchfork leaning on a fence post? I could close the book for a moment or for a week, and when I look at it again, that page will have the same picture. Similarly, when you describe what you see on that page, it will match the one that I had described. Since Berkeley denies the existence of mind-independent objects, it's difficult to see how your mind and mine (and mine at different times) manage to have identical perceptions of what is on that page. This sort of experience of continuity suggests that the external world exists as more than just perceptions in my mind or yours.[9]

Despite Berkeley's really clever argument, few (if any) people take idealism to be true. That it is "all in our heads" is a bit hard to swallow. As importantly, idealism suffers from the same very big problem as any empirical theory of knowledge: how to justify the inference from the perception of Mrs. Umbroso hanging laundry to her actually doing so? Empiricists assert that what is perceived is caused by reality, but simply saying that it is so doesn't make it true.

Non Sense Knowledge

Cogito, ergo sum ("I think, therefore I am").

—René Descartes

Rationalism shares empiricism's commitment that our knowledge needs to rest upon a set of foundational beliefs but holds that at least some of our beliefs can be wholly justified by our rational intuitions. That is, we can (and do) know things without relying upon any specific sensory experience. Rationalist claims to knowledge are justified *a priori*,[10] meaning that we can have knowledge before our interaction with any particular empirical evidence. A priori knowledge is usually contrasted with empiricism's *a posteriori* knowledge[11]—knowledge attainable only after interaction with sense-based evidence.

Perhaps the most famous example of a priori reasoning is found later in René Descartes's consideration of the "evil genius hypothesis." Recall that given the genius's power of deceit, we would not be warranted to claim knowledge of even simple things about the world, such as that grass is green or that we have bodies (or that grass and bodies exist at all). In this thought experiment, Descartes recognizes that even if he must doubt that he is embodied and that he knows the color of grass, he is undoubtedly doubting—that he is doubting could not itself be doubted. As doubting is a kind of thinking, and thinking requires a thinker, Descartes proclaims, "*Cogito, ergo sum*"—I am thinking, therefore I exist.[12] He understands that the nature of "thinking" is such that for it to occur, a thinker is required. So, since Descartes is thinking, Descartes must exist—a conclusion that can be reasoned to without relying upon sensory experience. Similarly, when Marco talks about the Thing-A-Ma-Jigger, "A fish that's so big, if you know what I mean, that he makes a whale look like a tiny sardine!" (Pool), we can know a lot of things even if we've never had any experience with a Thing-A-Ma-Jigger, a whale, or a sardine. For instance, we know that if they exist they are the sorts of things that can be measured; we can rank them by relative size and we understand the concept "fish," so a Thing-A-Ma-Jigger is some sort of creature that lives in an aquatic environment. Other examples of a priori knowledge include our knowledge that 3,977 is not the largest whole number, that all points of a circle are equidistant from the center, and that the Thing-A-Ma-Jigger cannot be simultaneously purple all over and yellow all over.

Another way to draw out the distinction between rationalist and empiricist theories of knowledge is by understanding the difference between "necessary" and "contingent." Mrs. Umbroso claims that "lungfish breathe." This is the sort of claim the truth of which is necessary. Given the nature of what it is to be a lungfish, to not be able to breathe is to violate what it is to be a lungfish. Similarly, "all bachelors are unmarried men" and "triangles have three sides" are necessarily true, given the nature of bachelors and triangles.

Suppose instead that Mrs. Umbroso made the claim, "To get to McElligot's Pool, Eskimo fish travel farther than Tibetan parachuting fish." The truth of this claim is contingent. Its truth is dependent upon a number of factors: the least of which is that Eskimo fish do in fact travel farther. But its contingent nature runs far deeper than that. Let's say that the Eskimo fish begin their journey at the southern tip of Baffin Island while the Tibetan parachuting fish begin theirs in a stream in the exact center of Tibet. Other things being equal, the statement's truth depends on just where McElligot's Pool is located. Imagine three worlds just like ours except that McElligot's Pool is in a different place on each one: in Norway, in Myanmar, and at an unnamed university in central Arkansas. The truth of "Eskimo fish travel farther than the Tibetan parachuting fish" changes depending upon which of the three versions of earth we are considering. This sort of "possible worlds" consideration is just as useful to pinpoint necessary truths: could the Thing-A-Ma-Jigger simultaneously be yellow all over and purple all over in any possible scenario? No—because the meanings of "simultaneously," "all over," "purple," and "yellow" doesn't change with the move from world to world. Similarly, the aforementioned triangles will have three sides in every world, and in each bachelors will still be unmarried. Statements like those concerning the Thing-A-Ma-Jigger's color, the number of sides to a triangle, and the marital status of bachelors are called "analytic truths"—statements that are true simply in virtue of their meaning. By contrast, statements that are not are called "synthetic truths."[13]

For rationalist epistemology, a very practical problem is that the knowledge attained is not always particularly interesting: "triangles have three sides," "fish are animals," "something which is all yellow cannot at the same time also be all purple," "bachelors are unmarried men," etc., can only get you so far. While the rationalist may know these analytic truths, they are at a loss when we consider access to knowledge of synthetic truths—propositions that we must empirically test. Claims like "universal health care will raise the average quality of life," "Dr. Seuss draws funny-looking animals," and "hot dogs are made largely of waste swept from the slaughterhouse floor" seem to require an empirical investigation to establish their truth (or lack thereof), and this is not a tool in the rationalist's toolbox. And so, the rationalist would be unable to know any of these things.

Rationalism, like idealism and empiricism, is an attempt to escape from the clutches of skepticism. Each seems to be a coherent but less than satisfactory attempt to ground our knowledge in some set of foundational beliefs. While wrestling with these issues remains a large part of contemporary epistemology, a small but growing number of philosophers—particularly feminist epistemologists in recent years—have found themselves critiquing the presuppositions of epistemology's status quo.

Knowledge in a Different Voice

This pool *might* be bigger
Than you or I know! (Pool)

The epistemologies above dominate the Western philosophical tradition. While each has its own strengths and weaknesses, there has also been a counter-tradition arguing that the assumptions underlying these theories of knowledge are seriously flawed. To borrow from philosopher Robin May Schott (1954–),

> Feminist epistemologies are typically critical of the presuppositions of mainstream theories: (1) That the subject of knowledge is an individual who is essentially identical to and substitutable with other individuals; (2) That the object of knowledge is a natural object known by propositional knowledge, expressed in the form S-knows-that-p; (3) That objective knowledge is impartial and value free.[14]

Consider each of these criticisms in turn.

(1) [Mainstream epistemologies presume] that the subject of knowledge is an individual who is essentially identical to and substitutable with other individuals.

As we have discussed epistemology thus far, the person doing the knowing seems to lack any identity beyond that he holds a true belief that is justified in the correct way (whatever that happens to be). This "generic person," though, lacks something important that each of us has and that participates in our having knowledge. He lacks actual experience of the world with its range of differing qualities; we vary in our psychology, in our physical bodies, and in our cultural norms and practices. These differences matter. Put simply, "knowers" are inescapably embodied, social creatures. This "situatedness" is not to say that the world is different for each viewer, but rather that each of us sees the world partially and through our own differently tinted glasses. Marco cannot help but to come to know things with a body and mind shaped by circumstances: he's a boy, is literate, has leisure time, and was born in a particular place at a particular time to particular people.

To have experiences upon which to base our knowledge requires that we perceive with our senses and that our minds give meaning and order to that information. Comprehension is the result of these mental concepts mixing with our perceptions, what philosopher Immanuel Kant (1724–1804) calls "intuitions." Our concepts require experiential content on which to work, and that information is gibberish without concepts to order it. According to Kant, "Thoughts without content are empty, intuitions without concepts are blind."[15] Our concepts can't be separated from our lived experiences, so this experience shapes and colors our "knowledge."

(2) [Mainstream epistemologies presume] that the object of knowledge is a natural object known by propositional knowledge, expressed in the form S-knows-that-p.

The form "S-knows-that-p" does capture much of what we call "knowledge"—you know that you are reading, I know that snow is white, the farmer knows that when people have junk they throw it in McElligot's pool. In fact, a person may not only know something but may also know that she knows it (You know that you know you are reading!). Given this ability to reflect, even if we could list all the things we know, we certainly could never list all the things we know that we know or know that we know that we know or . . . you get the idea.

An epistemology that structures knowledge in this way makes knowledge an all-or-nothing matter: Marco either knows that the residents of Sneeden's Hotel play croquet or he doesn't. And yet often our knowledge of the world is partial or "in progress." One simply doesn't always have or not have knowledge: a month prior to a recital we might say that the pianist doesn't know how to play Beethoven's *Moonlight Sonata*. To gain this sort of knowledge requires practice in the first instance and experience in the second. Similarly, brand-new parents may rush their infant to the hospital each time she cries, but those same parents will quickly learn that some kinds of crying are not signaling a medical emergency but rather that the baby is hungry (or just needs a good belch).

(3) [Mainstream epistemologies presume] that objective knowledge is impartial and value free.

We must remember that it's only within the context of social beings that judgments regarding matters of knowledge can be made. Given we are the sorts of creatures we are, evidence offered to justify a belief is both a matter of discovery and of decision. That we have a gender and are born into a particular socioeconomic class and that we have (or lack) healthy bodies and are the products of unique histories means that our differing values are going to impact our knowledge as well as our theory of knowledge. As the far-from feminist Friedrich Nietzsche puts it in his *On the Genealogy of Morals*,

> Let us, for now on, be on our guard against the hallowed philosophers' myth of a "pure, will-less, painless, timeless knower"; let us beware of the tentacles of such contradictory notions as "pure reason," "absolute knowledge," "absolute intelligence." All these concepts presuppose an eye such as no living being can imagine, an eye required to have no direction, to abrogate its active and interpretive powers—precisely those powers that alone make seeing, seeing something. All seeing is essentially perspective, and so is all knowing.[16]

Despite rejecting the idea that knowledge is something impartial and value free, recognizing this social aspect of epistemology may actually increase our chances of gaining objective knowledge. Recognizing that we each have a perspective means that each of these different sets of eyes sees something a little bit differently, and it may be through the integration of these differing bits that we can have objective knowledge. As with the old story from the thirteenth-century Persian poet Rumi, in the night each man who touched the elephant reports something very different about the thing they have touched: one says a pillar, another a water spout, a third a fan, a fourth a throne. As Rumi writes, "The sensual eye is just like the palm of the hand. The palm has not the means of covering the whole of the beast."[17] While the poet left it unstated in his "The Elephant in the Dark," were these men to share their impressions each would gain fuller knowledge of what he had experienced. After experiencing Marco's point of view the farmer at the end has a look, as if maybe there might be fish in McElligot's Pool. Similarly, Marco has already expanded his own understanding of the possibilities in his situation by reading the book, and his optimism might be tempered a bit by discussing the pool's condition with the farmer.

Or Even a Fish Made of Strawberry Jelly

For there is only one sort of ill fare—the deprivation of knowledge.

—Plato, *Protagoras* (345b)

In this chapter, we have mostly concerned ourselves with normative epistemology; theories of knowledge that take the quality of the justification as what makes knowledge out of our "mere" true beliefs. While empiricism and rationalism dominate the study of knowledge, there are other foundational approaches that were not touched upon, such as Plato's theory that we are born already in possession of the basic foundational blocks for knowledge and through proper education we come to remember these things.

A very different approach to epistemology that has gained traction recently is called "naturalized epistemology." This holds that a belief counts as knowledge if it is the result of an appropriate causal history. In other words, the process by which one comes to have a belief is essential for knowledge. Credited largely to philosopher W. V. O. Quine (1908–2000), naturalized epistemology is in part a response to the failure of various normative epistemologies to answer the problem of skepticism. Quine suggests that epistemologists alter focus from "is there a proper supporting relation between evidence and belief?" to "How does the one cause the other?" According to Quine: "The stimulation of his sensory receptors is all the evidence anybody has had to go on, ultimately, in arriving at his picture of the world. Why not just see how this construction really proceeds? Why not settle for psychology?"[18] In other words, the process by which one comes to have a belief is essential for knowledge. Sketching in just what these proper causal conditions are is a large part of this approach to epistemology. Given the correct conditions, reliable sources may include sense perception and reasoning as with empiricism and rationalism, as well as testimony from a sufficiently reliable authority, like the book that mentions underground brooks.

One might say that epistemology is a history of responses to skepticism. Skepticism—taken seriously—would seem to lead to a certain detachment from the world; that is, to solipsism. Solipsism is the idea that the self is the only thing that can be known, essentially that "I am reality." This denies one's place as a member of a community of persons. Persons who also are wrestling with the human condition: a condition that demands we make sense of the world around us but offers few hints as to where to begin, no signs at the many forks in the road, and no guarantee that anyone has a chance of getting anywhere despite our best and sincerest efforts. Epistemology at its best is hardly a remedy for the human condition, but it can be a foundation for good analysis, better decisions, and right action along the way. Or, as Marco reminds the farmer,

And that's why I think
That I'm not such a fool
When I sit here and fish
In McElligot's Pool!
Any kind! Any shape! Any color or size!
I *might* catch some fish that would open your eyes! (Pool)

CHAPTER SEVEN

On Beyond Modernity, or Conrad and a Postmodern Alphabet

Jacob M. Held

It's always dangerous to summarize a trend or tradition in philosophy, especially in one short chapter. It would be equivalent to explaining Dr. Seuss to the uninitiated with one stanza of one work and a paragraph of explanation. Simply stating that *The Lorax* is about environmental responsibility and then quoting *The Lorax* once or twice can't do justice to the work or Dr. Seuss. But summaries are this way; they must convey a great deal of information in a small space. Authors of summaries know they will fail to convey the necessary depth or breadth for a thorough or perhaps even adequate understanding of the material they wish to summarize. The goal is almost merely to not fail too spectacularly. A summary in philosophy is especially difficult. In order to summarize a tradition of thought one must presume a continuous thread of reasoning or shared pool of ideas among a disparate group of thinkers, each with a unique perspective. In what follows I am going to attempt to provide a quick introduction to Postmodernity, and I only hope I don't fail too egregiously, but if I do at least there'll be some Dr. Seuss sprinkled throughout.

To put it simply, Postmodernity is a movement, one marked by an "incredulity toward metanarratives."[1] If one understands this phrase, one grasps a major thought that defines the postmodern—the driving force according to which I will define it. So this chapter will focus on explaining what it means to be incredulous toward metanarratives by defining metanarratives and "the modern" and then explaining and motivating incredulity, or disbelief.

And although there can be debate about who is postmodern, I will focus on two prominent thinkers with unimpeachable postmodern credentials: Jean-François Lyotard (1924–1998) and Michel Foucault (1926–1984).

So Now I Know Everything Anyone Knows

The subtitle for this section is taken from Dr. Seuss's *On Beyond Zebra!* In this book we follow the narrator and his little friend Conrad Cornelius o'Donald o'Dell. Conrad has just mastered the alphabet. He knows each letter; the sound it makes and what it stands for. "The A is for Ape. And the B is for Bear" (Zebra). He knows all the letters this way, and so he claims to know everything anyone else can know. Why is Conrad so confident? Well, if there are only twenty-six letters, and they are rule bound to make certain sounds and stand for certain things, then knowing them all and their rules would mean one knew everything anyone could possibly know about the alphabet. There would be nothing else to know beyond "Z is for Zebra." The alphabet and its rules, therefore, form a kind of metanarrative, the rules from which all other statements, utterances, or games with letters must follow. If you want to play "I Spy," the rules of the alphabet dictate what letter you'll pick. You can't spy something that begins with "C" and a dog at the same time. All games using the alphabet will follow the alphabet's metanarrative, even if they have their own rules. But it's not just the alphabet that is like this; all language is rule bound and so all discourses, all discussions, are merely so many language games. Every statement is a move in a game. And each game has rules about what can be said, and when, and how it will be understood. Consider Conrad's insight, "So now I know everything *anyone* knows / From beginning to end. From the start to the close" (Zebra). What we can know, that is, what we can legitimate as knowledge is determined by what we can say, and what we say is determined by the kind of language game we are playing. So the rules of the language game, the rules of our discourses, determine what our world is allowed to look like and consist of. If there is one overarching rule for all the games, it is a metanarrative.

A metanarrative is the set of rules or guidelines for legitimating any utterance or statement. As such it would determine how all the other narratives or stories of our lives could be told. It's the mark of modernity to maintain that there is a metanarrative, one Truth that governs all other statements. It's this belief in one Truth that Lyotard wants us to doubt. The existence of or demand for a metanarrative is the demand to subsume all truths under one standard, under one set of rules, and Lyotard finds such a project problematic. Just as the narrator of *On Beyond Zebra!* refuses to be constrained by Conrad's twenty-six letters and makes up his own to go beyond Zebra to Yuzz, Snee, and Floob, so does Lyotard want to expand language beyond its borders to allow for the expression of things currently inexpressible. "The postmodern would be that which, in the modern, puts forward the unpresentable in presentation itself . . ."[2] Assuming there were animals like the Yuzz-a-ma-Tuzz, Glikker, and Wumbus, then the letters Yuzz, Glikk, and Wum would be all that allowed us to express their existence and natures. Without these letters they would be unpresentable; we wouldn't be able to say anything about them, not even that they exist. To restrict our language to twenty-six letters would be to close ourselves off to the reality of Yuzz-a-ma-Tuzzes and their cohorts. If we stopped at twenty-six letters we'd never be able to discuss them, to think about them, to know them. Our world would be smaller and more limited due to our language's inability to capture or express the nature of these things. Our language would fail to express the fecundity of our world. Now we know there are no such things as Glikkers, Wumbuses (or is it Wumbi?), and so forth. But there are experiences people have, there are things they feel, value, or conceive, that they may want to give voice to but can't because our current language lacks the phrases or idioms by which they could express these things. The claim that one narrative, one story could encapsulate and communicate the totality of human experiences greatly underestimates the depth and breadth of the human condition. But to really begin understanding the importance of the function of metanarratives and the need to go beyond them, let's look at the tradition to which Lyotard is responding: modernity. And let's focus on one of its most prominent thinkers: Kant.

Z Is as Far as the Alphabet Goes!

If modernity is marked by the existence of "any science that legitimates itself with reference to a metadiscourse . . . making an explicit appeal to some grand narrative,"[3] then Kant is an exemplar of modernity; a systematizer who sought nothing less than to categorize all areas of human knowledge, evaluation, and judgment in order to provide a coherent, orderly, and exhaustive view of the world.

Immanuel Kant (1724–1804) is most famous as the author of his three critiques of the various faculties of reason: *Critique of Pure Reason*, *Critique of Practical Reason*, and *Critique of Judgment*. Each of these critiques dissects a particular faculty of reason in order to discover its limits and thereby the bounds of human knowledge and experience. As Kant succinctly puts it, "All the interests of my reason . . . combine in the three following questions: 1. What can I know? 2. What ought I to do? 3. What may I hope?"[4]

Kant's goal is laudable. He wants to clearly set the limits of human understanding so we don't persist in error and make unjustified claims so that we can better grasp and thereby navigate the world around us. Each of these areas is fundamental to our lives. Knowledge, ethics, religion, and art are essential to the human experience. One can't do without any of these areas of study, so Kant wishes to clearly delineate their limits so that we conduct our inquiries well, within the natural and inescapable limits of the human mind.

Kant's first critique, the *Critique of Pure Reason*, is about knowledge—what can we know. This critique aims to explain the very conditions under which we can know anything. Kant seeks what he terms the transcendental preconditions for knowledge. That is, what conditions are necessary in order for us to know anything, or in a more simplistic even if anachronistic fashion, how is our brain wired and how does its wiring determine what we can know. According to Kant, the human mind is built in such a way, hardwired so to speak, as to categorize our experiences in certain ways under various concepts such as time, space, and causality within a singular consciousness, or "I." All knowledge comes from our experiences, but all of our experiences come to us through our mind. So our world and everything we can know about it is filtered through our mind first. The basic structure of our mind, therefore, determines the nature of perceived reality or the phenomenal world as Kant denotes it. This process categorizes and connects our experiences according to innate concepts of the understanding, making sure our experiences are coherent, but also by determining that only certain kinds of thoughts will be thinkable. The long and the short of it is, we can only know things we can experience and our experiences are a result of how our brain works. So our brain determines what we can know through determined concepts and categories. Only certain things are knowable because only certain things are thinkable. Anything beyond the limits of the human mind, beyond its concepts and categories, beyond possible experiences, is unknowable.

Consider Conrad. His world is only comprised of twenty-six letters because that is as far as his alphabet goes. It can't go further, and anything beyond Z is pure nonsense, and will remain so as long as he remains within his limited alphabet. This means that Conrad's world is limited to only those twenty-six letters and what he can say with them. His experiences must fit within that framework in order to be coherent, and so knowable. Anything beyond them is unable to be said, unthinkable, and so unknowable. Kant claims to have done nothing short of having defined the alphabet of the human mind and thus the limits of all possible knowledge. Thus he has claimed to have found the limits of our world, our experiences, and basically our lives.

The consequence of Kant's theory of knowledge is significant. If we can only know things of which we could have a possible experience, then the majority of our lives occur on the margins of knowledge. Consider that most of your life is not simply about facts and observations but evaluations built on things like God, souls, free will, dignity, or beauty; things we can't experience and so can't know. For Kant you can't know any of this stuff, not like you can know the sky is blue. For some this isn't problematic. They will just do as they always have done without any worries. But Kant, and philosophy, isn't for these people. Philosophy is for thinkers and people who care about why they believe what they believe and wonder whether they should believe it. For them, this result is devastating. The issues that determine the meaning of our lives are according to Kant unknowable, and this poses a problem—can we speak about right and wrong or religion and beauty with any authority if it's the kind of thing that can't be known? Kant answers with his second and third critiques, *Critique of Practical Reason* and *Critique of Judgment*. Beyond Z there may be certain letters that we are permitted to utter, but they are few and far between and still regulated by laws.

List of Ideas for People Who Don't Stop at the First Critique

We've done plenty of Kant for a Dr. Seuss book, so I'll only worry you with the second critique, the *Critique of Practical Reason*. In the second critique, Kant seeks to ground ethics. This is problematic for Kant since ethics implies free will, and the freedom of our will is not provable. But without free will we can't be held accountable for our actions, and ethics is all about praise and blame. So we need to be able to make claims about our freedom at some level. According to Kant's framework we can't know that we are free. In fact, the more we learn about ourselves the more it seems we're determined by material processes and are in no way free. We're constantly finding new laws of behavior, chemical processes that determine brain states, moods, and so forth. It seems the more we learn the more we appear to be nothing more than complex machines, and machines run on programs over which they have no control. You can't blame a computer, so if we're computers you can't blame us. As we learn more about how we are determined by our material circumstances, do ethics go out the window? Not for Kant.

Kant famously claimed, "I have therefore found it necessary to deny *knowledge*, in order to make room for *faith*."[5] Some things can't be known, but that doesn't mean they are pointless or meaningless. There are certain concepts, certain ideas we are warranted in believing because a holistic, comprehensive, and coherent worldview demands and depends on them. According to Kant these ideas include things like free will and God.

Free will is the idea of an activity that is spontaneous, that has no cause, that isn't guided by the laws of physics, chemistry, or biology, operating within you. If it were rule or law bound you'd be determined by those laws, the mere end result of a series of physical processes determined by the laws of nature. But for ethics we demand freedom; namely, that you can spontaneously do whatever you choose. When we think about ourselves we think about ourselves as law governed, as material beings made up of synapses and serotonin that operate according to the laws of nature. But we also think of ourselves as free; that is, as beyond any laws or determinism. So how can we make these views compatible? Does it make sense to think of ourselves as simultaneously determined material organisms and free? Let's hope so, because without freedom there is no ethics—in fact, there would be no value in the world whatsoever.

Free will, as a concept, seems obvious to all of us. In fact, we may think we experience our free will whenever we choose. We believe that for any action we could've done otherwise. And we feel this quite strongly. But prove it. Prove you could have done otherwise in any circumstance. Prove you could've not read these words. You can claim you could've done otherwise, but there's no way to prove it, and there's no way to experience or verify free will since we only experience the effects but never the spontaneous cause. All we have is the hollow claim, "I could've done differently." But it's impossible to experience our freedom, and so it's impossible for us to know we are free. But yet we believe it to be so, and for Kant this belief is warranted. Why? Welcome to the noumenal world, a world populated with things that not even Dr. Seuss could've imagined, literally.

Since our minds create our experiences by processing data according to its inherent schematic, that means there is a world behind our perceptions that is unknowable, the noumenal world. There is the world we see, that we know, the phenomenal world, and there is the world behind that one. A world we can't see because our minds aren't set up that way. Just as we can't see things in the infrared spectrum even though things exist in it, so does noumenal reality exist even though we can't experience it. This world is unlike anything you can imagine, since all of your imaginings are governed by the laws of your mind, laws like causality. But these laws are just mental constructs our mind places on perceptible reality to give it coherence; they don't really exist. The noumenal world is unlike anything you can imagine or comprehend. Even Dr. Seuss's world looks tame in comparison. All his creatures, kings, and lands, all his oddity and silliness is still law bound. If it weren't it wouldn't make any sense and no one would buy his books. Even beyond Zebra, the Spazzim, Itch-a-pods, and Yekko still exist in space and time, are bound by the laws of causality and possess determinate qualities. They have to. If we are going to have an experience of them, then these experiences will be structured according to the format of our brain. So we can know what the Yekko's howl sounds like, or whether the Itch-a-pods are currently here or there. But noumenal reality is the term given to describe that which lies beyond possible experience, a reality that must exist but which we can't know or even conceive. Whatever noumenal reality is—whatever really lies behind our perceptions—it needn't be law governed, it needn't be bound by cause and effect, it could be spontaneous, it could be free. Free will could exist in the noumenal realm. And just like the rest of reality, at root we, too, are noumenal. We may perceive our bodies as physical and law governed, but that is just the phenomenal reality of our selves; behind that is the noumenal reality we can't experience or know, and that self, our noumenal self, is free. We are free and culpable for our actions, whatever psychologists want to say. And thank goodness, for if freedom goes so does the value of human existence.

Once we get ethics by means of freedom, all sorts of other stuff follows for Kant. The soul allows us to envision our eventual moral perfection, and God and heaven allow us to believe not only that perfection is possible but also that our rewards in the afterlife will be consistent with our deservingness. Thus our ultimate good, happiness in accordance with virtue, toward which we are all naturally driven, is achievable and we can be motivated to be good, even if this life currently is full of pain and suffering. So in addition to freedom we are allowed to believe in God, rewards in heaven, and our ability to earn them as free and infinitely perfectible souls.[6]

Kant doesn't maintain we have to believe this stuff; we're not compelled to since it's not knowledge. But we are warranted to believe it, and if we are going to believe any of it, our beliefs must fit within this framework. He has thus clearly delineated and strictly limited the discussion of ethics and religion according to his epistemology. This is Kant's modernity. This is a metanarrative. What we can know, what we ought to do, and for what we may hope is outlined, restricted, and clearly defined. No one can go beyond. As soon as they do they are speaking nonsense or unjustified and unjustifiable claptrap. This is the modern mind-set that Lyotard and Postmodernity so vehemently oppose. Some wish to go beyond Zebra, beyond Kant to find what lies beneath, behind, or beyond.

Yet for all Kant accomplished, his discourses on the true, the good, and the beautiful were incommensurable. The language you use when talking about knowledge doesn't translate into talk about ethics, and the same goes for beauty and art. So each area, each game, gets its own language and follows its own rules. But what rules you pick for each game and how you interrelate them is a matter of choice. Kant chooses to view humanity as free. He is allowed to and warranted in doing so, but he isn't compelled to. He needn't believe we are free. Rather, if he wants our lives to look a certain way and contain certain values, then he will presume freedom. But that is a choice. That is one way to view the world. It is not the only way.

Lyotard wants greater choices, more diverse perspectives. He wants what he terms the justice of multiplicity and a multiplicity of justices. One finds justice or fairness or respect for all peoples when one opens up possibilities and recognizes the diversity of choices that lead to alternative evaluations of life—new games—and thus alternative meanings for human existence. Such a notion of justice is rooted in incredulity toward the metanarrative offered up by modernity.

For Postmodernity, Kant's values and rules aren't laws of nature beyond which we are incapable of going, they are a chosen way to view the world, one perspective among many. These rules are also limiting. They limit our choices and determine our social reality in a way that can make those on the outside or at the fringes constrained in ways detrimental to them. The Zax are forever stuck because the southgoing Zax can't get past what he was taught in southgoing school, and the same goes for the northgoing Zax. Each is stuck in a worldview about which path is best and how one ought to travel, and because of this their lives are mundane, to say the least. The Yooks and Zooks likewise are caught up in a system of values, bread-buttering values, that cause them to devalue their neighbors and leave them on the brink of annihilation. The Star-Belly Sneetches are caught up in a classist, materialistic worldview that excludes their fellow Sneetches and ultimately leads to poverty and exploitation. Gertrude McFuzz bought into the vanity propounded by her culture and suffered for it. Horton and the *Whos*, the pale green pants, and countless other Seussical creations suffer similar fates. These creatures must either acquiesce to the values handed them or suffer a great deal when transgressing or going beyond the status quo. If they could go beyond they'd find it was a much wider and richer world than they could've ever imagined.

What Do You Think We Should Call This One?

Up to this point we have stuck with Lyotard as our postmodern representative. And Lyotard is really good at pointing out the issue of modernity and the goal of Postmodernity. But there are others who illustrate the value of transgression, of going beyond, quite well. Michel Foucault, taking his lead from Friedrich Nietzsche (1844–1900), does so by placing ideas and narratives within their historical contexts. In so doing he is able to demonstrate that these ideas, taken as eternal truths by their proponents, are just blips on the radar of human culture, contingent aberrations that can and ought to be gone beyond.

A great deal of Nietzsche's work is about discrediting the arrogant claims of philosophers, claims to absolute knowledge. He does so by laying bear the conditions under which this knowledge was generated, accepted as truth, and maintained supremacy. The gist: most of the time claims to truth are nothing short of cloaked assertions of power and mechanisms of control. He uses this method to proffer accounts of Christianity, morality, political values, and other normative, evaluative schemas that have historically been used to ground and value human existence. Nietzsche referred to his methodology as genealogy. He sought to show the lineage of modern ideas so that we could contextualize them in order, ultimately that we might cast them off as antiquated notions of bygone days. It's this project that Foucault continues in his postmodern critique of modern narratives on normalcy from sanity and mental health to criminality and sexuality.

The crux of the genealogical method is the idea that by tracing out the historical foundations and roots of certain truths one is able to show their contingent origins. Our systems of knowledge and understanding as well as our systems of evaluations and standards are shown to be accidental, things could've been otherwise. If things could've been different, then they still can be, and this is important. This is the insight of the narrator in *On Beyond Zebra!* Although his buddy Conrad is a master of the twenty-six-letter alphabet, there could be more letters, there could be new letters, and these new letters could express new ideas, truths, and perspectives on the world. "You just can't spell Humpf-Humpf-a-Dumpfer" (Zebra) without HUMPF. And once one realizes this one realizes there is so much they don't and can't know when they refuse to go beyond Z. To stay within the given twenty-six-letter alphabet is to stay within somebody else's view of reality, a limiting and narrow view at that, one without the Wumbus and Umbus, one without Quandary and Thnadners. For Foucault, as for Nietzsche before him, life is about experimentation and ought to be lived dangerously, on the borders. Now we can't find Wumbuses, but we can go beyond Kant to perceive our world outside of or beyond his system, beyond modernity and its truths and values.

Consider one of Foucault's favorite topics: the medicalization of our lives. As Foucault points out, all we do and all we are is defined and redefined by various medical professions until we become nothing more than a list of disorders, dysfunctions, and prescriptions. One need only read *You're Only Old Once!* to get the gist of the problem. We're continually poked and prodded and told what is wrong with us; we're all given our "solvency" tests. Then we're prescribed a regimen of "pill drills" in order to get us in line with the current standard of health. And this is our permanent state until "at last [they] are sure [we've] been properly pilled" (Old). But we're never properly pilled because they always seem to find new disorders and develop new pills for these new problems. Now, clearly, for some things like cancer this is true. Cancer is bad. But what about other areas of our life, areas with no obvious standard or clear better or best? What about mental health or sexuality? How sad is too sad? How happy is too happy? What spectrum do you fall under and where? Is your place on this new scale a disorder that needs to be fixed? Are we "fixing" you merely so you can function in a society you've been thrown into, a society that itself might be sick? Are you too creative, too hyper, too independent, or simply too spirited to be able to sit still for eight hours a day doing mundane tasks for no clear purpose? If so, it's not your environment that's out of whack, you're the problem. But don't fret. They'll fix you right up. Dr. McMonkey McBean will diagnose your "disorder" and then he'll throw handfuls of pills at you, pills produced by an industry that oddly enough had a hand in discovering, defining, and describing the very "disorder" you now seem to have. And this procedure will continue until you're an adequately functional member of society, even if that means a dull and listless human being.

But what does it mean to be "functional" anyway? Do they just want you to behave within standard parameters so you can hold down your humdrum workaday job and life, or perhaps perform well at the standardized mind-numbing tasks that occupy the majority of the school day? Should this be the standard we live our lives by? There are so many questions and too many people ready to give us answers. Maybe it's time we ask some questions: Who put you in charge? Why is your way the best?

Or consider sexuality. Now obviously Seuss didn't deal with this issue in any of his books. I can only imagine the puns, word play, and menagerie that would attend a Seussian dialogue on sex and gender. But maybe that is how we ought to think about this topic. One thing Foucault is adamant to point out is that the very idea of gender and sex is a result of medicalizing human behavior. We diagnose you as straight or gay or bi. We demand that you categorize yourself, so we can prescribe the appropriate behaviors or condemnations. We figure out how you ought to behave, what is healthy, normal, and well adjusted. But gender is a construct. The idea that girls do one thing and boys another is so preposterous that its prevalence can only be explained as a mechanism of con-trol reinforced and maintained because we refuse to stand up against it. As one scholar noted, "One is not born, but rather becomes, a woman. No biological, psychological, or economic fate determines the figure that the human female presents in society; it is civilization as a whole that creates this creature."[7] It's not the case that all women are or need to be any particular way. The same goes for the rest of us. The world is populated by individuals. The group or categories we lump them into are often artificial creations that can and ought to be fought against. People are too different, too diverse to be categorized so simply as this or that gender. Such a simple construction is the result of simple minds, not evidence of a simple, ordered universe. So maybe a Seussian sex menagerie, as odd as it would be, would be enlightening and more a mirror of reality: ambiguously gendered creatures that float between and within catego-ries, each its own unique being navigating a maze of roles and positions in order to merely be the kind of thing that it is, regardless of whether it can be easily compartmentalized. Girls who like girls, and boys who like boys, or girls who like boys who like girls who like toys.

An additional point Foucault makes with respect to sexuality is how our discourse on it controls it. We don't control sex by not talking about it. Rather, we control sex and behavior by talking about it a great deal.[8] How we talk about it is a way of controlling it. We delineate what can and can't be said, what is appropriate behavior and what not, a knowledge, or science, a discourse on sexuality that exercises control over it and thus control over us. Talking about things is how science or discourses of knowledge categorize and understand them in order to control and regulate them. Now there is a lot of politics in Foucault and I could go on and on, but I think I've made his point for him: knowledge is power, power over the world, and so liberation or freedom comes from refuting and rejecting such systems of knowledge, systems that seek to control us but which are historically relative. The world can be otherwise.

On Beyond Metanarratives

We all live within boundaries. Geographically, we live in cities in states in countries on earth. With respect to the values by which we judge, value, and live our lives we also live within boundaries, conceptual boundaries. We have expectations and evaluations foisted on us as men or women, moth-ers or fathers, sons or daughters, expectations based on our faith traditions, conceptions of health, sexuality and gender, occupation, culture, and so on. Insofar as these values are constitutive of who we are and are important to our sense of self, we follow the instructions of doctors, teachers, lawyers, parents, priests, accountants, and society in general. We do so hoping that we will live a highly, or adequately, functioning life. All these boundaries serve the same purpose—they organize and categorize the world around us and thereby our lives.

To some these boundaries are comforting. They provide meaning and purpose. They are comforting because they provide security so long as we stay within their limits. Conrad can know everything in his world so long as he stays between A and Z. How nice to know everything, how safe. And he'll be told he's smart for knowing all there is to be known, and he'll be rewarded when he says "A is for Ape." He'll never have to be uncertain, uncomfortable, or confused again. Boundaries let us know what we ought to do, and being told what to do is comforting and probably important at some level. Kids need boundaries in order to feel safe. But the purpose of making a child feel safe is so that they can feel secure while exploring and growing. So boundaries can be beneficial, but they aren't impregnable. Once we have grown it's time for us to explore, and that means going beyond Z, past our boundaries.

Conrad realizes the benefit of going beyond Z once the narrator drags him from his dull classroom into a limitless world. There will be challenges beyond Z. New things require new skills, and sometimes we'll fail. Beyond Z lies Zatz, which is used to spell Zatz-it, and "If *you* try to drive one / You'll certainly see / Why most people stop at the Z / *But not me!*" (Zebra). Conrad can't know what a Zatz-it is, nor can he drive one. But his world is broader for having added Zatz to his alphabet, and zatz the point. Postmodernity shows the limits of our world so that we might transgress them. We see the boundaries so we know where we can go when we choose to venture out into the wilderness.

Lyotard discusses the border lands as the *pagus*, that place where the village ends, a place of boundaries, ceaseless negotiations and ruses.[9] As pagans we recognize a multiplicity of justices and the justice of recognizing multiplicity. "Justice here does not consist merely of observance of the rule; as in all the games, it consists in working at the limits of what the rules permit, in order to invent new moves, perhaps new rules, and therefore new games."[10] Foucault makes this multiplicity real by showing us alternatives, or rather the fact that boundaries are traversable. Things could've been otherwise, so they still can be. So we should be incredulous when someone says this is the way it is and always has been, or this is the only way it should be. In the end isn't this also why we read Dr. Seuss, and especially why we read him to children. We want our children to be questioners and adventurers, not automatons, a child that simply meets everyone else's expectations.

Postmodernity doesn't seek to discover and communicate eternal truths. Postmodernity expresses a perspective, a point of view of a doubter, questioner, and adventurer. The Postmodern is about limitlessness. This perspective is often uncomfortable for the same reason Socrates' questioning was unsettling; it requires that we always admit our ignorance while valuing the journey. It takes courage to walk beyond the boundaries and begin negotiations with the unknown. But this approach makes up for its lack of certainty with its beauty, a style of life worth living. It's okay to head straight out of town and into the *pagus*; remember, "it's opener there in the wide open air" (Places).

~

CHAPTER EIGHT

From There to Here, from Here to There, Diversity Is Everywhere

Tanya Jeffcoat

So often, when people talk about diversity they immediately start worrying about political correctness and thought police. But respecting diversity is about recognizing the cultural diversity surrounding us and analyzing the ways we treat people who are in any way different than us. And those differences are often so slight that strangers might not even recognize the distinctions—after all, to a stranger a Sneetch is a Sneetch. But within Sneetch society, the presence or absence of a star becomes a marker that determines the lived experience of each individual Sneetch. Whether according to skin tone, nationality, gender, sexuality, or possessions, humans exhibit the same sort of in-group/out-group behavior as the Sneetches. And, as Frantz Fanon so vividly points out,[1] there are physical as well as psychological ramifications for those deemed as out-group, far beyond "moping and doping alone on the beaches" (Sneetches).

Too often, the anger and depression associated with being a member of the out-group becomes desperation to join the privileged, even if it means forgetting (or despising) what we are. The Plain-Belly Sneetches modify their bodies to fit the ideals of the Star-Belly Sneetches, and humans likewise turn to a variety of "Fix-It Up Chappies" for alterations toward some total-izing norm or standard against which we must conform. Some turn to skin lighteners or plastic surgeries, while others attempt to purge their accents or deny their sexual preferences, and yet others sacrifice their families and their health in their attempt to climb the socioeconomic ladder, but, to one extent or another, all have fallen prey to the totalizing, one-size-fits-all tendencies and the normative hubris of the status quo. Dr. Seuss recognizes the harms that humans visit upon one another based upon such beliefs, yet still finds hope that "We can . . . and we've got to . . . do better than this."[2]

If we're to do better, then we must determine what stands in our way. The first obstacle is normative hubris, which is the arrogance that assumes that one way—OUR way—is the best way, not only for ourselves but for everyone else. Every society has norms or standards; without them, societies couldn't function. But there is a difference between noticing that different communities drive on different sides of the road and making the claim that WE drive on the correct side of the road (or the more logical or morally superior side) and that everyone who does differently is wrong, illogical, mentally warped, or immoral, even if their way of doing things works just fine.

We see normative hubris in *The Butter Battle Book*, as the Zooks and the Yooks both are absolutely certain that their way of buttering bread is the best and only way to do so. Each group assumes the other is somehow inferior for having made a different cultural choice: The Yooks go so far as to claim that "you can't trust a Zook who spreads bread underneath! / Every Zook must be watched! / He has kinks in his soul!" (Butter).

Normative hubris thus provides the first stumbling block to doing better, but it sets the stage for totalizing tendencies to develop within people. Once people decide that their way is the best way and that those who don't agree are somehow essentially inferior, it becomes all too easy to justify discrimination and persecution. The most obvious examples of this totalizing tendency are probably political and religious persecution, but we find it whenever people are discriminated against for not living up to societal ideals of masculinity or femininity, for instance, or for refusing to stay in the closet and pretend to be something they are not. It occurs when those in authority or in the majority tell minorities that they are somehow inferior because their culture and ethnicity does not fit the norm but that they *might* be better accepted if they did a better job of conforming. In all these cases, one group—the one with power—insists that others either conform or be shunned or persecuted.

But Seuss provides another option to totalizing tendencies. Even in *Happy Birthday to You*, Seuss emphasizes the importance of recognizing that "I am I," different and vital in a unique way from all those other individuals in society, or as he proclaims, "There is no one alive who is you-er than you!" (Birthday). In doing so, Seuss promotes a pluralism that encourages the individual to be something apart from those totalizing tendencies that continually try to mold people into a preset pattern and reject anyone who appears different than the norm. The lesson is an important one to learn because, for each of us, life is a continual encounter with the Other, individuals and groups who aren't just like us.

Caught in the Snide: Encountering the Other

As we go through our lives, we often meet people who seem different than us, and many times our hearts start thumping and we try to get away as quickly as we can, even if it means losing our Grin-itch spinach, spending the night getting Brickel bush brickels in our britches, or trying to hide in a Snide bush (Scared). But there are other options we have when we encounter the Other. We can shrink back in fear and work to maintain our distance, but we can also realize that perhaps we aren't as different as we first imagined, or at least that we can still form friendships despite our differences, even if the Other is a pair of empty, pale green pants. Unfortunately, we can also think of ways to exploit the Other, perhaps by treating the Other as a thing or an object for our benefit. When we do so, we form an I-It relationship because we aren't treating the Other as fully human and deserving of the same considerations we expect for ourselves.[3] In treating the Other as somehow less than, we take the first step toward exploitation and dehumanization. Slavery couldn't have been possible if the slaveholders truly believed that the people enslaved were equal. Similarly, King Yertle, in forcing his subjects to function as his throne, treats them as objects instead of citizens and proves that he doesn't care that they "are feeling great pain" and doesn't believe that those "down on the bottom . . . too, should have rights" (Yertle). Yertle shows that he is interested only in his own power and status and is willing to use those he sees as Other as a means of securing both, no matter how his pursuit might undermine the happiness and possibilities of those he rules. This attitude appears in many types of discrimination, but all types start with someone believing that someone else is different and somehow deserves less because of it.

So dehumanization (an attempt to strip away someone else's humanity, human dignity, and/or human rights) is one possible response to the Other, but so is humanization, which Paulo Freire calls humanity's vocation, or calling. Freire also believes that the people who have been dehumanized are the ones best able to see the need for social changes; after all, they are the ones most directly damaged by dehumanizing conditions. When you haven't been on the receiving end of discrimination, it's easy to underestimate its harm, or even to assume that it doesn't exist, at least not anymore. There is a certain blindness of the privileged that must be overcome if we are to act in humanizing rather than dehumanizing ways. The Star-Belly Sneetches, with their beach games and frankfurter roasts, took no notice of the Plain-Belly Sneetches around them and thus didn't realize the alienation and despair that the others felt. It is only when they lost their status (and money to Sylvester McMonkey McBean) that they begin treating everyone as equal. Until then, they took their privilege for granted, assuming that they were deserving of special treatment and that the others were not.

Peggy McIntosh takes up the problem of blindness and attempts to find ways of seeing better in the hope of thereby doing better. She claims that one reason we don't pay more attention to the discrimination around us is because most of us are taught *not* to see it or the ways that we have privileges that others do not share. Most of us are taught that there is equality of opportunity, but when we look closer at society, we can see problems with this belief. Some of us, like the Star-Belly Sneetches, are born into wealthy families, while others of us are so poor we don't have enough food to eat. Do the children born into poverty have the same opportunities as the kids of the superwealthy? McIntosh doesn't think so. Instead, she argues that it's like we each wear an invisible knapsack containing items that help us out and that unfairly privilege us over others. For instance, she thinks that because she's white and heterosexual, she hasn't faced the types of discrimination faced by those who aren't. To better help her understand discrimination and privilege, McIntosh has written lists of things she doesn't have to worry about, simply because of her race and sexuality. As an example, McIntosh says that unlike many homosexuals and racial minorities, she "can be reasonably sure that [her new] neighbors . . . will be neutral or pleasant"[4] when she relocates. Because of her privilege, she has a mobility that others lack. Like the Star-Belly Sneetches, she has both access and acceptance into places where others are shunned. But until she slowed down, paid attention, and wrote her lists, McIntosh wasn't aware of the extent to which she was privileged and others were disadvantaged. This is the blindness that Freire points to, and it is one of the problems that the philosophy of diversity attempts to address.

Being on the receiving end of discrimination causes a number of problems; for instance, the Plain-Belly Sneetches were unable to join in with the elite of Sneetch society, and they suffered both physically and psychologically because of it. Frantz Fanon speaks as someone relegated to the status of the Other, and he details the oppression that results. In particular, he describes the anger, fear, depression, and alienation that so often accompany discrimination, and he expresses the need for what he calls disalienation, which is the process of overcoming alienation.[5] Drawing upon Fanon, Sandra Bartky discusses the psychic violence done to those deemed Other, arguing that the psychologically oppressed internalize the negative stereotypes and assumptions about themselves in ways that are "dehumanizing and depersonalizing."[6] For instance, "suppose that I, the object of some stereotype, believe in it myself—for why should I not believe what everyone else believes? I may then find it difficult to achieve what existentialists call an authentic choice of self, or what some psychologists have regarded as a state of self-actualization."[7] We have all seen children who have been shamed and ridiculed to the point that they refuse to participate in activities that might lead to further abuse, regardless of their actual abilities, something we see in "The Sneetches" as the Plain-Belly children stand back and watch the Star-Belly activities that they know they can never join. The children's own anxiety, depression, and self-blame will keep them from putting themselves into positions where they might fail. Until they overcome the "internalization of intimations of inferiority,"[8] they will continue to "exercise harsh dominion over their own self-esteem,"[9] and their lives will suffer because of it. Psychological oppression functions this way, with individuals absorbing negative views about themselves and living truncated or limited lives because of it.

One possible outcome of such psychological oppression is self-commodification—the packaging and selling of oneself—as a means of becoming acceptable to those in power. When we do this we are no longer alienated from just the larger community; we become alienated from ourselves because we no longer behave according to what we are and what we want, but what society wants us to be. We see this in the Plain-Belly Sneetches' eagerness to alter their bodies to gain access to social privilege. Sylvester McMonkey McBean preys upon their feelings of inferiority and convinces them that by buying stars and altering their bodies they can buy the status they crave. They discover, however, that such self-commodification rarely works, since those in power will simply change the rules so they can keep their status. In turning to self-commodification, the Plain-Belly Sneetches embrace stereotypes and behaviors that undermine actual equality and empowerment. Only when those in power lose their status (by losing their money) are the Sneetches able to create a just society.

We see all these problems and more in *Daisy-Head Mayzie*. In this story, Seuss presents the typical ways in which people respond to the Other: horror (the teacher, who snatches up the little girl and rushes her from the classroom), problematizing (the principal, who decides Mayzie is a problem to be fixed), "scientific" objectification (the scientist, who forgets Mayzie's humanity as he reduces her to a mere object of study), persecution (the mayor, who wants her driven out of town), normalization (the florist, who wants to prune her back to the norm), and commodification (the agent, who sees her simply as a means of making money). No one asks young Mayzie what she wants, and in response to her new status as Other, Mayzie herself exhibits the very behaviors philosophers concerned with diversity describe: alienation, depression, and self-commodification.

Hearing the Other:
A Person's a Person, No Matter How Small

But there are other possible responses to encountering the Other. Horton the elephant, despite his own size and power, hears the plight of the Whos and recognizes that "a person's a person, no matter how small" (Horton). He decides that these "little folks [h]ave as much right to live" (Horton) as anyone else, and he devotes himself to saving the Whos from the best efforts of all those around him. In standing firm against the animals of Nool, Horton exhibits the true generosity that is so rare among those not subject themselves to discrimination and persecution.

Of course, just as society shuns the Other, it also tends to turn on those who stand with the disenfranchised. The animals of Nool quickly decide that Horton is "out of his head" and must be stopped from his "irrational" behavior of protecting the dust speck that serves as home to the Whos. They move to rope and cage Horton, and it's only the unification of Who voices that allows them to be heard. Horton, despite his size and power, cannot save himself or the Whos once he becomes their ally, not until the people of Nool are forced to hear and acknowledge the Whos. Once the Whos unite their voices, they exhibit the "power that springs from the weakness of the oppressed."[10] They are powerful because they know what is at stake, which enables them to put all their energy into their fight for justice. In doing so, they fight not just for their ideals but their very survival. It's this power that is "sufficiently strong to free both" the Whos and Horton, as well as releasing the people of Nool from their own arrogant assumptions.[11]

The Lorax provides another example of someone who speaks for those unable to speak for themselves or be heard.[12] When the Once-ler first starts cutting down Truffula Trees, he sends shockwaves throughout the entire area with his biggering and biggering. The Lorax, who speaks for the trees and for all those creatures interconnected with them, shouts out his warning until the last Truffula Tree falls, long after the Brown Bar-ba-loots, Swomee-Swans, and Humming-Fish have migrated in search of healthier climes. It's the Lorax who understands with Martin Luther King Jr. that "We are caught in an inescapable network of mutuality, tied in a single garment of destiny."[13] When the Once-ler takes the Truffula Trees, the damage stretches far beyond the individual plants. Like the Once-ler, we too often segment the world and ignore the network of mutuality in which we exist. When one portion of our community suffers, the damage runs deeper and broader than it first appears. For instance, as poverty levels rise, so do crime and disease rates. Educational levels fall, exacerbating the problem even further. The social and economic ramifications spread into the larger community, and, in most cases, the process rolls on. Too late, the Once-ler realizes that "UN- LESS someone like you / cares a whole awful lot, / nothing is going to get better. / It's not" (Lorax). Seuss, like King, knows that "[i]njustice anywhere is a threat to justice everywhere,"[14] and Seuss's stories show a belief that we can act with an eye toward justice and build a better world.

You Do Not Like Them. So You Say. Try Them! Try Them! And You May (Eggs)

It's easy to fall into the trap of normative hubris because most of us don't really pay attention to the people around us or even to ourselves. We don't slow down and think about the stereotypes that we believe or pay attention to the implications of our own words and actions. We don't learn about those people that we consider the Other. Most of us don't want to know about the violence and discrimination in our local communities, so the victims become almost invisible—about as difficult to spot as the *Whos* down in *Who*-ville. We assume that our way is the best way because we don't *really* know of any other way. Honestly, for most of us, we don't know our way very well either. We just do what we've always done, which is to conform to the status quo, or the way things already are. Philosophy focused upon diversity makes us slow down and pay attention to these elements that we so often ignore. In doing so, it attempts to replace hubris with a humility that recognizes that all of us, as individuals and as communities, have something unique to offer, that there are times when we all fall short of our ideals but that we can do better if we're willing to try.

Another way in which the philosophy of diversity undermines norma- tive hubris is by emphasizing the fact that American society has been mul- ticultural from the beginning. Because of this, understanding ourselves as Americans means examining the ways in which various groups have come together and contributed to the building of this country. We're a country of many types of people, people with different political and religious views, different cultural identities and races, sexual orientations and social classes, educational levels and favorite sports teams. Given our differences, it becomes ever more difficult to support the belief that there is one way that is THE WAY for everyone.

Besides highlighting privileges, discrimination, and minority contributions, the philosophy of diversity often examines our ideals and how we have both lived up to and have unfortunately fallen short of them. Our Declaration of Independence sets forth the basic creed of our country: "We hold these truths to be self-evident, that all men are created equal; that they are endowed by their Creator with certain unalienable rights; that among these are life, liberty, and the pursuit of happiness." And the plaque upon the Statue of Liberty captures our recognition of ourselves as primarily a nation of immigrants: "Give me your tired, your poor, / Your huddled masses yearning to breathe free, / The wretched refuse of your teeming shore. / Send these, the homeless, tempest-tossed to me, / I lift my lamp beside the golden door!"[15] Our national ideals call upon us to live lives devoted to equality and openness, yet we often fall short of this calling. When we examine our heritage—our ideals, our successes and our failures, and the diversity from which we spring—we see more clearly and are hopefully better able to avoid the normative hubris and totalizing tendencies that undermine the very values upon which this country was founded. Then we can start building a community that recognizes and respects us all, Horton and Wickersham, kangaroo and *Whos*.

Stewing a *Who*, or Isn't It All Relative?

Many people claim that respecting diversity makes it impossible to make moral claims, especially across cultural lines. After all, if we want to avoid normative hubris and totalizing tendencies, who are we to say that someone else's practices are wrong? Some of us are vegetarians while others are omnivores. In Star-Belly circles, it seems obvious that the Plain-Belly Sneetches are inferior, and Horton wants to protect the *Whos*, even when all of his neighbors think he is insane. If we are supposed to respect diversity, what's wrong with Sneetch culture uplifting the Star-Bellies or with the people of Nool stewing the *Who*?

Two types of relativism are relevant here. Descriptive relativism simply notes that different cultures have different practices. Some cultures strive to achieve gender equality, while others explicitly state that women are subordinate to men, for instance. But normative (or moral) relativism goes further by claiming that cultural norms are culture specific and cannot be adequately judged outside of that particular milieu. However, does a respect for diversity mean that we must accept moral relativism? Even if my basic understanding of myself is that "I am what I am," does this mean that whatever I think is good is in fact good for me or that I don't have a responsibility to be better than I am? Seuss doesn't think so. For instance, despite Jo-Jo's preference for yo-yoing, he must set aside his toys and work to save his community when it is endangered, and Mayzie, that fun-loving fowl, loses all claim to her child when she abandons her egg in favor of sun and surf. We exist in a world that requires moral decision making, and the philosophy of diversity must address this need while trying to avoid normative hubris.

Two approaches seem to allow for moral decision making while respecting diversity. The first is captured by the Universal Declaration of Human Rights, which states that "[a]ll human beings are born free and equal in dignity and rights. They are endowed with reason and conscience and should act towards one another in a spirit of brotherhood."[16] Because all humans have inherent rights, we can stop practices that undermine those rights. While this work expresses a respect for cultural differences, it also allows us to make moral judgments against those practices that undermine individual rights without necessarily falling prey to normative hubris. For instance, ending slavery did not destroy Southern culture, but it set in motion changes to better ensure that everyone's rights were valued. Southerners still drink iced tea and have biscuits and gravy for breakfast. Pickup trucks and cowboy boots aren't going anywhere. But now a group of people who had no recourse can demand that their rights be respected, just as the *Who* now have a voice among the citizens of Nool.

A second approach appears in John Dewey's discussions of morality and growth. Dewey (1859–1952), an American Pragmatist, rejects the idea that rights are unalienable, arguing that the rights of humanity have instead resulted from social development as individuals have become dissatisfied with tyranny and have struggled against it. By viewing rights as inherent, we can easily lose sight of our need to continually work toward ideals of social justice. According to Dewey, this work must center upon our daily activities, for he defines democracy as "a personal way of individual life."[17] In Dewey's day, as well as our own, people claim to believe in democracy while living lives out of step with democratic ideals, and oftentimes in ways that undermine democratic values: "Intolerance, abuse, calling of names because of differences of opinion about religion or politics or business, as well as because of differences of race, color, wealth or degree of culture are treason to the democratic way of life."[18] Each of these activities divides communities and undermines civility, critical inquiry, and communication, all of which are necessary components of democracy. If we want healthy communities, we must work to ensure that the individuals within them can thrive. For Dewey, those activities that undermine individual and community flourishing should either be discarded or reconstructed, and those people who perform such activities should be found blameworthy.

Because we are tied together, the consequences of our ethical choices extend into the larger community. Some place more value on the environment, while others value economic growth, and regardless of our policies, all are influenced. Becoming aware of and respecting diversity does not mean that we can dismiss ethical considerations as simply being a matter of opinion. As Anthony Weston points out, "Even if moral values vary all over the map, there is no way out of some good hard thinking."[19] The philosophy of diversity and the works of Dr. Seuss call into question the normative hubris and totalizing tendencies so often present when we avoid this thinking, and in doing so they promote values of equality and openness to other ways of living without falling into relativism. Dr. Seuss's works continually remind us of the richness of human experience. As he reminds us in the voice of Marco, "This [world] *might* be bigger / Than you or I know!" (Pool).

~

CHAPTER NINE

What Would You Do If Your Mother Asked You? A Brief Introduction to Ethics

Jacob M. Held and Eric N. Wilson

Many of Dr. Seuss's stories illustrate aspects of our moral lives. It's not hard to see the moral messages reflected through the Sneetches, Horton the elephant, the Lorax, and many others. These works, as overtly ethical yet accessible to even the youngest readers, help illuminate various aspects of philosophical ethics. And the connections among many of Seuss's stories and classical ethical theories are illuminating insofar as they help readers of all ages make sense of often difficult or seemingly impenetrable moral quandaries.

Philosophical ethics itself is the study of right and wrong. It's our attempt to answer the question "What should I do?" There are innumerable answers to this question. For those familiar with ethics, it often seems as if there are as many ethical theories as there are ethical theorists. There are so many theories, in fact, that it can appear at times that there is no one answer that will suit all people or that could possibly be the best among so many choices. In what follows we are only going to look at a few. We'll look at the deontology of Immanuel Kant, John Stuart Mill's utilitarianism, and the virtue ethics of Aristotle. But even this diversity may raise an eyebrow or two. After all, if powerhouses like Kant, Mill, and Aristotle each have their own theory, how are we supposed to decide among them? These are supposed to be the best and brightest in the philosophical canon and they can't agree, so how are we supposed to solve the problem? What hope is there for us?

This kind of doubt and skepticism that there is a right or wrong is often given voice in our lives when we hear someone ask "Who's to say?" or "Who gave you the right to judge?" These types of questions evince the attitude that there is no right or wrong, it's all just personal. This is an easy attitude to fall into; it's all relative.

Does It Matter on What Side I Butter My Bread?

In ethics, there has been a commitment to discovering and defining "the good." The good, for a philosopher, is synonymous with defining a fundamental set of rules or principles that equally apply to all people. Discerning right and wrong for the philosopher depends on determining the underlying structure of morality and bringing it out in the open. Thus, a defining feature of ethics is the discovery of those characteristics of the moral life that are representative of and applicable to humanity as a whole. However, some have claimed that such a task is by its very nature limited or even doomed to failure. Their reasoning often depends on the fact that at some point when two cultures or two people (or two Zax) whose core beliefs are fundamentally different meet there is an intractable disagreement about those core beliefs and values. Because both parties seem to be fundamentally at odds with each other and neither is in a place of authority, there is no way to decide between the two, thus, we are forced to admit that both sets of beliefs or values are equally valuable (neither the northgoing nor southgoing school being the "right" school to attend) and our only recourse short of forcing our view on the other is tolerance and respect (or even standing still). Variations among peoples and differences between cultures and countries lend evidence to such negative approaches. And history bears witness to the problem of asserting via force that our view is best, as any native people can attest. The theoretical approach to ethics that maintains that there is no answer to what is right or wrong that applies equally to all people is known as *relativism*. And there are two principle types of relativism: cultural and normative.

Cultural relativism, as its name suggests, claims that morality is limited to the scope of a specific culture. Central to the idea is the claim that an individual's beliefs can only be understood or evaluated in relation to their culture and that each culture is its own source of legitimate ethical claims. No one culture is better than any other, so no culture needs to justify itself to some universal moral code. In fact, the very existence of such a code is argued not to exist. Consider the example in *The Butter Battle Book*.

The Yooks and Zooks have a long-standing divergence of opinion, to put it lightly. They disagree on which cultural practice is superior. Each side sees their practice as morally superior and the other's as morally bankrupt. As the grandfather iterates, "It's high time that you knew of the terribly horrible thing that Zooks do. In every Zook house and in every Zook town every Zook eats his bread with the butter side down! . . . we Yooks, as you know, when we breakfast or sup, spread our bread . . . with the butter side up. That's the right, honest way!" (Butter). So he concludes, "You can't trust a Zook who spreads bread underneath! Every Zook must be watched! He has kinks in his soul!" (Butter). This disagreement about a seemingly innocuous cultural practice leads ultimately to a stalemated nuclear arms race, with each side poised to annihilate the other.

We can glean two important points about cultural relativism from this example. First, this practice, like so many others that people engage in, doesn't seem to matter. It doesn't matter on what side you butter your bread. Buttering bread is trivial, so there is no good reason not to tolerate it. It doesn't inhibit the ability of the practitioners to function well, nor does it harm anyone else. The Zooks seem perfectly happy eating bread butter side down, and the Yooks do well with theirs buttered topside. The cause of conflict in this story is one group trying to force the other to change their cultural practice, and for no other reason than that they think theirs is best. Secondly, often trouble and strife, even war can result from an intolerance of other's beliefs and practices. So respect and acceptance may be the best order of the day. This message permeates many of Seuss's stories. Yet there seems to be a limit to our tolerance. Should we tolerate Sour Kangaroo's desire to boil the Whos, or the Sneetches discriminatory social structure? Should we sit back and watch, refusing to judge the Once-ler as he destroys the environment or Yertle as he oppresses the turtles in his pond?

Cultural relativists rely on the claim that cultures are separate, self-justifying sources of valid ethical claims. But in the age of globalization there is no such thing as an isolated culture. We are interconnected, for better or worse. The Sneetches, denizens of Nool, and Yertle's subjects don't live in a vacuum. As one scholar notes, "Morally, as well as physically, there is only one world, and we all have to live in it."[1] Part of our job as reasoning, judging creatures is to make do in this one world as best as we can. So to refuse to judge is to become complicit in evils that are directly and profoundly linked to each of us. If we are motivated by respect, or tolerance out of respect, then we must make evaluations and judgments about cultural practices that seem to disregard the concerns or interests of those people we are trying to respect through our tolerance. Some things shouldn't be tolerated. But then some things should be. It's hard to know the difference. But just because it's hard doesn't mean we give up, it means we keep trying.

Yet some take the problems of cultural relativism to demonstrate not the need for a universal ethical system but a broader understanding of relativism, one that pertains to each individual's moral judgments, not just cultural practices. This view is sometimes termed normative relativism.

Normative relativism says that a person's beliefs are justified only in relation to a self-imposed framework, making ethics something akin to a matter of taste. No two people can be measured by the same principle due to the fact that each individual is different, and the rules that each adopts are specific only to them. Central to understanding normative relativism is that no single person has an incorrect view about ethical reasoning, there are only different views. Values are a matter of personal opinion or individual perspective. We hear this view given expression when someone says, "Well that may be true for you, but . . ." The idea that it is merely "true for you" implies that we each have our own view and each ought to be respected as much as every other because all views are equally "true." This is the reaction many get when they judge a friend's action to be faulty. For example, you confront your friend the Once-ler about his unethical business practices and he claims, "Well, you can agree with that Lorax fellow if you like, but I'd prefer to make Thneeds and money. We're each allowed our own opinion." To an extent he is right; we are all allowed our own opinion. But that doesn't mean all opinions are equally supportable. After all, some people hold the opinion that Sneetches without stars are second-class citizens. This belief is not only unsupportable insofar as a measurement of moral worth will equally apply to starless and starred Sneetches but also it harms starless Sneetches in a demonstrable way. Opinions have impacts, and we can't turn a blind eye to the effects of ignorance and moral bankruptcy.

Consider Horton the elephant. Horton both hatches an egg abandoned by a slothful, derelict parent and protects the Whos from the shortsightedness of Sour Kangaroo, the Wickershams, and all the other animals in the jungle of Nool. In each case Horton had to maintain an ethical ideal. In the case of the egg it was fidelity, being faithful "one-hundred percent" (Hatches). With respect to the Whos it was respect, the belief that "A person's a person. No matter how small" (Horton). These are values that Horton demands others abide by as well. In fact, we as readers are disgusted by the practices of Mayzie the lazy bird and all the residents of Nool because they are violating these basic moral principles and in each case great harm would result if Horton didn't hold firm; the egg would perish and the Whos would fall victim to Sour Kangaroo's final solution.

If Horton had turned a blind eye, he would be as blameworthy as the others. And we should recognize that often our motivation to turn a blind eye

may be more an example of our cowardice or our unwillingness to be persecuted than a principled stance for tolerance.[2] Those who demand not to be
judged are usually those most guilty of moral turpitude, those that couldn't
pass any type of moral test or assessment. Of course, they wouldn't want a
standard applied to them; it would shed light on their shoddy practices and
profligate life. We can easily imagine Sour Kangaroo demanding not to be
judged, and in disbelief inquiring who is Horton to tell her how to live her
life or run the jungle. Whereas Horton wouldn't mind so much being judged
by his peers. He has nothing to fear, and nothing to be ashamed of. Tolerance is too often the easy way out of having to do the heavy lifting of ethical thinking or the hard work of ethically living. Although tolerance may
be warranted in some cases, it isn't an absolute command. And really, who
should tolerate *Who* genocide or the plight of an abandoned child? To put it
bluntly, refusing to judge is a cowardly act. Refusal to judge is not an act of
neutrality but to choose for the existing evil. But if relativism is untenable,
what are the alternatives?

Kant:
Respect One-Hundred Percent and No Matter How Small

German philosopher Immanuel Kant (1724–1804) is considered one of the
greatest moral philosophers of the modern era. At the same time, he is considered one of the most notoriously difficult. Thankfully, we don't have to
try to grapple with Kant alone; we can enlist the aid of Seuss's paragon of
Kantian morality, Horton the elephant. We'll begin with Horton's famous
credo, "A person's a person. No matter how small" (Horton). Here, Horton
is promoting the view that all people matter. All people possess an inherent,
inviolable value beyond any price or measure; all people possess dignity. Kant
couldn't have said it better.

According to Kant, the value of persons stems from their status as rational
beings, a status that allows us to postulate freedom, and people are valuable
as the possessors of freedom. Kant states: "Every being that cannot act otherwise than *under the idea of freedom* is just because of that really free in a practical respect . . . I assert that to every rational being having a will we must
necessarily lend the idea of freedom also, under which alone he acts."[3] But
freedom itself cannot be proven, for it cannot be experienced. Rather, it is
through our awareness of our capacity to give ourselves a moral law to which
we are bound in virtue of being rational that we are able to postulate our freedom. Our ability to give ourselves the moral law demonstrates our freedom,
and our freedom makes our adherence to the moral law possible.[4] Insofar as

people are free they are the wellspring of value; that is, they are that which is valuable in itself. Everything else in the world is valued merely as a means to some further end. Kant declares, "*Honeste vive* (live honourably), i.e., truly honour what universally has worth. What necessarily has a worth for everyone possesses dignity, and he who possesses it has inner worth."[5] Likewise, "that which constitutes the condition under which alone something can be an end in itself has not merely a relative worth, that is, a price, but an inner worth, that is, dignity . . . an unconditional, incomparable worth; and the word *respect* alone provides a becoming expression for the estimate of it that a rational being must give."[6] Insofar as human beings possess dignity, they are owed respect. Respect is a moral relation between all rational, free beings and it is a relation demanded by our status as dignified. "There rests . . . a duty regarding the respect that must be shown to every other human being."[7]

In Kant's ethics respect for oneself and others is shown via adherence to the categorical imperative. In two formulations we are shown how living rationally—that is, morally—we demonstrate both respect for ourselves and respect for others. We offend the dignity of others and shame ourselves when we fail to uphold the moral law.

Yet it can seem odd to claim that we are only free when bound by a law. Being bound by laws seems to be the opposite of freedom. Isn't freedom doing whatever we want? Well, since we are not perfectly good wills but are tempted by our inclinations and desires, we need to be assisted to obey the moral law. The moral law, in the form of the categorical imperative, provides a rule by which we direct our activities so that we might approximate better a moral life. "All practical rules consist in an imperative which says what I ought to do. They are meant to signify that a free action, possible through myself, would necessarily occur, if reason were to have total control over my will."[8] Yet we are not purely rational, we are also full of urges, desires, and whims. Sometimes these take hold of us, and sometimes they are quite powerful. The moral law affords us guidance and makes sure that we do the right thing for the right reason and don't get carried away by our inclinations or bodily desires.

The first formulation of the categorical imperative states: "Act as if the maxim of thy action were to become by thy will a Universal Law of Nature."[9] In other words, act only in a way consistent among all rational beings, or do not act in a way that is self-defeating. The first formulation emphasizes consistency. But why be so concerned with consistency? After all, most people's lives are riddled with inconsistencies and contradictions. For Kant, consistency is all about rationality and freedom. As rational, we recognize that actions are only free; that is, self-imposed, if they are not the result of external forces, such as inclinations or desires. Somehow we need to check to see if our actions are free of outside influences. Well, one way to check is to see if everyone else could consistently do what I wish to do. Since all people are at root rational, then whatever applies to me must apply to them as well. If, however, I can't will that they do exactly as I, then I must be treating myself as an exception, which is akin to relying on something other than reason, which we all share, and this other thing would be inclinations or external considerations. If I can't universalize my maxim, then I am acting as an exception to reason, and so I am not acting freely or as a dignified being ought to. Consider *The Cat in the Hat*.

In *The Cat in the Hat* we witness the hijinks of the Cat along with Things One and Two. It seems good, harmless fun and surely a needed break in the monotony of a rainy day. And there seems to be no overt moral message or quandary in this piece, until we get to the end. The book ends with the children's mother returning home and asking what they did all day. A question is then posed to the reader, "What would you do if your mother asked you?" (Cat). Would you lie? Mom will never find out, the cat was thorough, and your sibling isn't going to rat you out since that would implicate her as well. The temptation to lie is strong. You can avoid a scolding from mom, and no one is harmed in the process. From the perspective of self-interest lying seems the obvious choice. But are there other factors that should be considered? Kant would ask us to consider whether our practice of lying could be universalized, and if not, what would that mean.

If you try to make lying a universal law, you can see the inconsistency. If lying were a universal law of nature, then in this circumstance mom would never ask the question in the first place; she'd know she couldn't trust any answer. She'd know that you, just like everyone else, will lie to get out of trouble. So whether the cat had destroyed your house or not, your answer will always be the same, "We did nothing, mom." Lying only works in a culture that presumes truth-telling to be the norm. If lying were a universally recognized practice it would no longer be effective since the precondition needed in order for a deception to work would not exist. So not only would lying not work on mom, since she wouldn't trust any response you give her, but also she probably wouldn't have left you alone in the first place. If you universalize lying, then lying ceases to work. The fact that you can't universalize the practice of lying proves it is generated not out of reason, which we all share and so is a universal trait, but something peculiar to you, something exceptional about yourself. Lying only works if we treat ourselves as exceptions to the rule and so as an exception to everyone else. But the only things exceptional about us are those external factors (inclinations) that shouldn't motivate the behavior of a dignified, free human being. Lying is an undignified practice, one that also disrespects those to whom one lies.

Let's look at another formulation of the categorical imperative: "So act as to treat humanity, whether in thine own person or in that of any other, in every case as an end withal, never as means only."[10] Here Kant, like Horton, demands that we respect each person, no matter how small. In our actions this means treating people as valuable in themselves not as a means or a way to achieve some end or project that we want. Consider the kids in *The Cat in the Hat*. If they lie to their mom, they are using her. The point of the deception is to avoid punishment, to pull the wool over her eyes so their project of self-satisfaction can be achieved. In order to do so they must use her by deceiving her. She is a pawn in their attempt to secure as much happiness for themselves as they can. In effect, lying is akin to telling someone they are not worth the truth and you don't trust what they would do with it, so you'll withhold it from them in order to make sure you get what you want. You also disrespect them by depriving them of their ability to make fully informed choices. If the children lie to their mother, they withhold from her the knowledge she needs to make an informed and free decision, and they do this out of pure self-interest. So lying is wrong, always. Since we can't escape our rationality and thus the demands of freedom and dignity, we are always bound by the moral law whether we like it or not. Moral rules are absolute.

The ramifications of such a theory cannot be ignored. Horton, in order to respect the lives of the *Whos* and to uphold his promise to Mayzie the lazy bird, sacrifices a great deal and puts himself in grave danger. Horton put his entire life on hold and even faces death in order to maintain his moral principles. Not everyone can do this, nor do many think it is necessary. As a result, it is easy to understand the downside of a Kantian ethic. The demands it places upon each of us are absolute, and many may believe it is far removed from one of the most important characteristics of being human—our satisfaction or happiness. There is a serious question that the Kantian must give a response to, and that is whether or not the hardships we may endure in upholding the moral law are worth it. This concern for well-being or happiness leads many to favor an ethical theory that focuses on consequences.

Sorry Thidwick, but the Good of the
Many Outweighs the Good of a Moose

While Kant focused on freedom and respect, the philosopher John Stuart Mill (1806–1873) focused on the consequences of our actions, specifically the amount of pleasure or happiness that they generate. Whereas Kant found

the font of value to be located in each person's dignity, Mill sought to demonstrate that happiness was the ultimate good toward which we all strive,
and so it is the value against which all of our actions ought to be measured.
His procedure for demonstrating this is pretty straightforward. Consider any
action you are doing and ask why you are doing it. For example, if you are a
Bingle Bug, ask why you want to ride on a Big-Hearted Moose's horns. You
might respond, "It's such a long road and it's such a hot day" (Thidwick)
that riding would be easier. I can then ask why you want to travel the easiest way possible. You might respond, "I'd prefer to relax, rather than walk."
I can keep asking "Why?" all day if I choose and eventually your response
will be, "because it will make me happy." If I then ask why you want to be
happy we can see that we'll be at the end of my inquiry. You want to be
happy because happiness is good, period. Happiness is not pain. If anyone
needs to know why one is preferable to the other they need merely experience some pain, and they'll quickly come around. Happiness is therefore the
only thing good in itself, and it is the ultimate good toward which we strive.
So happiness, not dignity, will be the metric against which we evaluate our
actions. But notice, this means *happiness* is good, not just my happiness. The
goal then is to generate as much net happiness in the world as possible. So
if now a Tree-Spider, Zinn-a-Zu Bird, and his wife and her uncle want to
ride, so be it. The more the merrier. Their happiness counts in the equation
as well, and if we are trying to maximize happiness in the world, it being
the ultimate good, then we should try to maximize it wherever we find it.
"The creed which accepts as the foundation of morals, Utility, or the Greatest Happiness Principle, holds that actions are right in proportion as they
tend to promote happiness [pleasure], wrong as they tend to promote the
reverse of happiness."[11] Moral assessments thus proceed as a kind of pro/con
analysis whereby for any action we look at the potential good or pleasure
that it will produce, the potential harm or pain it may lead to, weigh them
against each other, and should the predicted or probable good outweigh the
predicted or probable bad the action is the right thing to do. This seems like
common sense. We do this all the time. Should I wake up and go to class or
sleep in? Should I scrimp and save or should I just go out and buy that new
thing-a-ma-jigg? Should I lie to Gertrude about the attractiveness of her one
droopy-droop feather or tell her my real opinion, that she looks dull and
lackluster? We often come to a decision based not on respect or duty as Kant
would hope but on the amount of pleasure, ours and others, that a considered
action is likely to produce. Often we even make these decisions not based
on producing pleasure but simply avoiding pain, as in lying to Gertrude. If
she asked us what we thought of her dull behind, most of us would probably

respond as did good Uncle Dake: "Your tail is just right for your kind of bird" (McFuzz). Even if we didn't believe this to be so, even if we thought her tail was an abomination, we would lie or otherwise avoid the truth and deceive Gertrude in order to spare her feelings. Gertrude's spared feelings count more than whatever might motivate our desire to tell her exactly what we think. In fact, if we told her the brute, honest truth, as we saw it, and caused her great pain and body image issues, her friends and ours would probably think we had acted callously or even sadistically. Our appeal to the categorical imperative and the duty to always tell the truth and thus act in a consistent and dignified manner would not spare us their harsh assessments. So Mill is onto something. But it's not quite as simple as just finding more pros than cons for any moral problem with which we're faced.

Calculating possible pleasures and pains is a tricky matter. Are all pleasures of equal importance? How much does each weigh? And according to whose scale? According to Mill, some pleasures are of greater value. Mill differentiated between pleasures by calling those of greater importance the higher pleasures and those of lesser importance the lower pleasures. Higher pleasures emphasize special characteristics unique to humanity, ones that ought to be promoted above the base and bestial. As Mill claims, "It is better to be a human being dissatisfied than a pig satisfied; better to be Socrates dissatisfied than a fool satisfied."[12] Both eating a chocolate sundae and getting a college degree produce some pleasure in us. But one produces a sustained pleasure unique to humans; the other a short-lived animalistic pleasure, one a human wouldn't be fit to define her life by. Some pleasures are more befitting a human life and produce a greater deal more pleasure in terms of quantity and quality. This seems right. Some pleasures do seem more potent and durable than others, and if we are maximizing pleasure in general, then although we don't want to ignore lower pleasures like food, sleep, and sex, we should aim toward the higher ones—for example, art, friendship, and education—and try to maximize these for everybody.

Yet, the disadvantages of utilitarianism are significant and demand careful attention. Consider poor Thidwick. Before he is able to shed his horns and free himself from his oppressors, Thidwick is encumbered with five hundred pounds of pests on his head. All of his free riders are perfectly happy. So what if one moose is dissatisfied, the happiness of all the other creatures outweighs his discomfort. More people are happy exploiting Thidwick than are unhappy, so for a utilitarian the equation works out, the greatest happiness of the greatest number is produced through the apparent maltreatment of Thidwick. Even more problematic, this harsh treatment of Thidwick isn't immoral since it produces the greatest good. Thidwick is merely one among many, the goal of which is maximal happiness. Thidwick is simply a cog in a happiness-producing machine, and so long as the output is the maximum possible happiness, it doesn't matter if a cog gets worn out in the process. The problem is obvious. If the only goal of a group of people is to maximize happiness for the greatest number of participants, then it is quite likely that some are going to be sacrificed for the sake of the rest. The concern that utilitarians can find it justifiable to accept even seemingly horrific atrocities so long as the eventual output is positive is often expressed by the question, "Does the end always justify the means?" Shouldn't there be a limit to what we are allowed to do to maximize happiness? Shouldn't there be an upper bound limit to what we are willing to do, even if we have the satisfaction of the masses as our goal?

The usual criticism against utilitarianism is that basing the morality of an action or rule on the promotion of some consequence is going to permit the abuse of some part of the population at the expense of the majority who are benefitting. Consider that if Thidwick had not escaped his "guests" his life would have been plagued with a seemingly unending chain of exploitation. These moral hang-ups bring into question whether or not consequences are all that matter. Clearly, utilitarians are not oblivious to these difficulties, and a great deal of ink has been spilled dealing with them. But for us the important point is that if utilitarianism is found to be lacking, there is still another alternative. It may be that the consequences of our actions are only a part of the moral life, and pleasure alone cannot be the sole measure of them. Is the answer to go back to Kant and the absolutism of his duty-based theory? Well, there are other options. The good life may not be determined by either duty or pleasure.

Aristotle's Great Balancing Act

The question central to Kant and Mill could be phrased as "What is the right thing to do?" Their moral philosophies depended on being able to differentiate between actions that are good and bad. Aristotle (384–322 BCE) thought differently. Focusing on actions was too narrow. Instead of worrying about what specific thing you ought to be doing, he believed we should be asking, "What kind of person should I be?" Aristotle thought that what really mattered was a person's character. Therefore, Aristotle had to figure out and define what mattered in our moral composition.

Aristotle understood the behavior of animals and objects as fulfilling certain functions. A good hammer was one that did what a hammer was supposed to do, and did it well. Similarly, a good person was one that did what a person was supposed to do. And in order to be a good person, to do our job as people well, we needed certain dispositions or habits. Just as a hammer must have a long enough handle to generate sufficient momentum, a head denser than the material it hammers, and not be so hard as to be brittle in order to be an effective hammer, so must a person have states of character appropriate to fulfill the end of human life; namely, flourishing or living well. These states of character are the virtues.

A virtue, at its most basic, is any trait that is functionally beneficial. It is a perfection of the person, a state of one's character that assists one in achieving her excellence. Among these Aristotle included generosity, truthfulness, modesty, courage, and temperance. His lists vary throughout his work, and none ought to be considered exhaustive. But regardless of the content of the list, being virtuous meant maintaining the virtues consistently and applying them appropriately in our decision making. No single action could be good or bad independently of the person who performed it, their intentions, and the circumstances in which it was performed. All factors had to be considered. The idea is that we call a person good because they tend to act in a way that is like a good person. Someone who has spent their entire life stealing is not suddenly a good person because they don't steal in one circumstance. Nor should they be praised for finally exercising self-control. This one instance of honesty is an exception to their greater tendency to steal. Only if they refrain from stealing for the right reason and consistently over time can we say that they have become a better person. Moral character is developed through good habits. Through habituation one trains oneself to routinely do what is best or most admirable and thus develops a disposition or character toward the good. This disposition reinforces itself as we routinely act properly, and so we develop our characters. But this is always a work in progress.

In trying to determine what type of person we should seek to be or what would be a virtuous action for each person, Aristotle notes that as in nature, the good lies in the mean—that is, the middle. Just as too much water will drown a plant and too little dehydrate it, so the same is true of our virtues. Too much of any character trait is bound to be harmful, just as too little will equally inhibit our ability to function optimally. We need to seek the mean. But each person will have a different mean, since each person begins from a different place. The mean will always be relative to us. Consider the virtue of courage.

Courage as a state of character is a predisposition toward danger, fear, and obstacles in general. There is no hard and fast rule about what it is or how to be courageous. Yet through self-reflection and assessment we can come to an informed decision regarding our behavior. The courage of a soldier in the heat of battle and the courage of a child contemplating a ride on the Ferris wheel are different. Yet each is guided by the mean. If the soldier is too courageous he will be foolhardy and put himself and others in unnecessary danger. Likewise, although there may be truth in the cliché that "those that fight and run away live to fight another day," if all the soldier does is run away, he will not develop as a soldier or person. He needs to fight at the right time in the right proportion; determining when this is will be a continual project of self-discovery. Likewise, the child must find his mean. If he is fearless, then he will not only ride the Ferris wheel without a second thought but he may also be willing to accept every foolhardy dare with which his peers challenge him. Fear and caution aren't cowardly when they evince prudence. Yet if he cowers and refuses to ride the Ferris wheel he not only deprives himself of a fun experience but also sets a pattern of behavior in which he hides from or avoids everything that makes him even the slightest bit uncomfortable. Doing so would significantly inhibit his growth as a person. Foolhardy, careless people as well as cowards fail to flourish. We can see this exemplified in the story of Thidwick. Thidwick's tale is one of exercising generosity in the proper proportion. If he is too generous, being hospitable to each and every "guest," then he can no longer function as a moose. Likewise, if he refused even the most innocuous Bingle Bug's request for a brief ride he would quickly be seen to be a petty and selfish moose, and this won't help him on his life's journey any better.

Virtues are character traits that assist us on our life's journey, and since all of our journeys begin from different places and have unique destinations there will be no one right answer that suits everybody, even if there are general guidelines that equally apply. We know certain dispositions—honesty, generosity, courage, prudence, temperance, etc.—facilitate growth, and that the mean is wherein success is to be found, even if we're not sure exactly where that is. We know we should strive to be courageous, but what this means for us in our lives is going to have to be figured out by trial and error.

The culmination of the virtuous life is a state of being Aristotle called *eudaimonia*. Roughly translated, *eudaimonia* means "flourishing." Such a rendering hints at the activity that *eudaimonia* describes and how it is an ongoing effort by the individual, not an accomplishment to be reached. One does not have it one day and not the next. It is fostered and maintained through caring for oneself and one's moral development consistently over a complete life. Dr. Seuss reiterates the Aristotelian ethos, reminding us to "Step with care and great tact and remember that Life's a Great Balancing Act" (Places). That is, a successful life requires constant care and maintenance through self-reflection. Life is indeed a "great balancing act," and so we need to cultivate those skills and character traits that help us to be "dexterous and deft" as we travel the wiggled roads of life. Will we succeed if we take the advice? Dr. Seuss answered with a resounding, "Yes! You will indeed! (98 and 3/4 guaranteed)" (Places). Aristotle would most definitely agree.[13]

But obviously we can't end here. Just as with all ethical theories, virtue ethics will have its detractors. The faults of Aristotle's virtue theory can best be shown by means of the advantages of the act-based theories of Kant and Mill. They offer clear edicts or rules for calculation that guarantee a set answer to any moral quandary. Aristotle is ambiguous. He never tells us exactly what it is that is good. It is supposedly relative to the person and the context. But as Thidwick found out, it is difficult to know what to do when the time arises. A person may know that he should not be rude or that "a host, above all, must be nice to his guest" (Thidwick). But that alone will not provide Thidwick with the information he needs. In Thidwick's case, it may have been beneficial to have some clear-cut way to know what to do, when to be hospitable and when not to. Thidwick left to his own devices is at a loss. Thidwick's life might've been significantly easier if he'd known with certainty what to do. Perhaps Kant or Mill could've told him. "These animals are using you, Thidwick. It is disrespectful and they ought to be evicted." Or, "Don't you see the joy your horns bring so many of nature's creatures? Just suck it up, Thidwick, you bring them great happiness." But when he is on his own and trying to figure out the right proportion of hospitality to show his "guests," he is lost. Eventually, his horns made the choice for him by molting. So the lack of any set criteria in a virtue-based ethics appears for some to be a shortcoming. Yet this may also be its strength. After all, life is not black-and-white, so a moral theory that asks us to continually reassess and correct the trajectory of our life may be more true to our lived experiences as human beings than theories based on cold calculations or absolute decrees.

The Places We Will Go

Aristotle wrote, "It makes no small difference, then, whether we form habits of one kind or of another from our very youth; it makes a very great difference, or rather *all* the difference."[14] He meant that the most important and critical time to morally educate somebody was during childhood. The focus on early childhood is not without warrant. Aristotle realized that if a person developed a bad habit early on in his life it was much harder to get rid of later. So, being able to successfully teach the virtues and relate them to children in meaningful ways at a young age was of utmost importance. If the virtues are taught at a young age, then one could aid in their continual development. Yet, conveying virtuous behavior could not be done through explanation or lecture alone. It had to be shown and practiced. And all parents know children learn more from examples than lectures. They also learn quite well when entertained and when their lessons impact them in a fundamental way, when it becomes an experience. Perhaps this is why Dr. Seuss is so popular and poignant. He communicates, entertains, and transforms us through his stories; stories that don't tell you what is right or wrong but which begin the process of moral education through the presentation of scenarios and laudable and shameful characters.

It could be argued that the best examples to teach and convey meaningful ideas to our children are the stories we give them. If it really is the examples that matter, then we are rich in the tools to do so. Herein is the ongoing relevance of Dr. Seuss and the importance he may hold to our children. In his stories the parts that are of utmost importance are exaggerated, and the relationships that exist between the characters provide a working model by which we can compare our own actions. It is not that any singular story conveys a lesson of importance over the others. It is that together the works of Dr. Seuss develop and illustrate a multitude of ideas and situations, and this diversity is representative of the variety of situations that we will inevitably encounter throughout our own lives. It is doubtful anyone of us will ever have it all figured out, knowing exactly what is right and wrong in each and every circumstance. But this life is too vast, too open, and too messy to be so easily deciphered and conquered. What we can hope for, and what we can accomplish, is to garner a deeper understanding and appreciation for this life, and through continued questioning and investigation live honorably. And whether we are just beginning our journey or already well on our way, we can all learn from the courage and fidelity of Horton, the trials and tribulations of Thidwick, and the arrogance of the Zooks, Yooks, and Zax.[15]

~

CHAPTER TEN

Horton Hears You, Too!
Seuss and Kant on Respecting Persons

Dean A. Kowalski

Devout Dr. Seuss fans can recite the opening lines of *Horton Hears a Who!*: "On the 15th of May, in the Jungle of Nool, in the heat of the day, in the cool of the pool . . ." (Horton). However, not everyone remembers that Dr. Seuss introduced Horton fourteen years earlier in *Horton Hatches the Egg*. The moral messages of Dr. Seuss and his iconic elephant are best appreciated by studying each story in turn. This kind of procedure, fortuitously enough, is analogous to standard investigations of Immanuel Kant's two categorical imperatives. Kant never wrote books for children. In fact, his prose is complex and foreboding; however, some of his ideas—like Dr. Seuss's—are immanently intuitive, bordering on common sense. Indeed, the moral messages of Dr. Seuss and Kant tend to converge, especially with respect to the ethical importance of personhood and human dignity. This essay proposes to capture both levels—the Kantian complexity and the Seussian obviousness—in order to help the reader achieve a deeper appreciation for each.

Philosophical discussions about the value of personhood and human dignity cannot begin without Kant. His ideas in this regard have been seminal. However, few philosophers agree with all facets of his view, his staunch commitment to moral absolutism being one notable example. For the past two centuries or so, philosophers have attempted to retain the intuitive heart of Kant's ethical ideas but rework some of the details for the sake of overall plausibility. A careful interpretation of Dr. Seuss's heroic elephant suggests one such revision. It will be argued that *Horton Hatches the Egg* and *Horton Hears a Who!* powerfully convey the moral importance of personhood but without obviously affirming Kant's position that moral rules hold without exception. The very fact that Horton's behavior is *heroic* holds the key to this revision of Kant.[1]

I Said What I Meant, and Meant What I Said

In *Horton Hatches the Egg*, Mayzie the bird is tired and bored of caring for her egg and seeks a bit of rest. Horton strolls by, and Mayzie pleads with him to take her place. Horton thinks the idea is preposterous; he's an elephant after all! But Mayzie presses: "I know you're not small . . . Just sit on it softly. You're gentle and kind. . . . I won't be gone long, sir, I give you my word" (Hatches). Horton agrees to assist her, and he fortifies the tree to support his great bulk. But Mayzie doesn't return quickly. In fact, winter passes. But through it all, he remains diligent, affirming, "I meant what I said, and I said what I meant, an elephant is faithful one-hundred percent" (Hatches). This slogan, never appearing in *Horton Hears a Who!*, clearly conveys the moral ideal that we should be faithful to our word.[2] Horton is faithful to what he said; Mayzie is not. Seuss's moral message is clear: Horton is commendable for keeping his promise to Mayzie, but she is blameworthy for lying to him. So, *Horton Hatches the Egg* seems to convey the moral importance of keeping one's word.

Kant introduces his categorical imperative in a way that also highlights the moral importance of keeping one's word. Its initial phrasing is known as the "universal law" formulation. It reads, "Act only according to that maxim by which you can at the same time will that it should become a universal law."[3] Admittedly, it's not initially clear how this pertains to truth-telling. Kant intends his categorical imperative to serve as a general principle from which more specific moral obligations can be deduced. Nevertheless, scholars agree that the moral force of the universal law formulation is most obvious in cases that involve making a lying promise.[4] Let's begin unpacking Kant's categorical imperative by clarifying its terms.

By the term *maxim*, Kant meant something like an implicit, general rule to be followed. So, with respect to any action we are about to undertake, we must be cognizant of its corresponding implicit rule (and the intention from which it's made). Articulating the implicit rule is merely a matter of gener-alizing or universalizing: whenever someone is in circumstances relevantly similar to mine, that person should act as I do (or am about to do). Once the maxim is carefully articulated, Kant intended to put it to a kind of two-part test. This is captured by his phrase "will that it become a universal law." Kant's usage of "will" here implies that you, as a rational or reasonable person, would be willing to accept your rule upon its being universalized. So, the first part of the test comes in the form of a question: could you reasonably or rationally accept that everyone follow the implicit rule that you are about to enact? Would you be willing that everyone do as you are about to do? Upon asking yourself this, the second part of the test is to answer it. The key to its answer again relies on the idea of reasonability or rationality. If there would be contradictory or self-defeating results were everyone to do as you are about to, then you cannot reasonably or rationally accept your implicit rule. You would not be willing that it become a universal law. In such cases, the answer to your question is "no"; a negative answer in the second part of Kant's test is definitive evidence that the act you intend is impermissible (morally wrong). You, as a rational agent, are about to perform an act that you would not be willing others do in that situation. In this, you are being inconsistent or irrational, allowing an exception for yourself that you are not willing to grant others, even though they are exactly like you in every relevant way. This, concluded Kant, provides you sufficient reason not to perform that act.

How Kant's universal law formulation forbids making lying promises (and dishonesty generally) is now clearer. Kant used the example of securing a loan that you had no intention of repaying. Remember the specifics of the situation matter very little. It could be a Wickersham looking to start his own banana farm or Vlad hoping to expand his "business." The crucial feature is the maxim. Accordingly, if the proposed action is to be universalized, then we have: whenever a person (you, a Wickersham Cousin, Vlad) is in need of money, he or she should make a lying promise to secure the desired funds. It's pretty clear that this maxim has contradictory or self-defeating results. Dishonesty only achieves its intended goal in a culture that presumes truth-telling. Were everyone to make lying promises whenever in need of money, then people would cease to lend money. So, if everyone were to act as you intend, you couldn't secure any funds, which entails that no reasonable or rational person could accept its implicit maxim. You would not be willing that everyone obtain a loan in the way you intend. So, if you proceed, you are making an exception for yourself that you are not willing to allow others, even though they are in your exact circumstances.

Sometimes the contradictory or self-defeating nature of the maxim lies in its intention. Consider the prospect of shirking your civil obligations. Perhaps you don't wish to pay your taxes. Perhaps a bit like Jo-Jo (the young twerp), you do not wish to engage in civic responsibility simply because you don't feel like it. According to Kant, it's not the prospect of the *Whos* being dunked in hot Beezle-Nut oil that makes Jo-Jo's choice impermissible, it is simply that such a maxim cannot be universalized. Consider that if everyone were to act in your mindless "Jo-Jo yo-yo bouncing fashion," then society would no longer function smoothly. After all, no one really likes serving jury duty, not to mention paying taxes. But, presumably, the whole idea behind your intention—shirking your civic responsibilities—is to benefit from everyone else's conscientious efforts. *They* will keep society running smoothly, while *you* laze around as an anonymous freeloader. But if everyone were to act as you, then society would break down, thereby contravening your initial intention. You wouldn't benefit at all but rather place yourself in great peril (Beezle-Nut oil or no). Thus, your maxim has contradictory or self-defeating consequences; no rational person could reasonably accept that everyone act on it. You intend to grant yourself an exception you would not be willing to allow others were they in your situation.

Clearly, Mayzie provides Horton a promise that she has no intention of keeping. She tells him that she will return shortly, but she fully intends to take a long vacation in Palm Beach. She was gone for fifty-one weeks, and only met up with Horton and her egg again via crazy, random happenstance. If everyone made lying promises to their neighbors because they were bored and tired of upholding their personal responsibilities (which includes raising children), no one would believe anyone and society would crumble. In this way, Mayzie's proposed maxim suffers the ill effects of both the "lying promise to secure funds" and "social freeloader" examples. Because Mayzie knowingly enacts a maxim that cannot reasonably be universalized, she acts impermissibly. She makes an exception for herself that she could not willingly afford others. Were she so willing, it would be impossible for her to secure her selfish goal.

An Elephant Is Faithful . . . One-Hundred Percent [?]

Dr. Seuss thus clearly sides with Kant on the importance of promise keeping and honesty generally. Kant, in fact, believes that you should *always* be honest—that is, faithful to your word—regardless of any seemingly negative consequences. Moreover, Kant believes our moral obligations hold without exception, making him a moral absolutist. Because we have a moral duty to tell the truth (as the opposing maxim fails the universalization test), it follows that there are no circumstances in which we may permissibly break our word or practice dishonesty. This remains so even if our proposed dishonesty has no other goal than protecting innocent persons. In "On a Supposed Right to Lie from Altruistic Motives," Kant writes, "To be truthful (honest) in all deliberation, therefore, is a sacred and absolute commanding decree of reason, limited by no expediency."[5] The idea seems to be that just as there are no exceptions to the principle that the sum of the interior angles of a triangle is 180 degrees, there are no exceptions to the principle that making lying promises is always wrong. Both are grounded in rational or logical considerations, and principles so grounded hold without exception.

But many scholars find moral absolutism to be implausible. Kant was not unaware of such concerns. To bolster his position, he considers a dilemma involving a murderer looking for his next victim. Assume that a known murderer approaches you and inquires about the location of his next intended victim, an innocent neighbor of yours. Only moments ago, you saw your neighbor frantically enter the front door of his home. What should you do? Assuming no viable third alternative, should you lie to the murderer to protect the life of your innocent neighbor or report your neighbor's location truthfully, knowing that this will undoubtedly get the innocent man killed? Kant was clear: morally speaking, you must answer the murderer truthfully, thereby disclosing the neighbor's location. Your duty to tell the truth is absolute.[6]

The debate emerging here is not whether it's ever permissible to lie for selfish or personal gain. Should Horton break his word to Mayzie simply to avoid the ribbing of his jungle friends, he acts impermissibly. Rather, worries about the moral absoluteness of honesty are grounded in situations when moral duties conflict. We have a duty to tell the truth and a duty to protect the lives of innocent people (insofar as we can), and in this Kant agrees. However, what should we do in situations where we must choose one over the other? All systems committed to moral absolutism, Kant's included, are conceptually precarious because they seem ill equipped to reconcile such moral dilemmas. After all, imagine the following alteration to the lying murderer case. Assume that you had promised the neighbor that you would not disclose his location to anyone, but especially the sociopath chasing him. When the murderer inquires about your neighbor's location, what should you do? Keep your promise to your neighbor or answer the murderer's question honestly? Alternatively, let's say that your other next-door neighbor performs a kindness to you and, out of gratitude, you promise to repay it whenever he needs it. Let's further say that he requests you to repay the kindness by assassinating his professional rival. Horton is laudable for keeping his promise to Mayzie. But should you keep your promise and assassinate the rival? Doesn't it seem just as plausible (if not more so) to break your word so as to not end the life of your neighbor's rival?

The force of these questions speaks against Kant's blanket insistence on truth-telling. Fortunately, many scholars also believe that Kant's absolutism is unnecessary; his larger project of grounding moral duties in what rational agents can consistently will arguably remains intact.[7] So long as the person pondering the exception to the rule can consistently accept that everyone act as he is considering, then his act is permissible. Nevertheless, this remains a bit contentious. It might be argued that qualified maxims, those about being honest with the built-in exception to save the life of innocent persons, become self-defeating if universalized. Insofar as murderers may no longer believe those they question, the maxims lose their efficacy. Yet, intuitively the alleged self-defeating result isn't as obvious as lying to a bank manager to get a loan (that you never intend to pay back). *Would* the relevant maxim, if universalized, negate the intended purpose of attempting to nonviolently protect the life of an innocent? Furthermore, note that the agent is not making an exception *for* herself, which seems to be a staple to deeming maxims impermissible.

Without definitively resolving this debate, note that the interpretation proposed here highlights (or safeguards) the heroic nature of acts that agents undergo in the face of extreme adversity. The most natural view to take about Horton is that he is a hero. He kept his word to Mayzie even though the three hunters were about to mortally wound him. He remained resolute when they instead decided to sell him to the circus (and off they all went with Horton being unhappy 100 percent). However, Kant seems committed to holding that Horton is morally required to keep his word in even these extremely dangerous, life-threatening circumstances. According to Kant, were Horton to leave the nest, he would be acting impermissibly. But is this plausible? Can agents be seriously required to keep their word in each and every situation, even if doing so means giving up their lives? A more plausible approach is to label such choices heroic. Acting heroically means going above and beyond what is required. In this way, perhaps Horton ought to be praised as a hero but not blamed were he to leave the nest when his life was threatened. No one can be blamed for not being a hero.

In portraying Horton as a hero, Seuss's story invites us to rethink some of Kant's ethical ideas. Perhaps the genius of Dr. Seuss is that he invites each of us to reexamine ourselves and our moral commitments. Seuss agrees with Kant that keeping our promises is extremely important. If you knowingly give your word then you ought to keep it, even if doing so causes you the inconvenience of indefinitely sitting on an egg in a small tree or dealing with the ribbing of friends. But we may demur from Kant's insistence that we must be faithful to our word 100 percent. Those that do so keep their word, at least if that means giving up their life, are heroes. Yet, so many of us become unfaithful to our word too soon. We often give up when the going gets the slightest bit rough. This is a moral failing, and in this regard we should be more like Horton.

A Person Is a Person, No Matter How Small

The next step is getting clearer about how exceptions to general (Kantian) moral rules might be crafted. What constitutes the difference between praising morally heroic behavior and blaming someone for not doing enough? Answers to these questions begin to emerge upon examining *Horton Hears a Who!* and Kant's "ends in themselves" formulation of the categorical imperative, especially when the latter is interpreted via the former. The idea of human dignity or personhood holds the key. In fact, Kant believed that this idea resides at the very core of all ethical behavior. Kant's "ends in themselves" formulation reads: "Act so that you treat humanity, whether in your own person or in that of another, always as an end and never as a means only."[8] This version of the categorical imperative clearly conveys—in a way that the "universal law" formulation doesn't—the idea that persons themselves possess a certain kind of unique worth or value. Kant labeled nonpersons "things." Roughly, it's always impermissible to treat a person as if she were only a thing.

Accordingly, the conceptual differences between a person and a thing are crucial. Things are objects that have purposes or goals put upon them. They are used as a means to achieve some project. Persons, however, are sources of value insofar as they (we) independently implement purposes or goals into (or onto) the world. Persons, but not things, possess the ability to universalize and contemplate implicit maxims, recognize the difference between right and wrong, and grasp the significance of that difference. Persons, but not things, can perform actions because they are right and refrain from actions because they are wrong (not that we always do). Persons, but not things, are appropriately praised or blamed given how they choose with respect to the moral knowledge they possess. Persons are therefore sources of moral behavior, and, in a way, of morality itself. Kant labels these morally significant features of personhood "being autonomous." For Kant, the fact that persons are autonomous—rational agents, possessed of volition (free will) and foresight—is the crux of all moral value and ethically significant judgments.

This also begins to explain why Kant believes that persons possess unconditional and intrinsic moral worth. Persons possess a kind of inherent dignity that is beyond or above any price. This dignity may not permissibly be sacrificed or traded for any (other nonmoral) goal or project exactly because it is beyond or above any such goal or project. When a person's dignity is so sacrificed, implicitly the person who fails to recognize the dignity of the other implicitly affirms, "You, fellow person, are not as important or deserving as me; I am more deserving or important than you and thus am at liberty to treat you as a mere tool (means) to achieve my personal projects." Such affirmations implicitly condone treating persons like mere things. Failing to treat persons with the dignity they inherently possess—and the respect they thereby deserve—is to make the gravest of moral errors.[9]

Horton clearly saw the difference between persons and things. Horton surmised that the floating dust speck, even though as small as the head of a pin, somehow contained persons; it commanded his attention and demanded his respect. The speck was unusual; he had "never heard tell of a small speck of dust that is able to yell" (Horton). Nevertheless, Horton was perceptive enough—with his inordinately large and sensitive moral ears—to realize that the inhabitants of that speck were very small persons requiring his assistance. Horton learns that the speck denizens are called "Whos," living in Who-ville. They have houses, churches, and grocery stores. The mayor of Who-ville, on behalf of all the Whos, expresses his gratitude to Horton for the elephant's careful assistance. Furthermore, that the Whos are persons entails that Horton cannot put a price on their well-being—their dignity as persons is beyond all price. Regardless of how much trouble Sour Kangaroo and the Wickershams cause him, recognizing the Whos' inherent moral worth— respecting their dignity as persons—is more important. In fact, nothing could be more important than protecting persons in serious need, especially if providing aid presents no serious harm to you. Horton indeed affirms, "I can't let my very small persons get drowned! I've got to protect them. I'm bigger than they" (Horton).

For Kant, anyone who willingly fails to observe the respect due to a person or themselves acts impermissibly. Moreover, the moral duties owed to persons entails that we must not treat others as a mere means even if upholding those duties is inconvenient or bothersome. And sometimes this can be downright difficult. After all, it would have been much easier for Horton to ignore the speck's faint yelp on that fifteenth of May. He could have gone back to his splashing in the cool of the pool. He wouldn't have had to suffer Sour Kangaroo's disparaging "humpfs" and verbal assaults. His reputation would not have suffered. The Wickersham Uncles and the Wickersham Cousins would have left him alone. But Dr. Seuss provides the reader with someone—Horton—who does the right thing despite all the troubles it entails. Horton goes so far as to spend all day searching three million flowers to find the misplaced Whos. Indeed Horton is willing to sacrifice his personal safety to the extent of being lassoed (with ten miles of rope) and caged by

Sour Kangaroo and her cronies. Such is the extent of our obligations to our fellow autonomous persons (no matter how small).

I'll Stick by You Small Folks through Thin and through Thick!

It seems intuitive that we cannot be morally required to sacrifice our own life for another. This contention is supported by the "ends in themselves" formulation. We are to respect humanity, including that of our own person. Each of us is due equal respect insofar as each of us is autonomous. This entails that no person can be morally required to sacrifice himself or herself for another. Taking action that sacrifices your life, like a parent for a child, is invariably heroic. The lengths to which Horton goes to protect the *Whos* also borders on heroic sacrifice. He might be suffocated by the ten miles of rope or find himself in the Beezle-Nut stew! But remember that heroic behavior is above and beyond the call to duty. Heroic acts are thus not morally required.

This interpretation has some interesting implications. First, it provides insights into how Kantian rules might be recrafted generally. Consider again the inquiring murderer. The dilemma is that you are duty bound to protect the life of your innocent neighbor but also duty bound to answer the murderer's question honestly. No matter what you do (assuming no third alternative and that your beliefs regarding the inquirer's murderous intentions are well justified), something morally unfortunate will result. Here, Kant advises you to tell the murderer the truth; he requires you to disclose your neighbor's whereabouts so as to allow the murderer to make his own autonomous decision, about which you are absolved of the consequences. However, this leaves us with no principled way to deal with conflicts of duties generally. On the interpretation proffered here, and even if Kant would disagree, it seems that you should allow the "ends in themselves" formulation to trump the "universal law" formulation. So, the rule of thumb here might be: whenever faced with two conflicting (Kantian) duties, always perform that action that disrespects persons the least. Telling a solitary lie to the murderer is not as serious as giving up the life of your innocent neighbor. Furthermore, you might now derive a new maxim, one more sensitive to the circumstances: whenever someone can tell a small, isolated lie to save the life of an innocent person (especially if you are quite certain that you will be believed), then one ought to tell the lie. Not only does this revision pass the "end in themselves" requirement but it also (arguably) passes the maxim test because it doesn't obviously have the self-defeating ramifications of a more expansive policy of dishonesty (at least in terms of making an exception for yourself that you wouldn't be willing to grant others).

Second, this interpretation helps to clarify the thorny issue of determining the extent to which we are duty bound to provide assistance to others in their attempt to lead autonomous lives. Our negative duties—what we ought not to do—are rather well-defined in Kant's system; however, our positive duties—what we ought to do—are not. What lengths are we required to go in offering aid? Reconsider Horton. Surely he is obligated to find the speck a safe resting place as he splashes in the pool. His obligation is not obviated by the mere fact that some gossipy denizens of Nool find him eccentric for carrying around a speck. None of this presents any great danger to Horton. However, as we just saw, it's not clear whether he's obligated to protect the speck if it requires him to be tortured to death with hot Beezle-Nut oil. Thus, the rule of thumb is that you, as an autonomous person, cannot be obligated to become a mere tool or means to another person's autonomous projects. Your autonomous projects are just as important as theirs. Drive an injured friend to the doctor when you're not doing anything? Yes. Donate a kidney to your brother when both of his are failing and you can live with one? Probably. Subsequently donating your only remaining kidney to your sister? No.

Third, this interpretation interestingly conveys the conceptual benefits of combining Kant's two categorical imperatives. Recall the maxim test from the "universal law" formulation: if an implicit maxim, once universalized, has contradictory or self-defeating ramifications, you may not do the action you are considering. Also recall the only explanation for why you would be willing to employ such a maxim: you must allow an exception for yourself that you would not be willing to grant others. If you allowed the relevant exception generally, your maxim becomes unworkable. This uncovers the irrationality of your proposal. But the core *moral* reason why you ought not to proceed with your act is solidified once we supplement the "universal law" formulation with the "ends in themselves." By allowing the exception only for yourself, you are implicitly saying that you are more important than everyone else. You are deserving of the exception, but no one else. But what makes you *alone* morally deserving of this benefit? Aren't you simply one autonomous person among many? Aren't you just as, but no more so, deserving as anyone else? The relevant rational error you make is that you are placing yourself morally above others, even though you have absolutely no good reason for doing so. In addition, by treating yourself as an exception you're basing your decision on that which makes you exceptional—not your reason, but your desires or inclinations. Acting on these alone, for Kant, is undignified. You're not behaving as a free, rational being; that is, autonomously. Instead, you are treating yourself as a mere thing, acting solely from bodily whims and desires. Thus, acting contrary to the "universal law" formulation proves you are acting irrationally and thus contrary to the "ends in themselves" formulation as well. This behavior not only disrespects others, it disrespects you as well.

We can now better understand the depth of Dr. Seuss's moral insights via Mayzie's failings and Horton's heroics. On the one hand, Mayzie not only acted on a maxim she couldn't universalize but also she used Horton as a mere prop or tool in her selfish project. Her ploy would only succeed if she kept from Horton the full truth about when she intended to return. She failed to provide Horton the respect due to him. She might have asked Horton for help with full disclosure about the facts and her intentions, but she chose not to, thereby disallowing any chance Horton had to respond as an autonomous person. Treating Horton with respect "as an end unto himself" entails that he be allowed to autonomously choose whether to aid Mayzie in her project, thereby adopting (or coadopting) her project. Of course, Mayzie would expect that others so treat her, which again explains how she illicitly makes an exception for herself.

Horton, on the other hand, makes it clear just how important human dignity is. Yes, what Mayzie did was wrong, but Horton's interactions with the *Whos* provide the underlying reasons. Furthermore, Horton's example makes something else clear: oftentimes, we fail to offer aid to others in need simply because we are lazy or apathetic. Many of us hide behind the excuse that keeping a promise or doing a chore is asking too much. At best, this is mere self-deception. At worst, this is an implicit affirmation of selfishness. Too often, we behave as Mayzie—on some level we falsely believe that our (nonmoral) projects are more important than those of others. Consequently, Horton's heroism lies not in the fact that he was willing to become an ingredient in the Beezle-Nut stew but rather in the fact that he was not quick to shirk his responsibilities. In this sense, Seuss and Kant agree. Horton was willing and able to keep his word insofar as he could. If that is all it takes to be a hero, implicitly argues Dr. Seuss, then all of us can be that sort of hero. We should be more like Horton (and less like Mayzie). Dr. Seuss convincingly demonstrates this by furthering the story of Horton—from faithful egg sitter to courageous *Who* protector. By reexamining the "story" of Kant's categorical imperatives—from the "universal law" to "ends in themselves" formulations—we can better appreciate the depth of Dr. Seuss's moral genius. In this way, these two literary greats reciprocally facilitate an enriched appreciation of the ethics of respecting persons.

We Are Here! We Are Here!

It's true that Horton's heroism causes unrest in Nool, at least temporarily. However, Horton's neighbors are to blame for the disruption. They are the ones who have failed to properly investigate the facts. Indeed, note why we see Sour Kangaroo as the antagonist: by single-mindedly valuing her personal project—even one that brings general harmony to Nool—over the *Whos* well-being, she fails to respect their inherent worth as persons. She thereby affirms that the denizens of Nool and the contentment they enjoy are more important than the *Whos* and their livelihoods and, indeed, their very lives. Therefore, although hers is not a completely selfish project—unlike Mayzie's—she still commits the gravest of Kantian moral errors. However, upon realizing her error, she quickly makes amends. She exclaims to Horton "from now on, I'm going to protect them with you!" ("And the young kangaroo in her pouch said, ME TOO!") (Horton). Sour Kangaroo changes her ways because of the obviousness that "a person is a person, no matter how small."

That the temporary civil unrest in Nool was caused by willful ignorance highlights an important feature of doing moral philosophy: one must be sufficiently informed by getting the relevant facts straight. Horton and Sour Kangaroo disagreed about what ought to be done with the speck because they disagreed about whether it contained persons. ("On that speck—as small as a head of a pin—persons never have been!" [Horton]) But once the *Whos* "yopped" loud enough and Sour Kangaroo was sufficiently attentive, her disagreement with Horton disappeared. Ethically speaking, they didn't disagree. Both agree with Kant that persons are of utmost moral value and deserving of respect.

Unfortunately, civil unrest caused by disagreements about the facts is not reserved to Dr. Seuss stories alone. The dignity of actual persons has not always been, nor is today consistently, respected. Blind (and willful) ignorance is often the root cause of the injustices associated with not respecting the inherent worth of persons. Those in the Jungle of Nool were blind to the *Whos* due to the fact that *Whos* can't be seen with the naked eye. But we must remember that Dr. Seuss published this story in 1954, in the midst of the controversies of the civil rights movement. Although African American civil rights activists like Martin Luther King Jr. did their best (like the Whoville mayor) to organize chants akin to "We are here! We are here!," all their "yopps" to achieve social recognition went unheard for far too long. Many Americans remained "blind" to the plight of African Americans. At least Sour Kangaroo couldn't see the *Whos* standing in front of her. Yet, people in this country could obviously see African Americans and the injustices they faced. Horton pleaded with Sour Kangaroo to try just a little harder—listen just a little more carefully—if her eyes failed her. Perhaps Dr. Seuss was pleading with his readers: just look and listen a little more carefully to what is going on right in front of you. So, perhaps the real beauty of *Horton Hears a Who!* is that once you realize that *Whos* are persons, you can better see that persons are "Whos." As "Whos" and not "Whats" or "Its," persons are deserving of your respect because they possess inherent worth. When "Whos" are treated like things, this is the gravest of moral errors.

Accordingly, what grounds the importance of human dignity is that human beings are *persons*. What Seuss recognized so clearly is that being a person—being a "Who"—is not merely a biological category. It is a moral category. In this sense, all the inhabitants of Nool are persons. Yes, they look like animals and insofar as they are kangaroos, monkeys, elephants, and eagles, they are animals. But they are also persons because they represent creatures who are autonomous—rational agents possessed of volition and foresight. In ways that only Dr. Seuss can, he was reminding us that persons come in all shapes, colors, and sizes. Claiming that color, shape, or size does morally matter is to fail to recognize that persons are "Whos." Horton recognized that the *Whos* are persons. He listened, he heard, and he acted—heroically. In doing so, he hears me and he hears you. We, too, are "Whos." We, once again, should be more like Horton the elephant.

⌒

CHAPTER ELEVEN

Pragmatist Ethics with John Dewey, Horton, and the Lorax

Thomas M. Alexander

Pragmatism is an unfortunate term, especially when it comes to the subject of ethics, for its popular sense connotes someone who is self-centered and shortsighted whereas the philosophical version means just the opposite: developing long-range, shared goals and ideals that expand meaning in our lives. While both William James (1842–1910) and Charles S. Peirce (1839–1914), the founders of pragmatism, had important things to say about ethics, it was John Dewey (1859–1952) who developed the most encompassing and profound ideas on the subject. Ethics, for Dewey, blended in with his whole social philosophy, which included his theory of the role of education in democracy and his view of democracy itself as social intelligence applied to all aspects of life.

Dewey's ideas were frequently misunderstood—to the point of being taken as saying the opposite of what he meant (as in the case of the term *pragmatism* itself). He was accused of denying there were any intrinsic values, of making success the end of life, of advocating whatever was crudely expedient, of being a nihilist and believer in social Darwinism. Each one of these claims is perfectly false; Dewey rejected these notions and affirmed their exact contraries. Part of the reason for this misjudgment was that people had such a fixed idea of ethics as a set of absolutes that any other view was thought to come down to "nature red in tooth and claw." People often want a feeling of security in the values they prize the most. Many such people did find

Dewey's ideas threatening, especially those who thought that ethics had to be a preordained set of fixed beliefs and an infallible way of discerning good from evil—that is, people who turned to a dogmatic outlook as a way of not having actually to *think* about the complexity of existence. Like Socrates, Dewey thought that morality was all one with what he called "reflective conduct." People who view ethics as unquestioning obedience to commands (either God-given or coming from social institutions or traditions) exhibit what Dewey called "the quest for certainty." Not only did he think this quest futile but also he thought it actually made people less able to deal with ethical issues as they arose in life. Such people, after all, are like the German soldiers at the concentration camps who pleaded they were "just following orders." The ethical life, for Dewey, was one of constant reflection and risk. Neither obedience nor good intentions were enough to help us evade the responsibility of moral reflection or the possibility of tragic error.

So, what is ethics concerned with? Dewey affirms that there is no separate sphere of our existence that is "ethical"; that is, ethics is concerned with *all* forms of conduct, or is so at least potentially. To use one of Dewey's examples, it may seem outside of the concerns of ethics to decide to open a window to get fresh air. But if there is a sick person in the room, someone with asthma, say, whether to open a window or not might well be a decision to reflect upon. Nor is Dewey saying that each and every decision we make is of equal moral value—this would make us as incapable of action as Hamlet, riddled with existential anxiety about each choice. One of the features of ethics, says Dewey, is being able to distinguish between relatively important matters that do call for reflection and relatively trivial matters that do not. But this ability is the result of experience, not a function of a prefabricated formula, and it is fallible.

Besides rejecting the idea that there is a special domain of "the ethical" marked off from other pursuits, Dewey rejected the idea that ethics was something imposed from outside, something not only set apart from nature but also fundamentally at odds with it. Such views like to see human existence as constantly challenged to choose between following "natural desires" or to obey what conscience or God dictate. There is an episode in the film *The African Queen* in which Katharine Hepburn's character, Rose Sayer, a teetotaling missionary, objects to Charlie Allnut's drinking. Charlie wakes up to see the last of his liquor being poured overboard. "Aw, miss," he says, "It's only human nature to want a drop now and then." "Human nature, Mr. Allnut," Rose replies, "is what we are put in this world to rise above." Or we can think of the story of the prophet Elijah in I Kings 19: having defeated the priests of the god Baal, Elijah flees for his life to Mount Horeb (i.e., Mount Sinai, where Moses received the Ten Commandments). There, alone, he finds God not in the wind and storm, but in the "still, small voice" within himself, asking, "Elijah, what are you doing here instead of doing My work?" This story could be read as Elijah struggling to overcome his "natural" desire to live in order to obey the call of conscience. Dewey would say that the call of conscience, like temperance, is *also* part of human nature, and what the voice within him was doing was limiting a very narrow, selfish desire with a desire for a more inclusive good and higher value. If we cut off morality from human nature, we turn the whole moral life into one of conflict; if, on the other hand, we have a complex and broad view of human nature we can see ideals growing naturally out of our daily experience, capable of being encouraged, modified, or, if necessary, countered with other forms of conduct.

This, in fact, is how we grow up. A small child may selfishly claim a toy as hers and refuse to share. A parent could simply order the child to share and threaten punishment if she did not. What the child learns in that case is fear of punishment and blind obedience. Instead, one could try to teach the child to imagine what it is like for other children never to get to use the toy. What the child may learn then is to use her imagination in order to understand how other people feel; the child may develop sympathy and kindness. From the act of sharing the child may learn to play with others rather than alone and so develop a more complex and social personality. New values, like friendship, emerge to limit the earlier desire to keep the toy. This, in turn, gives the child a broader range of experience by which to judge actions and options in the future. In *Green Eggs and Ham*, Sam's friend has the initial belief that he dislikes green eggs and ham. This judgment is changed by the simple experience of trying them. New experiences can be the basis of new "prizings," but they can also make us reevaluate our old beliefs. If we see human life as the ground from which such new and richer values can grow, we cease trying to "master" a resistant nature and learn to cultivate fertile ground.

Such a picture, however, should not be taken naïvely. All sorts of values can spring from experience. One child may discover a capacity for empathy, but another may discover the pleasure of bullying others or torturing animals. A child who breaks a glass may discover the courage to be honest when asked "Did you break this?," but she may also discover creative talents in lying and the power to deceive. Dewey does not shy away from the difficulty of this reality; this is precisely why the moral life must cultivate virtues of thoughtful reflection and critical reevaluation. He would point out to those who would unequivocally say that empathy and honesty are good and bullying and deceit are bad how ambiguous our moral existence really is.

Is telling the truth *always* right? The German philosopher Immanuel Kant (1724–1804) said "yes." Kant's test for a moral act was whether we could universalize the "maxim" or rule of action implied in it without contradiction. And indeed one can consistently universalize the maxim "always tell the truth" into a law for all rational beings; no contradiction follows. One cannot do so for lying—a world of universal liars is logically impossible. But would you honestly tell an enraged, drunken husband that his estranged wife was staying in your house? During war, skilled "liars" are employed to deliver false intelligence to the enemy. Likewise we may ask: is empathy *always* good? We may empathize with someone in such a way so that she remains dependent and focused on her weaknesses or develops into a hypochondriac. "Tough love" at times may be better.

It was Dewey's refusal to pay lip service to empty absolutes, so useless in practice that so often scandalized people who wanted morality to be a simple set of dictates, a chart of right and wrong actions that would get them off the hook of thinking for themselves. This does *not* mean Dewey thought *every* response to a moral problem of equal value or as being "right for the one who made the choice." That is a position known as "relativism," a view that goes all the way back to the Greek philosopher Protagoras (490–420 BCE). But there is a vast difference between the relativist, who says all values are arbitrary, subjective matters of taste, not capable of being criticized, and what we might call the "relationalist" or "contextualist." A relational view of value sees it as a function of our being caught up in a world and interacting with it; we are always in a context—but a context with a history and with possibilities. The context calls for reflection and inquiry beyond any subjective response. It is true that we may have an immediate, unreflective response of liking or disliking something. Dewey tends to call such instances "prizings" or "values"; but the story doesn't end there. If we simply respond to them, experience may teach us to stop and think next time. Such prizings may be reevaluated in the light of other values. Prizings, or immediate likes and dislikes, need to be distinguished from the process of *valuation*, the reflection upon the situation and its possibilities for conduct. The *meaning* of the initial like or dislike becomes enlarged and so puts the value into a different context: it is "reevaluated." Thus the challenge Dewey sets up is not between "absolute" versus "relative" (i.e., subjective) values but between developing a *morally thoughtful* or a *morally thoughtless* character. The subjective relativist is content merely to undergo whatever feeling comes his or her way. The contextual relationalist seeks to develop and grow through being attentive to experience and its possibilities.

To return to our example, we may have been raised to think that being good means being obedient until the day we realize with horror what "following orders" can mean. In 1968, during the Vietnam War, a helicopter pilot, Hugh Thompson Jr., witnessed the My Lai Massacre in progress and halted it. He and his two crewmen saw American soldiers shooting unarmed civilians, many women and children. He landed his helicopter and threatened to shoot the American servicemen if they continued. They were carrying out the orders of their commander, Lieutenant Calley. Calley himself defended his actions by saying he was only "following orders." Thompson's courage was only officially recognized many years later, while in the meantime, in the passion of the moment and in the military's attempt to hide such atrocities, he was castigated as disloyal and unpatriotic. In 2009, Calley finally said he was "sorry." Following orders or obeying superiors does not necessarily ensure one is doing what is right or that one is thereby a good person. Lieutenant Calley is an extreme example of moral thoughtlessness.

If one expects ethics to be a list of simple rules to solve all the moral dilemmas of life for us, then Dewey's approach will be disappointing indeed, for Dewey stresses that the moral life must be one of constant reflection, questioning, exploring, and endeavoring to create and follow worthwhile ideals. It is the endeavor to live *thoughtfully*. This is a process one does not carry out alone but in constant interaction with others. Ethical thinking is not simply the internal, private search for what the voice of conscience says. It is often carried out in discussion with friends and others so that we may have an enhanced view of the situation and ourselves. Indeed, we have the capacity for deliberating privately because as children we were gradually *taught* to be reflective. "We deliberate with ourselves because others have deliberated with us," says Dewey. It is certainly one of the main themes of Theodor Geisel's—Dr. Seuss's—books to help children begin to deliberate morally and sensitively about their world.

Before discussing Dewey's views of moral deliberation and what it is to have a moral character, it would help to contrast Dewey's approach with the two dominant schools of ethics, utilitarianism and deontological ethics.[1] When one takes a course in ethics, frequently these two approaches are the only ones extensively discussed and contrasted. Utilitarianism says one should act for the greatest good (happiness) for the greatest number. It urges taking consequences into account. Deontological ethics says simply do what is right; do your duty and the consequences be damned. Both approaches try to interpret *all* moral values in light of *one* supreme value (happiness or duty), and both try to provide a universal rule of conduct by which any and every action may be judged. Dewey's ethics provides a different approach, one that refuses to reduce all moral values to one supreme value or that believes ethics is a matter of judging individual actions by universal rules. This contrast helps explain Dewey's ethical thought and distinguishes Dewey's views from utilitarianism, with which it is often confused.

Utilitarianism, best represented by British philosophers Jeremy Bentham (1748–1832) and John Stuart Mill (1806–1873), picks on one value, happiness (which they understood as pleasure), and came up with a fixed rule: Always act so that your action realizes the greatest happiness for the greatest number. Or, in simpler terms: all values ultimately come down to pleasure and pain; all one must think about in moral conduct is how to maximize pleasure and minimize pain in general, not just for oneself. Mill complicated this somewhat by saying there were different *kinds* of pleasure of higher or lower quality: one would prefer to be "Socrates dissatisfied" than "a fool satisfied." But the utilitarians urged that one must always look beyond one's own immediate desires and consider the consequences at large. Hence this view is often described as "consequentialism." Since Dewey's approach also insists on taking consequences into account, it is frequently treated as a form of utilitarianism when acknowledged at all.

The relation of utilitarianism and Dewey's position might be illustrated by the story of *The Lorax*. In Dr. Seuss's story, once there was a land with lots of beautiful Truffula Trees until the old Once-ler comes along and discovers he can make Thneeds from their soft tufts. He chops down a tree, and immediately the Lorax pops out of the Truffula stump: "I am the Lorax. I speak for the trees. I speak for the trees for the trees have no tongues. And I'm asking you, sir, at the top of my lungs . . . *What's that THING you've made out of my Truffula tuft?*" (Lorax). "Thneeds can be very useful," the Once-ler says, "It's a shirt. It's a sock. It's a glove. It's a hat. But it has *other* uses far beyond that. You can use it for carpets. For pillows! For sheets! Or curtains! Or covers for bicycle seats!" (Lorax). The Thneeds turn out to be popular, and the Once-ler and his family begin to manufacture them, cutting down more and more trees. The Lorax keeps warning the selfish and shortsighted Once-ler. He speaks for the poor Brown Bar-ba-loots "who played in the shade in their Bar-ba-loot suits and happily lived, eating Truffula Fruits" (Lorax). But the Once-ler enlarges the factory: "I meant no harm. I most truly did not. But I had to grow bigger. So bigger I got. . . . I went right on biggering . . . selling more Thneeds. And I biggered my money, which everyone needs" (Lorax). More and more creatures are affected. The Swomee-Swans can't sing because of the pollution. The Gluppity-Glupp from the factory is "glumping the pond where the Humming-Fish hummed" (Lorax). Soon the land is a waste, and the Lorax leaves only a pile of rocks with one word: "UNLESS" (Lorax).

In one sense, the Once-ler can be portrayed as the classic utilitarian. He is attempting to act to increase happiness in himself and the consumers of the Thneeds: the more Thneeds, the more happiness, and the Truffula Trees are the means to that. But what the story shows, of course, is that the Once-ler is not really thinking about the long-range consequences for everybody—for the whole ecosystem. The original environment supported a diversity of species: Brown-Bar-ba-loots, Swomee-Swans, and Humming-Fish. The quality of the air and water are affected. Although the Lorax is also thinking about consequences, he is thinking about the complexity of the world and the meaning of our actions in it. He is not motivated by "maximizing happiness" but by the ideal of acting responsibly for the sake of the whole environment. A utilitarian might argue that the Lorax is in fact just a better utilitarian than the Once-ler: the Lorax sees the long-range consequences better and is concerned for the happiness of other species. But the fact is that utilitarianism did promote rather narrow, materialistic values and supported the growth of capitalism with its vague ideas of promoting general happiness. A utilitarian would have *calculated* the maximum outcome of "happiness" rather than being genuinely *concerned* with the Bar-ba-loots and others. The Lorax *is* the voice of this general concern that overrides our desires. The Lorax, I contend, is actually a Deweyan ethicist, not least for his constant warning to "stop and think." He is concerned for consequences, but not in the utilitarian sense at all. He engages in what Dewey calls "reflective morality." He is concerned to show the *meaning* of the Once-ler's actions. Consequences are used to reveal the meaning of the *present* situation. The utilitarian, in fact, subjects the present to an imagined future that never really comes—it recedes as he approaches. And often in practice this means that immediate, shortsighted ends are pursued in the dim belief that they will automatically create happiness for everyone. John Stuart Mill defended the value of maximum individual liberty in the belief that personal self-determination was what made most people happiest. The standard creed of capitalism is, by allowing everyone to pursue his own self-interest, the market will grow indefinitely, creating more goods at cheaper prices and leading to the happiness of all. It's the "Once-ler philosophy." On the other hand, Dewey says we must try to understand the possibilities of the present and act in a way that a meaningful future grows from it, one that sustains a variety of values.

We can contrast the deontologist with the Deweyan by briefly examining the stories of *Horton Hears a Who!* and *Horton Hatches the Egg.* A deontologist acts for the sake of duty pure and simple—"deontology" itself comes from the Greek for "duty," *deon.* This was a central value in the ancient school of Stoicism and the Roman moralists. But the major representative is Immanuel Kant, whom we have already met. Evaluating consequences, Kant argues, are no guarantee one is doing what is right, nor are feelings of happiness or pleasure what gives worth to moral action or to a human life. Kant was concerned that an act, however noble it may seem outwardly, could ultimately be traced to self-love and seeking one's own satisfaction. I may be generous, but do I not love myself in my act of generosity? *Ought* I give a needy person money simply because it makes me happy? A mother may *feel* happy caring for her child—but what if she does not? She may be like Mayzie. Mayzie is a lazy bird tired of hatching her egg. She gets Horton to sit on her egg because she needs a rest, and off she goes to Palm Beach. She doesn't do her *duty*. So Kant is unimpressed by determining the ethical value of an action on the basis of what makes someone happy or not. It is the rule expressing the duty that determines if an act is moral. I must treat persons as beings of "infinite worth" and as "ends in themselves," says Kant; that is, as having intrinsic value and being endowed with rights. Kant believes that we should look to moral or "practical" reason: determine what the rule you are thinking of following in a present situation is. Universalize it as if it were a law for all persons and see if it stands the test of being self-consistent. If so, then it is right and the "voice of duty" or, in Kant's terms, the categorical imperative, enjoins it. But it is acting for the sake of duty, respect for the rule, not because of our feelings that is important.

In *Horton Hears a Who!* we have a story of a mindful elephant whose conscientiousness (and big ears) allow him to be aware of very small persons that others are not aware of at all. Because he alone can hear them, he makes a promise to protect them. One day as Horton is taking a bath in a pond, he thinks he hears a call for help. No one is around, but a small speck of dust, or rather someone on it, seems to be the source, "Some sort of a creature of *very* small size, Too small to be seen by an elephant's eyes . . ." (Horton). Horton thinks this person is afraid of being blown into the pool, and so he carefully places the speck of dust on some clover. It would seem Horton is a good Kantian: he is treating another person as an end in himself or as having infinite worth: "A person's a person no matter how small" (Horton). In trying to protect the speck from the other incredulous and careless animals, Horton hears the *Who*s—for that is what they are—tell him he saved a whole town, *Who*-ville. "You've saved all our houses, our ceilings and floors. You've saved all our churches and grocery stores" (Horton). Horton replies, "You're safe now. Don't worry. I won't let you down" (Horton). But keeping this promise turns out to be quite difficult. Devious monkeys, the Wickersham Brothers, steal the clover and give it to Vlad Vlad-i-koff, an eagle, who flies away with it. Horton laboriously follows only to see it dropped in a field of clover. But he goes through it, clover by clover, until he finds the *Who*s on the "three millionth flower." *Who*-ville has been badly shaken; everything needs repairing. But Horton promises, "Of course I will stick. I'll stick by you small folks through thin and through thick" (Horton). But the animals—including all the Wickersham relatives—find Horton, threaten to tie him up, and boil the clover. Horton pleads for the *Whos* to make as much noise as they can in order to prove they exist. They try but do not succeed in making themselves heard until the last little *Who* ("a very small, very small shirker named Jo-Jo" [Horton]) joins in and *"Their voices were heard!"* (Horton). Horton smiles, "Do you see what I mean? . . . They've proved they ARE persons, no matter how small. Their whole world was saved by the Smallest of All" (Horton).

As in the case of *The Lorax,* in which the Lorax could be read as a sort of utilitarian, one could make a case for Horton being a Kantian deontologist. He respects persons as beings of inherent worth "no matter how small" or inconsequential. He makes a promise and keeps it, come hell or high water, as he does in *Horton Hatches the Egg.* But I would like to urge that this, too, would be to force a narrow interpretation where a wider one, Deweyan, would be more appropriate. One of the things that Dewey sees as crucial in the moral life is developing habits of conscientiousness—of carefully reflecting on aspects of a situation that may not at first glance be obvious. We can call this "The *Who* Factor." The *Whos* are values that may easily be overlooked but which are as important as the evident ones. Like the Once-ler in *The Lorax,* the various disbelieving animals, like the Wickersham Brothers, are fundamentally *thoughtless* individuals. They act out of a narrow sense of what is and is not and do not go to the trouble of finding out if Horton is right before passing the judgment that there are no *Whos.* Nor does Horton carry out his duty with a cold rationality, doing duty for duty's sake. Horton acts because he *cares* for the *Whos.* Kant would find this problematic. Just as Horton cares for the egg in *Horton Hatches the Egg,* in *Horton Hears a Who!,* he is devoted to preserving something that others have disregarded so that, by the end of the story, the world is richer for his success. The world at the end of *Horton Hears a Who!* is changed because a new group has been discovered and acknowledged. Horton has moreover taught the value of *conscientiousness,* not of following rules for their own sake. Whereas Kant would be suspicious of Horton's feelings of concern and sympathy, Dewey would see them as good qualities of Horton's character. As we proceed to look at Dewey's analysis of moral deliberation and moral character, let us keep Horton in mind.

Unlike the utilitarians or the deontologists, Dewey does not believe that the spectrum of values can ultimately be measured in terms of *one supreme value* like pleasure or duty. He does not believe that ethics is concerned with *finding the rule or rules* by which each action may be morally measured. Ethics is woven into all aspects of human existence; we live ethical *lives* and this means that a variety of values enters in and that our life is the *expression of character*. One of the major problems we often face is in fact the *conflict of values* in our lives. For Dewey, we really are often in the situation of comparing apples to oranges or even to pineapples and cabbage. The issue is not capable of being reduced to so many units of happiness or pleasure, nor can it be solved by universalizing whatever rule we seem to be operating by because *duties themselves come into conflict*. One may try to figure out beforehand some artificial hierarchy of duties. But ethics cannot give us a little chart of which duty trumps which as if the moral life were a game of poker. Kant's ethics simply cannot handle the fact that our duties come into conflict and this is a central feature of our moral existence. The best we can do, says Dewey, is to try to integrate and harmonize diverse values. But ultimately what we are concerned with is deciding about what *meaning* our moral life will embody.

This struggle to deal with complex ranges of values that need to be harmonized and integrated or perhaps chosen or rejected altogether is what Dewey calls "deliberation." This was another term that made people confuse his thought with the utilitarians' emphasis on "calculation." But it is quite different, and in no way is it some sort of algorithmic calculus such as Bentham imagined possible. Deliberation relies on a body of experience and our web of habits in order to explore, prior to acting, the various possible ways of responding to a situation. Dewey sometimes calls this "dramatic rehearsal in imagination." In one of his major works on ethics, *Human Nature and Conduct*, Dewey keenly observes:

> The poignancy of situations that evoke reflection lies in the fact that we really do not know the meaning of the tendencies that are pressing for action. We have to search, to experiment. Deliberation is a work of discovery. Conflict is acute; one impulse carries us one way into one situation, and another impulse takes us another way to a radically different objective result. Deliberation is not an attempt to do away with this opposition by reducing it to one amount. It is an attempt to *uncover* the conflict in its full scope and bearing. What we want to find out is what difference each impulse and habit imports, to reveal qualitative incompatibilities by detecting the different courses to which they commit us, the different dispositions they form and foster, the different situations into which they plunge us. In short, the thing at stake in any serious deliberation is not a difference of quantity, but what kind of person one is to become, what sort of self is in the making, what kind of world is in the making.[2]

This key point is almost universally neglected when Dewey is seen as a "consequentialist" like the utilitarians. The moral concern in deliberation is uncovering the various meanings and values at play in a situation and thus providing us the basis for what this or that action will *mean* and *who* we shall become.

This passage also shows, by the way, how Dewey differs from the existentialist position of Jean-Paul Sartre. Sartre had argued that humans are radically free and we create our "essence" out of our existence; that is, we become what we are as a result of our choices. Choosing is our act of self-creation. But for Sartre this was an irrational act of pure will and something that each individual had to grapple with on his own. He gives the example of a young man, one of his students, who came to him during the war with a moral dilemma: should he join the *Résistance* (the "resistance" movement against the Germans) or stay at home and care for his aging mother?[3] Sartre's response was "I can't choose for you." Sartre regarded the young man as trying to evade his freedom; but even in the act of choosing to go to Sartre and not a priest, he had in effect chosen. What the young man was probably hoping for was someone to help him figure out the implications of each possible decision; that is, the *meaning* of each possible choice. It is too bad he was not able to go to Dewey instead of Sartre. For both thinkers we could say that when we choose we choose the self we will be, except that Dewey thinks this is a deliberative process, an exploration in thought and dialogue with others, while for Sartre it is a lonely and irrational act of will.

As we deliberate, the role of ideals becomes clear. Ideals are not pure fixed realities but genuine possibilities of the present. Insofar as an ideal becomes truly operative in our present situation, various aspects of the situation are transformed into what Dewey calls "ends-in-view." That is, the *meaning* of something in the present situation is transformed by the possibilities it has of realizing some ideal. Let us say I wish to befriend someone I like at work. The ideal here would be friendship—the enjoyment of companionship, enjoyment of each other's company, and sharing of interests. The means at hand—the ends-in-view—could be asking the person to join me for lunch or a cup of coffee, engaging in conversation that indicates interest in what he or she does or cares about or offering to do small favors. Another example could be that one's ideal is to build a house. At various stages pouring cement, setting up wooden frames, laying bricks, and so on would be the ends-in-view of the same ideal: the complete house. What Dewey wants to stress by this term is that nothing is a "mere means"; the end is the outgrowth of the means and in reflecting on the means, we need also to reflect on the end. Dewey is often thought to have held that we somehow seize on an end and then coldly use whatever can function as a means to realize it. This is the opposite of what he said. Dewey constantly emphasized not only that means and ends are woven together in intelligent conduct but also that ends themselves must undergo reflection and deliberation as they are realized. After all, the person one thought would be a good friend may turn out to be another sort of individual entirely; the actual house one lives in may be quite a different reality from the ideal one thought to bring forth.

Deliberation, then, involves the use of imagination to reveal the possibilities of the *present* situation and the various ideals or meanings it might come to embody. Dewey's ethics, then, is really an ethics of *meaning*. The environment in which we act is not merely the immediate physical one, here and now. The environment includes past history and future possibilities. Intelligence is our ability to interpret the present in light of those two temporal horizons. The more we grasp the past history involved in the present situation the more likely we are to understand better the conflicts it carries. Knowledge is a highly relevant aspect of ethics for Dewey. Knowledge does not simply give us the past history but provides a more accurate basis for projecting possibilities in the present. The more we grasp the range of possibilities for action, the more we might select a course of action that realizes value and meaning, harmonizing the conflict. Thus knowledge, imagination, and ideals work together to constitute moral intelligence. This is why the *popular* understanding of the term *pragmatist* is so inappropriate to Dewey's ethics.

"Morals means growth of conduct in meaning . . .," says Dewey. "It is all one with growing. Growing and growth are the same fact expanded in actuality or telescoped in thought. In the largest sense of the word, morals is education."[4] We can now see why Dewey thought education to be of such central importance to philosophy in general and ethics in particular. Strangely, he stands in company of only a few other major philosophers who have agreed on this point: Plato, Rousseau, and, perhaps, Aristotle (Aristotle's *Politics* breaks off just as he brings up the topic). Dewey is close to Aristotle, especially in terms of his view that ethics is ultimately about moral character. With Aristotle, Dewey assigned a central place in ethics to the formation of the right habits. Whereas Aristotle tended to focus on habits to discern the "mean relative to oneself," Dewey stressed the formation of habits of thoughtfulness, conscientiousness, and shared inquiry. This for him was the key to democracy—not a set of governmental principles. In a strange way Dewey is in agreement with Plato: the best society is that in which intelligence guides conduct. Plato, however, had indulged in a magnificent but dangerous hypothesis in his *Republic*. He had asked the question: "What would a society look like *IF* a science of justice existed?" He is often mistaken to have thought presumptuously *THAT* he actually possessed such a science, when it is absolutely clear he did not (*Republic* 506e). Dewey asks the question: "What habits should a society cultivate in which there is no finished science of morals?" His conclusion is, a society that is disposed to inquiry, exploration of possibilities, discussion, and criticism and reevaluation of prior ends in light of actual outcomes. It is a society that can grow intelligently.

The aim of moral education for Dewey is to become a moral self, to have a moral *character*. Insofar as the Aristotelian idea of "virtue ethics" has been a subject of philosophical interest in recent times, largely in light of the perceived dead-end debate between utilitarianism and deontological ethics, it would be more accurate to place Dewey along with Aristotle in the class of "virtue ethicists." Virtue ethics focuses on the ideal of moral character, not specific rules or specific actions. One may donate a large sum of money to a worthy charity, but if one does it by accident or in order to gain popularity, the act has different moral significance than it does if one does it from pure generosity and compassion. It is the *character* that reveals the meaning of the act. If the Once-ler had been convinced by the Lorax that it was in his economic self-interest to save the Truffula Trees, he still would have been acting out of a selfish motive rather than one taking into account the needs of other creatures and the welfare of the environment.

> The self should be *wise* or prudent, looking to an inclusive satisfaction and hence subordinating the satisfaction of an immediately urgent single appetite; it should be *faithful* in acknowledgement of the claims involved in its relations with others; it should be solicitous, *thoughtful*, in the award of praise and blame, use of approbation and disapprobation, and, finally, should be *conscientious* and have the active will to discover new values and to revise former notions.[5]

As for Aristotle, the self is the interwoven set of habits that provides the structure for our organized responses to situations. Habits are not passive tools but active powers; they project lines of action into the future. Some sets of habits simply replicate themselves in conduct. But other habits move us toward growth. Aristotle believed in a fixed essence of the species, whereas Dewey knew that life was an ongoing, open-ended process. Thus Dewey stressed the habits of growth as of key moral importance. The self is revealed in its actions; actions show what we truly and genuinely care about. Dewey dismisses the idea that haunted Kant: the possibility our most generous actions might spring from "self-interest." The self *is* its interests, says Dewey. The question is what *kind* of interests we have. If I care for my own immediate gratification over the needs or feelings of others, I am selfish; if I care for the needs and feelings of others, I am altruistic. The issue is not whether I follow or repress my "self-interest." The issue is whether I have a pinched and narrow self or a broad and sympathetic one. As Dewey says, "The real moral question is what *kind* of self is being furthered and formed."[6]

A final comment can be made about Dewey's concept of freedom. Too often freedom is simply treated as the absence of restraints. But as Plato well knew, we may be prisoners of ignorance and bad desires. Dewey would agree. The key to freedom is not simply doing what we want but being *able* to do what is good. A baby left alone at birth is not thereby "free"—it dies. It must be cared for and raised to become a full human being. Thus acquiring habits is a key to freedom: we could not speak English without having learned it; we could not play a guitar unless we had learned how. It is because we were taught a language in our past that we can go on and learn others. It is by learning how to play a guitar that I might go on and learn another instrument. Thus the education of desire is a key aspect of freedom; desires need wise habits, and wise habits help us to evaluate past desires. Once again, education becomes a central topic for Dewey: a culture that believes in freedom needs to believe in education, the sort of education that helps cultivate growing, reflective, thoughtful, inquiring selves.

"Pragmatist ethics," understood in its Deweyan rather than popular sense, offers an important alternative to most of contemporary moral theory. Dewey's ideas suffered an eclipse for nearly half a century until a growing number of scholars from a variety of fields began to rediscover them. In time, ignorant misconceptions may be replaced by sounder readings, and once again ethics may actually speak to what Dewey termed "the problems of men" and not the problems of professional puzzle solvers. With his emphasis on education, Dewey would have found Dr. Seuss's wonderful books as laying the foundations for the development of thoughtful, concerned moral characters.

CHAPTER TWELVE

~

The Grinch's Change of Heart: Whodunit?

Anthony Cunningham

In *How the Grinch Stole Christmas!*, we find a creature who experiences a remarkable *metanoia*, a profound change of heart. The same creature who would steal Christmas and delight in the stealthy scheme at the great expense of the *Whos* eventually returns all the trappings of Christmas and even carves the "roast beast" with the joyful denizens of *Who*-ville. By the end of the story, the Grinch is certainly a new and better Grinch. We have similar examples of such transformations for the better in other well-known stories. Like the Grinch, Charles Dickens's Ebenezer Scrooge experiences a Christmas conversion, turning from his miserly, misanthropic ways toward love, generosity, and good cheer. In much the same way, on his trip to Damascus to persecute Christians, the biblical Saul literally sees the light and becomes a new man.

Such dramatic changes are not confined to literature and biblical stories. Real-life cases are plentiful enough. George Wallace, the Alabama governor who defiantly stood in the doorway of the University of Alabama in 1963 to prevent Vivian Malone and James Hood from enrolling later renounced his staunch segregationist views and apologized to black civil rights leaders for his ways. Oskar Schindler, the crafty businessman who sought wealth and power and who was quite willing to exploit the lucrative opportunities that the war and the Nazi oppression of Jews offered in this vein, eventually spent his great fortune saving Jews from annihilation. Such stories are hardly the mundane stuff of everyday life, but neither are they exotic. They are simply famous examples on public stages. We certainly recognize them when we see them. The undeniable fact is that sometimes people, even everyday people, change profoundly for the better, and sometimes the change is less a matter of slow, gradual evolution and more a matter of virtual revolution. In the Grinch's case, this is precisely what we find—a sudden change of heart where he turns his back on his mean ways and embraces a new life and self.

We know that this kind of thing can happen, so by thinking about the Grinch and his kind, we are not just speculating on one particular make-believe character, a fanciful product of one creative man's vivid imagination. This sort of thing is not simply make-believe. Nevertheless, the phenomenon is always remarkable because, after all, people rightly say that it's hard to teach an old dog new tricks. Well-entrenched characters tend to resist amendment, gradual or otherwise. In this light, understanding how and why people might experience a profound change of heart can help put some flesh on the bones of a better understanding of something extraordinary about us—our capacity for change for the better against such tall odds. And this kind of appreciation might also say something meaningful about our ethical attachments and commitments in general. So with this in mind, let's see if we can understand the Grinch and his kind.

The Grinch's Change of Heart: Some General Anatomy

First of all, notice that we can separate some important elements of such stories. For one thing, changes can always vary greatly so far as the sheer extent of the change is concerned. In a word, people can change just a little, and they can change a whole lot. Obviously, the big changes are usually the most remarkable ones, but even small changes can be most welcome as an initial step in the right direction. As they say, long journeys start with the first step.

Moreover, aside from the sheer amplitude of a change, alterations can be a matter of degree or a matter of kind. For instance, if I've always given $20 a year to the poor and I suddenly increase my contribution to $20,000, the change is a big one, but it is fundamentally a matter of degree: In this case, I do more of what I've always done. However, if I have never given to the poor in my whole life and I suddenly change my ways, then the change is not just a matter of degree, but a change in kind: I do something different, something I've never done before, and not simply more of what I've always done. Notice that in the Grinch's case, the change is a change in kind *and* it's also a big one. He goes from hating a *Who*-ville Christmas to happily joining their celebration of the holiday.

Changes can also vary in terms of their pace. In this sense, think about human bodies. We certainly expect them to change. If we found a group of octogenarians who looked just like twenty-somethings, we'd be very surprised (and no doubt they'd be very pleased). On the other hand, if we suddenly aged twenty years overnight, we'd be shocked (and dismayed). Where the body is concerned, we expect most changes associated with aging to be fairly gradual, even if they are virtually inevitable. For the most part, we expect as much of human character, whether the changes are for the better or the worse. Rapid character changes tend to be the great exception, rather than the norm, particularly where changes for the better are concerned. This makes sense because, like a house of cards, it takes a lot longer to build character than to knock it down.

Notice that the most extraordinary changes of heart are like the Grinch's: profound changes in kind that take place over a relatively short period of time. In the Grinch's particular case, the change seems just shy of instantaneous. From the top of Mount Crumpit, he listens on Christmas morning and hears the denizens of *Who*-ville singing despite the fact that he has stolen all their presents and Christmas trappings. He puzzles over the paradox until his "puzzler" is sore because he was certain that his scheme would obliterate their Christmas. Finally he comes around to the idea that maybe Christmas doesn't come from a store. Perhaps, Christmas means a little bit more than just that for *Who*-ville, and this realization somehow induces a dramatic change in him. Hence, in almost no time at all, the Grinch comes to see the world in a radically new way. The creature who races down the mountain at breakneck speed to return all the presents, decorations, and Christmas goodies, and who eventually carves the roast beast, is a new Grinch so far as his character is concerned. Again, we know from real life that this kind of thing can happen, so the vital question is how and why.

The Grinch's Metamorphosis: Seeing the Light of Reason?

One possibility is that the Grinch suddenly grasps some truth that he didn't see or only saw dimly before. For instance, think of the way that geometrical or logical proofs can often work for us. As any student of math or logic can recall, you can puzzle over a problem for a long, long time, turning it around this way and that way, and then suddenly the solution can hit you spontaneously (or sadly, not). In this kind of case, your mind suddenly tracks the geometrical truth, and once it does, you see it all clearly. Reason somehow shows you the right direction, illuminating the understanding in a new way.

Of course, this geometry example is a case of abstract thinking, a case of what you might call theoretical reasoning, as opposed to practical reasoning about how to live and what sort of person to be. This difference might seem like a big one, but not all philosophers believe so. Immanuel Kant (1724–1804), the eighteenth-century German philosopher, acknowledged differences between theoretical and practical reasoning, but he thought that in the ideal, practical reasoning should heed the dictates of reason just as strictly as theoretical reasoning. As he saw things, the main difference between the two was that the former required the assistance of the will, while the latter didn't. Think of it this way. When you think about "7 + 4," your mind immediately goes to 11 as the correct answer. There is no two-step process where you think your way to 11 and then decide whether you are going to believe what your mind tells you. You simply see 11, and that's that. And if you don't come to 11, then you're simply not a very good mathematician. Of course, you might not want to give someone the right answer when questioned, so you might say the will could still be involved in this way, but this is a different issue. The will certainly plays a role in giving the right answer, but no role in arriving at 11 as the right answer in the first place. On the other hand, when reason tells you what you ought to do (practical reason) as opposed to what you ought to think or believe (theoretical reason), the will must join forces with reason to produce an action. Thought without the will would be inert. Thus, Kant thought that doing the right thing, as opposed to thinking the right thing, required reason and the will to join forces, with reason directing the will down the correct path.

Now if Kant were to think about the Grinch, he'd surely take him to task for his nasty Christmas scheme. Kant thought that the moral law commanded respect for each and every rational being. In one famous formulation of the law, Kant insisted that rational beings must always be treated as "ends in themselves," not as a means to our own ends: "Act so that you use humanity, as much in your own person as in the person of every other, always at the same time as end and never merely as means."[1] Hence, just as the Grinch wouldn't want the citizens of Who-ville to take his stuff and to revel in his unhappiness, neither should he treat them in this way. After all, they matter every bit as much as he does. Kant had various versions of his moral law, but he thought they all came to the same thing: A rational being must prize the inherent dignity of equally worthy rational beings. As a rational being, I must pursue my life, duly constrained by the moral law. I express my rational autonomy by choosing to follow the law, rather than being ruled by mere inclination. All sorts of creatures can have desires, but only a moral being has the capacity to evaluate those desires. The moral law serves as a filter by which we can live true to a vision of rational beings as free and equal beings.

What might get in reason's way in this regard? Well, human beings are not all reason. We have all sorts of inclinations that can pull us against reason, the better part of our inevitably mixed nature. Of course, we don't know for sure why the Grinch hated Christmas so much and why he so badly wanted to spoil the happy occasion for *Who*-ville. Maybe he envied their good cheer and fellowship. Maybe he saw all this fuss about Christmas as a pathetic, hypocritical farce begging to be exposed for what it truly was. Maybe he just never liked the *Whos* and simply wanted to hurt them for his own satisfaction. We can't say for sure, and to be honest, Kant wasn't all that confident about being able to plumb the depths of the human heart with any degree of certainty in this sense. As a matter of fact, Kant thought that the roads to perdition were many and varied, and they all passed through the darkness of our often-insidious desires and inclinations: We can want and feel all sorts of things that divert us from the moral law, and like a veritable slave to our own desires, we can give into them, thereby forsaking the higher moral law for the dictates of its lesser. Kant thought we could only be truly free when reason ruled us, when we obeyed the law of our higher rational nature.

If you think about real life for a moment, you may be tempted to say that Kant's presumable picture of moral change, some sudden rational apprehension of the moral law and a resulting correction to align oneself with that law, usually isn't very effective when it comes to stopping bad guys from mistreating others. After all, when the desperados knock down your door and break your glasses, all your plaintive (or self-righteous) cries of "But don't you see how wrong it is for you to treat me like this?" usually come to naught. Yet, maybe this undeniable fact of life simply reinforces Kant's vital point: When we are in the grip of such powerful desires and feelings (like the bad guys), they can hijack reason and keep us from seeing the world clearly. In this light, maybe a Kantian conception of a *metanoia* shouldn't be judged by its relative infrequency or lack of potency. After all, it can be really hard to achieve clarity when it comes to all sorts of instances of theoretical reasoning, so why shouldn't we expect the same with respect to practical reasoning? We can so easily be blinded by mad passion of one sort or another.

What would a Kantian explanation of the Grinch's change of heart look like? It could actually take more than one form. Or more precisely, there could be two elements to the moment of clarity and the resulting change of heart. For instance, the Grinch could suddenly come to see that the moral law actually commands him to live differently than he's been living to date. In this case, he might think all along that he was actually living an upright life, and in a moment of reflection or spontaneous clarity, he might come to see that he wasn't living true to his rational principles. In other words, he might somehow believe that he was doing the right thing by taking away the cheap and tawdry trappings of Christmas, and in a moment of crystal-clear vision, he might suddenly see that the moral law forbids such things. He might realize that he is actually disrespecting the *Whos* by stealing Christmas.

Then again, instead of realizing what the law commands in this specific instance, the Grinch might suddenly realize that he has allowed himself to be hijacked systematically by his wayward inclinations, not just episodically. Ultimately, an autonomous being isn't ruled by his desires, but rather, by the moral law that manifests his true dignity. In light of this realization, the Grinch might resolve anew to set himself aright by following the commands of the law.

Notice that these two elements, one being an instance of poor judgment and the other a matter of inadequate oversight, might also go together. The Grinch might suddenly realize that he has been fooling himself all along about his fidelity to the moral law because he was unwittingly feeding the fires of his wayward inclinations, and now that he sees his circumstances clearly, he might resolve to put himself back on the upright track. A particular episode like the sound of *Who*-ville singing might somehow alert him to the general shape and orbit of his own life, effectively driving home the realization that his life has been nothing short of a shameful sham. Awakened anew to the real meaning of equal respect for his fellow creatures, he might renew his resolve to put reason back in the driver's seat. Having drifted away from his deep respect for the moral law, he might come back home to reason, so to speak.

We don't have to work too hard to find examples from everyday life that seem to fit this general description. I am unfair to someone because I begrudge him his far greater success. My envy works around the clock to sow the seeds of seething resentment. If I can convince myself that he has wronged me or that his gains are ill gotten, I can take refuge in righteous indignation, something far more comfortable than a frank admission of my own inferiority in some respect or other. Maybe this is what happened to the Grinch. Maybe he was always something of a loner, living on Mount Crumpit and seeing the laughter and camaraderie of the *Whos* as something of a slap in the face. *Those* Whos *think they are so big, so much better than me. Well, they are all fakes and hypocrites. They don't really love each other. All they really care about is the Christmas loot. Take that away from them and then see how happy they seem. Yes, that's it! I shall expose those phonies for what they really are.* But when Christmas survives in spite of the Grinch's crusade, perhaps he sees not just the *Whos* but also himself more clearly. Maybe his change of heart is a case of his head realizing the twisted corruptions of his own heart.

As the Seuss story goes, "It could be that his head wasn't screwed on quite right" (Grinch), and maybe he suddenly sees the light, just as we can see the error of our ways when we are going the wrong way in a geometrical proof.

This is one way to look at the Grinch, and indeed, changes of heart in general—as instances of coming around to some important principle that we have ignored, abandoned, or just haven't noticed before. The emphasis in this case is on reason: The light we see is the light of reason making plain the undeniable truth, and once we see it, we cannot resist it, just as we can't ignore the truth about geometry or arithmetic.

The Grinch's Change: Bring Back That Loving Feeling?

Yet, consider another way to think about the Grinch's change of heart. One might contend that the Grinch doesn't suddenly grasp some new truth, but instead, he feels something new. Whereas Kant saw ethics in terms of rational moral laws, David Hume (1711–1776), the Scottish Enlightenment philosopher, looked to human sentiments as the ultimate source. As Hume saw things, reason must always be the slave of the passions in a fundamental sense. He regarded sympathy, our capacity, and indeed, our decided proclivity to participate imaginatively in the weal and woe of our fellow human beings, as the cornerstone of morality. Show Hume a Grinch who might not only wish to steal Christmas but also annihilate every last Who in the world, and he might say many bad things about such a mean fellow, but "irrational" wouldn't be one of them.

In fact, imagine for just a moment a Grinch who didn't care about anyone else in the whole wide world. As Seuss might say, "Not a bit, not a stitch, not even a sliver" (Grinch). As far as this Grinch would be concerned, Hume would say he'd have no reason to blink an eye, even if so doing might save a thousand little Cindy-Lou Whos from some grave threat. A Grinch who might stand idly by as the Whos starve or suffer Who genocide would be many things—cold, callous, cruel. But these vices wouldn't necessarily make him irrational. The road to change would not be paved by reason for Hume, at least not in Kant's sense. He would insist that you could never get this Grinch to care about even one Cindy-Lou unless you established a connection between little Cindy-Lou and something else he already cared about, or unless you said or did something that gave rise to a new desire to save Cindy-Lou.

You can easily imagine all sorts of desires that might fit into the former category. The Grinch might love chocolate chip cookies, and it might just so happen that nobody could possibly beat Cindy-Lou Who's cookies. Or the

Grinch could have all sorts of terrible aches and pains, and Cindy-Lou might be just the little *Who* doctor to cure him. If Cindy-Lou effectively spared her own life by convincing the Grinch that it was worth his while to keep her around, we wouldn't say that he really cared about her. In this case, he would simply see her as an instrument to satisfy his own desires. The kind of reasoning that she and the Grinch would engage in would be means-end reasoning by way of demonstrating a connection between her existence and something else that the Grinch really wants.

Of course, sometimes such discoveries about means and ends have very big effects on a life. If the Grinch really wants to make millions of dollars and finds out that teaching philosophy in a university is the best way to go, then this will be big news for him. But notice that the revelation about an effective means to his end would only induce a change in what the Grinch does, not a change in what he is, at least not in any deep sense. What he's really all about in this case is making a whole lot of money, and philosophy is just an effective means to the same. True enough, the practice of philosophy might eventually change the Grinch in some respects since form often follows function, but the piece of practical reasoning that brings him to a new end—whether this is teaching philosophy or saving Cindy-Lou Who—will hardly be something that constitutes a watershed in who he is. In this case, he's just a Grinch who figured out how to get what he really wanted all along.

Hume, like Kant, didn't think that this kind of indirect (instrumental) concern for Cindy-Lou could confer any genuine moral credit on a person. Both would agree that the Grinch would have to care about Cindy-Lou for her own sake, and not just as a means to satisfy some other desire. But here is where Kant and Hume would part company. Whereas Kant would frame moral goodness in terms of a principled respect for Cindy-Lou's intrinsic worth as a rational being, Hume would look to sympathy's fellow-feeling, where the emphasis really is on feeling. In other words, while Kant would look to the head, Hume would look to the heart by way of what amounts to love in some form or another. As Hume says in his *Treatise*, "Reason is, and ought only to be the slave of the passions, and can never pretend to any other office than to serve and obey them."[2]

When it comes to giving a person a reason to do anything in life, Hume thinks that justifications can only go so far. When accounting for what you did, you will always come to a reason for which you can give no further reason other than the sheer fact of your desire. *Why did you save your pennies for so long? To buy myself a fantastic violin. Why do you want a fantastic violin? To play beautiful music. Why do you want to play beautiful music? Because I do*. True enough, one might redescribe the desire in various terms (*Beautiful music makes me feel so good*), but the descriptions would ultimately go only so far and they, too, would be open to the very same line of questioning (*Why do you want to feel so good?*). In the end, you'd get to a point where you couldn't say anything more about why you want this rather than that.

Hume thought this was so for all things, including morality. One might make all sorts of fine-tuned moral distinctions about subtle concepts and perceptive observations about moral phenomena, but in the end, morality came down to the fact that human beings were psychologically disposed to experience certain kinds of feelings and desires about the weal and woe of fellow human beings. Show Hume a Grinch totally devoid of any care and concern for little Cindy-Lou Who and he might call him all sorts of bad names—cruel, callous, uncaring, selfish, brutish, insensitive. But he certainly wouldn't call him irrational.

Why does this detail matter? Well, for someone like Hume, a change of heart must always depend on a change of heart in the colloquial sense. Such a change is not some apprehension of a rational truth that might be dispassionately explained and appreciated. Instead, the change must be the birth or the rekindling of feeling, an affective reaction rather than an intellectual one. We might speak of a kind of seeing and knowing here, but not in the way that we speak of seeing and knowing our way to solving a geometrical proof.

We don't have to look very far to find all sorts of examples that fit this kind of description. Years ago, I watched one of my brothers die, and after I spent his last night alone with him in the hospital, I certainly emerged a changed person. Unlike the Grinch, I didn't do any complete about-face, but the experience left me a different fellow in key respects. How so? Well, I definitely didn't gain any deeper intellectual appreciation of the biological facts of death. My brother was there, and then he was gone. His heart was beating, and then it was not. His brain had electrical activity, and then it was all gone. I understood these biological facts going in, and I certainly understood them going out. But my appreciation of death was different, and the important difference had to do with the emotional experience of watching my brother die. The difference was a *feeling* one, not a dispassionate *thinking* one. The experience left a deep mark on my life.

If we return to the Grinch, his experience seems more like mine than it does like a Kantian change of heart. Seuss says that the Grinch's small heart grew three sizes that day, and the sense is that he feels something new, something that leaves him a changed Grinch. Hearing *Who*-ville singing without their Christmas presents and trappings put the Grinch on a serious wonder.

And the Grinch, with his Grinch-feet ice-cold in the snow,
Stood puzzling and puzzling: "How *could* it be so?
It came without ribbons! It came without tags!
It came without packages, boxes or bags!" (Grinch)

I don't think the Grinch reaches a new, dispassionate conclusion, the way we might about a geometrical or logical proof. Instead, I think he experiences a new kind of feeling toward the *Whos*, something that changes the way he sees the world; in the process, this change in sentiment changes who he is.

A Final Word: Who Gives a Grinch?

Let's suppose that I am right here about the Grinch. Again, Seuss tells us that the Grinch's small heart grew three sizes that day, so it seems we are on safe ground with this guess. Even if the Grinch's case is a change of feeling, this is just one fictional example, and it needn't say anything definitive about whether most changes of the heart are more about the heart than the head, so to speak. The example of the Grinch invites us to reflect on how reason and emotions figure in being good more generally. Kant was very worried about making moral goodness a matter of feelings in any important sense. After all, we cannot command ourselves to feel something in any straightforward way. As he saw things, moral goodness must be within our power, and indeed, must be equally so for all of us if praise and blame are to make sense. How could it make sense to hold people responsible for what they do or who they are if these things rely on feelings that they might or might not have through no fault of their own? He sought a foundation for moral goodness in reason, and he believed that reason could hit on right action not just by accident but by tracking the moral truth, just as theoretical reason tracks the truth in mathematics or logic. Ideally, feeling would run parallel to reason, but feeling on its own could never have any moral authority.

On the other hand, Hume saw what we think of as "morality" as a product of our contingent empirical psychology, not as the immutable workings of reason itself. Given the kind of creatures we are, we happen to feel certain things, and some of these things we feel so deeply and reliably that they are well-entrenched sentiments, not just passing fancies. Take these feelings away from us and we would be very different creatures. Indeed, take our capacity and proclivity for sympathy away and morality would be something else entirely.

Unlike Kant, Hume didn't worry about any necessary universal foundation for morality. He thought we were alike enough that one could make some meaningful observations about morality for humanity in general, but this had to do with the contingent fact that we happened to feel and want many of the same things, not because we absolutely had to feel and want them under pain of irrationality. As Hume said in his *Treatise*, "'Tis not contrary to reason to prefer the destruction of the whole world to the scratching of my finger."[3] Had he come across a Grinch who preferred to see the *Whos* destroyed in this fashion, he would have thought the Grinch a terrible, nasty fellow, but the flaw would've been a problem with his feelings, not his powers of reasoning.

A great deal hangs on this contrast between Kant and Hume, not just in cases of some dramatic change of heart like we see with the Grinch but in the more mundane shape and everyday orbit of human lives. The key question is whether Kant is right to put reason at the helm with the emotions playing a subsidiary role at best, whether Hume portrays us as we really are, as creatures whose ultimate ends are given not by reason but by feeling in one form or another, or whether there is some other middle way between these two very different views of human character and moral goodness.

~

CHAPTER THIRTEEN

Thidwick the Big-Hearted Bearer of Property Rights

Aeon J. Skoble

Moose have large horns. It's not unreasonable to wonder whether some of that space could be used for something. If a moose wanted corporate sponsorship, for example, one could place logos on the horns. In Dr. Seuss's story, *Thidwick the Big-Hearted Moose*, a different use is proposed, and disastrous consequences ensue. In a charitable gesture, Thidwick allows a Bingle Bug to ride on his horns. But the Bingle Bug then invites dozens of other creatures to establish homes on Thidwick's horns. They then claim to have formed a community, with an entitlement to property rights on Thidwick's horns. Their exercise of their alleged rights turns out to place Thidwick's life in jeopardy. In this essay, I will argue that the "guests" did not in fact have any rights to live on the horns and that Thidwick was mistaken in letting his big-heartedness be used against him by the other creatures. This will allow us to see something about the nature of property rights.

Would You, Could You, Get off My Head?

The plot follows the pattern of the slippery slope: the Bingle Bug, put out by it being a hot day, asks Thidwick for permission to ride on his horns. Thidwick reasons, correctly, that a tiny bug riding on his horns will not be an inconvenience at all, so he grants the bug's wish. But the bug invites more and more creatures until it really is an inconvenience for Thidwick. Thidwick feels as though he cannot protest the inconvenience on the grounds that "a host above all must be nice to his guests" (Thidwick). But this is where Thidwick's reasoning becomes flawed: they aren't his guests. The bug, not Thidwick, invites the other creatures, who themselves go on to take advantage. For example, the bug invites a bird, then the bird takes a wife, and then the bird asks both his wife and her uncle to move on as well. Thidwick is mistaken in regarding them as guests just as they are mistaken in thinking they are entitled to live there. But later, this mistake leads to further problems: when Thidwick decides to go to the other side of Lake Winna-bango, the creatures protest: "You've no right to take our home to the far side of the lake!" (Thidwick). This claim is flawed in three distinct ways.

First, even on their own terms, the creatures' protest is irrational. The reason Thidwick wants to go to the south side of the lake is that there is no more Moose-Moss on the north shore. If Thidwick were to starve to death, then the creatures would lose their home. But the other two flaws in their protest involve conceptual confusion. Calling it "our home" is to think that moving in uninvited establishes property rights or that mere occupancy creates a proprietary relationship. By that reasoning, there is no such thing as auto theft or theft at all. And saying that Thidwick has no right to take his own horns to wherever he chooses is to deny that Thidwick has a property right to his own self.

For a closer look at why these creatures are mistaken, let us consider the argument made in the seventeenth century by John Locke (1632–1704) in his *Second Treatise of Government*. Locke's argument is about human beings, of course, not moose, but since Thidwick is an anthropomorphized fictional moose, with rational self-awareness (and a good command of English), we can take him to be a person at least allegorically, and so Locke's argument works for Thidwick.

Locke's argument famously claims that the rationale for forming a government is the protection of rights that we have by nature, antecedently to the creation of any form of government. Locke talks about the protection of our lives, liberties, and property, but he clarifies that by "property" he includes our lives and liberties—in other words, a property right in ourselves. A central principle in Locke's argument is that since all people are moral equals, no one can have a natural claim of ownership over another. We therefore have a natural right of self-ownership. As Locke puts it, "Though the Earth . . . be common to all Men, yet every Man has a Property in his own Person. This no Body has any Right to but himself. The Labour of his Body and the Work of his Hands, we may say, are properly his."[1]

Thidwick, then, is the owner of his horns. The Bingle Bug acquires a right to ride on the horns by asking for, and receiving, permission from Thidwick.

This is not the same thing as acquiring a property right. The bug's request was for temporary occupancy—"would you mind if I rode on your horns for a way?" (Thidwick)—not to establish residence. But even if the request had been "Do you mind if I live here?," it still would not establish a property right in Thidwick's horns for the bug. The bug is, as Thidwick puts it, a guest. The idea of an "inalienable" right to self-ownership not only implies that it's wrong for others to enslave you but also that you cannot rightly enslave yourself. So while the bug is entitled to stay as a guest, if Thidwick consents, the bug cannot ever acquire a *right* to live there. If the bug had a right to live there, it would mean Thidwick had alienated his self-ownership right, which is impossible.

Most of the other creatures aren't even guests, despite Thidwick's referring to them as such. They are all invited by the bug without Thidwick's consent. As a guest, one does not acquire the right to invite other guests, at least not without clearing it with the owner. The so-called guests do not have proper permission, so their occupancy is illegitimate, even if Thidwick doesn't realize this. They consume resources that they feel entitled to, but are not. The Zinn-a-Zu bird, for example, plucks out 204 of Thidwick's hairs, which hurts the moose. The bird is not only unconcerned with the pain he is inflicting but also rationalizes the appropriation of the hairs by noting that "you can always grow more!" (Thidwick). The woodpecker destroys property that is not his by drilling four holes in one of the horns.

In a short time, the one invited guest has been joined by a spider, three birds, four squirrels, a bobcat, and a turtle. Each is a drain on Thidwick's resources—while the Bingle Bug by himself represents a negligible load for Thidwick to bear, the eleven-creature menagerie creates a considerable burden for the moose. Besides the weight he must carry, though, things are much worse: the eleven conspire to rob him of his liberty entirely. They claim that *he*, Thidwick, has no right to move to the south of the lake because that would entail moving "their" home against their wishes. At this point, Thidwick is functionally a slave: he is not permitted to use his own body for his own purposes but is obliged to use it to serve others. Again, it is just as wrong by a Lockean view for Thidwick to enslave himself as for him to be enslaved by others. Even though they are not physically coercing him, they are making a claim to the effect that he has no right to liberty, which he erroneously acquiesces in. Note, however, that his enslavement is the product not only of the other creatures' sense of entitlement but also to Thidwick's continuing to base his decisions on the premise that "a host must be nice to his guests" (Thidwick). This is a perfectly good principle as far as it goes; the mistake lies in thinking, one, that the eleven are his guests, and two, that being nice to them entails giving up his very bodily integrity.

One Vote, Two Votes, I Vote, You Vote

It does occur to Thidwick, at this point, to note the unfairness of his not being able to move to the south shore. The Bingle Bug's response is to put the matter to a vote, which Thidwick loses eleven to one. The Bingle Bug defines fairness in terms of the outcome of voting, but this begs the question. If Thidwick's fundamental right to self-ownership and liberty is subject to the majoritarian voting of others, then he doesn't actually have a fundamental right of self-ownership or claim to liberty at all. A voting procedure can represent fairness in certain circumstances; for example, when all parties are on an equal footing and have agreed to subject a particular decision to a vote (think of a group of friends selecting a restaurant or a town council voting on a date for a festival). But if a voting process can override fundamental liberty rights, as it does in Thidwick's case, then the premise of equality that democratic processes presuppose is undermined. This is incoherent.

To highlight the idea that democratic voting procedures cannot be understood as trumping fundamental liberty rights, Robert Nozick's thought experiment "The Tale of the Slave" is instructive.[2] Nozick describes a series of transitions whereby a slave gradually finds his master allowing democratic voting about how the fruits of the slave's labor are to be distributed and how the slave's free time may be spent. Even in the best-case scenario, the slave never actually enjoys real liberty and fails to have Lockean self-ownership. Nozick's point is that just because you use democratic voting procedures, it doesn't guarantee that you are protecting fundamental liberties, or indeed the moral equality on which a democracy is predicated. This is presumably the same rationale for the various antidemocratic features of the U.S. Constitution. Take, for example, the protections afforded by the First Amendment: rights to speak and publish freely are protected even if it thwarts the will of a majority. The founders had a clear conception of natural rights to basic liberties as being conceptually prior to and more fundamental than the administrative structures of the government designed to protect those rights and liberties.

After outvoting Thidwick, forcing him to remain on the north shore despite the dwindling supply of Moose-Moss, the eleven take steps to make sure they can continue to dominate Thidwick. They invite more creatures to take up residence on Thidwick's horns: a fox, a bear, three mice, an indeterminate number of fleas, and 362 bees. With over 379 votes, the menagerie will be sure to dominate Thidwick in perpetuity. As long as democratic voting overrides fundamental liberty rights, Thidwick's autonomy can never be restored, as he will always be outvoted by the parasitic creatures. This is a central insight of the "public choice" school of economic thought. James Buchanan, for example, notes that "those who expect to experience an increased flow of benefits from the government" will be sure to vote for policies that widen the scope of said benefits.[3] Buchanan's observations about the rich and poor are here analogous to Thidwick (who is "rich" in the relevant sense of owning a resource of potential value to others, via his body) and the "guests" (who, while they all have bodies of their own, perceive themselves to be poor in the sense that they don't possess Thidwick). The creatures claim to have formed a community, so in one sense it seems appropriate to institute democratic voting procedures. The problem is that they never actually acquired any right to live on the horns in the first place, so their voting about what Thidwick can do with his horns has no justification. They claim that the moose runs a "public hotel," implying that Thidwick has opened his horns to any and all creatures who wish to live there. But it is not Thidwick who has extended this offer. "There's plenty of room . . . and it's free!" (Thidwick) claims the Bingle Bug.

His Guests Are *Still* on Them

The creatures' exercise of their alleged rights turns out to place Thidwick's life in jeopardy; first, because of the scarcity of Moose-Moss on the north shore, but then, more dramatically, when Thidwick becomes the target of hunters. He tries to elude the hunters, but being weighed down by more than 379 other creatures—five hundred pounds worth—is a considerable hindrance. He realizes he could run faster without the extra weight, but he still thinks he must be "nice to his guests." Their guest status and Thidwick's "niceness" at this point are overriding even his capacity for self-preservation. Although he escapes from danger at the end, it should be clear that the "guests" didn't in fact have any right to live on the horns and that Thidwick was mistaken in letting his big-heartedness be used against him by the other creatures. Thidwick's property right in his horns is a logical consequence of his self-ownership rights, even if neither he nor the menagerie recognizes this.

Thidwick does save himself from the hunters, thanks to the serendipitous timing of his annual horn shedding. Just as he is cornered by the hunters (cornered because the creatures won't permit him to jump into the lake and swim away), Thidwick realizes it's time for the horns to come off. This allows Thidwick to regain his liberty and self-ownership: the horns, now discarded, can be kept by the creatures, and Thidwick is free to swim to the south of the lake. It's a pyrrhic victory for the creatures, of course: since the horns are no longer attached to a set of legs, the hunters may easily take the horns and all the creatures as their prize. The reader will typically agree with Dr. Seuss that the creatures got what they deserved—"stuffed, as they *should* be" (Thidwick). And we feel relieved that Thidwick's rediscovery of his fundamental right of self-ownership comes in time for him to escape the hunters and rejoin his friends. We see here an important aspect of Lockean self-ownership: without it, even self-preservation is difficult to secure. Thidwick knows he needs to leave the north shore, or he'll starve. He knows he could outrun the hunters bent on killing him if he didn't have five hundred pounds of pests on top of his head. But with his autonomy gone, he cannot act on what he knows to be the life-preserving choices.

Does Thidwick Need a Visa to Get to the South Side of the Lake?

Given current anxieties, some may be tempted to see *Thidwick the Big-Hearted Moose* as a parable about illegal immigration, with big-hearted Thidwick as the United States and the over 379 creatures as illegal immigrants. I would resist this interpretation. First of all, that interpretation only makes sense if Thidwick is seen as unaware that the creatures are moving in, which isn't how the story goes. More importantly, the analogy fails in that immigrants are primarily net gains for the economy, engaged in productive labor, whereas the creatures are not productive at all. This interpretation plays to fears that immigrants come just to go on welfare, which is not accurate. The idea of the story as a parable about the welfare state generally is a little more plausible—Thidwick's "big heart" having similarities to the epithet "bleeding heart," and the general laziness and parasitism of the creatures, whose draining of Thidwick's resources threatens to destroy both him and them, as representative of those that exploit such a system. Proponents of a universal basic income, for instance, argue that everyone is entitled to a minimal income provided by the society, regardless of whether they are employed at all. Critics of this approach argue that this perversely creates incentives to avoid work, which shifts an unfair burden onto those who do work. Thidwick could be seen as the one provider in the society while the "guests" are all getting a "free ride." While this isn't inaccurate, I think it misses the bigger picture: the nature of liberty and the foundation of rights.

It's worth reiterating that Thidwick's loss of liberty, his enslavement, is primarily due to his own mistaken conception of his duties toward others. Allowing the Bingle Bug to ride on his horns was not obligatory in the first place. Thidwick was happy to do this as a favor. While this didn't create any entitlements for the bug, it's understandable that Thidwick might feel that the bug is now a guest, and a host should be nice to his guest. But he should not have regarded any of the other creatures as guests nor felt any obligation to be nice to them, especially when their claims of entitlement trumped his own liberty and claims to self-ownership. Thidwick gets in a jam because he doesn't realize (or has forgotten) that he has a fundamental right of self-ownership, and it is his realization (or rediscovery) of the idea of liberty that gets him out of it.

One way to interpret *Thidwick* is as a cautionary tale to the effect that we can be complicit in our own oppression. When the Bingle Bug invites the Tree-Spider to move in, he claims that Thidwick won't mind. Thidwick acquiesced, even though he apparently did mind. How often do we acquiesce to encroachments on our freedoms because of perceived obligations that in reality are nonconsensual and thus nonexistent? Contrast Thidwick's predicament with that of Horton the elephant in *Horton Hatches the Egg*: Horton is taken advantage of by Mayzie, to be sure, but Horton did agree to take care of her egg. He feels he must honor an agreement he voluntarily made, even if it's true that Mayzie is irresponsible. Thidwick, on the other hand, never agreed to give rides to any of the creatures who came after the Bingle Bug. Thidwick's tale reminds us that we are self-owners and that we cannot acquire property nonconsensually. It also reminds us that we sometimes forget this and allow others to encroach on our freedoms. As Mack the turtle notes in opposition to King Yertle, "We, too, should [and do] have rights" (Yertle).[4]

∾

CHAPTER FOURTEEN

Rebellion in Sala-ma-Sond: The Social Contract and a Turtle Named Mack

Ron Novy

So Yertle, the Turtle King, lifted his hand
And Yertle, the Turtle King, gave a command.
He ordered nine turtles to swim to his stone
And, using these turtles, he built a *new* throne. (Yertle)

From atop his nine-turtle stack King Yertle claims dominion over all he looks down upon: "Oh, the things I now rule! I'm king of a cow! And I'm king of a mule" (Yertle). With two hundred more piled on, he proclaims, "I'm king of the butterflies! King of the air! Ah, me! What a throne! What a wonderful chair!" (Yertle). He estimates that by adding just a few turtles more (well, 5,607 turtles more), he will be king of the moon as well. But from below the growing pile of his fellow citizens, a plain little turtle named Mack cries out,

Your Majesty, please . . . I don't like to complain,
But down here below, we are feeling great pain.
I know up on top you are seeing great sights,
But down at the bottom we, too, should have rights. (Yertle)

It does not end well for King Yertle. He ignores the pleas of his subjects, and a revolt—a revolting burp anyway—brings down the great throne of unhappy turtles with a violent shake. Revolting against a government is a serious thing, so how might we justify the overthrow of King Yertle?

A Turtle's Life: Poor, Nasty, Brutish, and Short

If a covenant be made wherein neither of the parties perform presently,
but trust one another . . . it is void: but if there be a common power set
over them both, with right and force sufficient to compel performance,
it is not void.

—Thomas Hobbes[1]

So why is Yertle king and Mack his subject? One of the oldest and most
popular explanations for how we came together in civil society is called "the
social contract." While social contract theory varies as much as social contract theorists do, at its heart the social contract claims that for a government
to legitimately rule requires that it have the consent of those who are to be
governed. This consent is codified by their entering into literal or implicit
contracts with one another to create that civil society.

Imagine a time lost in the mists of history before turtles lived together
in little turtle tribes or big turtle nations—a time of not quite enough food
and too few livable ponds, a time with not enough resources for all turtles to
thrive. Since the turtles are all more-or-less equal in needs and abilities—for
instance, they all need the same sorts of things to eat and have the same sort
of capacity to find food—there is conflict; as philosopher Thomas Hobbes
(1588–1679) puts it, "They are in that condition which is called war; and
such a war as is of every man [or turtle] against every man [or turtle]."[2] Despite living in this state of war—what Hobbes calls "the state of nature"—
like us all proper turtles desire to live well and to avoid death, servitude, and
things similarly unpleasant. As reasoning and reasonable creatures, each of
the turtles recognizes that avoidance of death—a distinct possibility in the
war of all against all—and a chance at thriving—which is impossible due
to this struggle—may be accomplished by making an agreement with one's
neighbors: a contract in which they agree to treat each other in certain ways,
say, to share access to the delicious cattail roots at the north end of the pond,
and not in others, say, to not raid one another's earthworm supply.

Having an agreement among the parties is fine and good so far as it goes in
expressing our desires, but given Hobbes's assumption that all turtles are and
can only be self-interested, such agreements will hold only so long as each of
the turtle contractors benefits satisfactorily from the arrangement—after all,
trust can only get a turtle so far. Without some sort of mechanism that can
punish a turtle who fails to keep to her agreements, the combination of scarcity and the turtle's self-interested nature will lead to conflict over resources
and so a return to the state of nature. In this time before government, "there

is no place for industry . . . no arts, no letters, no society, and, which is worst of all, continual fear and danger of violent death, and the life of man [or turtle] is solitary, poor, nasty, brutish, and short."[3]

Yet each individual recognizes that a state of war with her neighbors is undesirable and puts her own life at risk; and so, she comes together with those neighbors to form a social contract—an agreement regarding how each is to treat the other contractors and the creation of a "sovereign," an entity that can enforce the agreement. Basically, the contractors grant the sovereign permission to punish them if they violate the agreement. With the ability to trust that your neighbor will not kill you in your sleep or steal your earthworm stash, the contractors can direct their energies toward living well and accumulating goods. In this way, our rational self-interest requires acceptance of the social contract; and, with this decision to submit to the authority of a sovereign, civil society is born.

For Hobbes, this sovereign must be an absolute authority to ensure the survival of society and so also its individual member turtles. To leave any power with the citizenry, Hobbes argues, is to give those with that power the ability to abuse the contract and their fellow citizens. Given the choice of abiding by the social contract or returning to the state of nature, no rational turtle would choose to abandon the contract and so willingly accepts rule by an absolute sovereign. A proper king, therefore, is necessary to secure and enforce the social contract. But a proper king does so to the benefit of those who created and granted power to the sovereign. If a king only rules for his benefit, if he neglects the welfare of his subjects, then as Bartholomew Cubbins would so elegantly put it, "He's no king at all" (Oobleck). The contract exists for our benefit, and the king exists to enforce it. And for Hobbes, this seems to work out pretty well.

Brussels Sprouts for All

Imagine turtle life in the state of nature: each turtle at war with every other, no law, no commerce, no public works, no libraries, no Internet, no fun. Suppose that Terri the turtle and her neighbor Arthur both really love Brussels sprouts, but only Terri is doing something about it: she has planted a garden. She tends the young plants for months until they are ready for harvesting. Arthur sees his chance, and late one evening he tiptoes into the field and takes all the yummy green orbs he can carry. Something that—while not very nice—isn't illegal, there is, after all, no civil society and so no law to violate. When Terri wakes she sees that her months of hard work are for naught and pledges to never commit so much of her time and resources to a project from which she can't be sure she'll benefit. Arthur feasts; Terri does not.

Suppose instead that Terri and Arthur have decided to pool their resources to raise the Brussels sprouts garden and to split the harvest between them. As the harvest approaches, can Terri be sure Arthur won't turn on her and take the whole crop for himself? After all, there is nothing guaranteeing either of them will abide by their agreement. Recognizing the possibility of betrayal, late one night, Terri sneaks into Arthur's house with a shovel and wallops him until he is dead. Terri feasts; Arthur does not.

Or imagine instead that Terri and Arthur each plant a private Brussels sprouts patch. Arthur is quite muscular and tills the ground extraordinarily well. Terri isn't quite so strong, so her plot is less well tilled. On the other hand, Terri is very experienced with keeping worms and other creepy-crawlies away from her plants, while Arthur hasn't a clue about this, so Arthur's plants are a bit scraggly and sickly. They both recognize that if they could combine their abilities, each would have a much better chance at a garden full of delectable little green cabbages. Each one's inability to do everything needed to ensure a good harvest fails to maximize the Brussels sprouts yield of either harvest. If only they could trust one another enough to combine their efforts, they'd be wading in a sea of vegetables.

What if they could trust each other? What if there was a mechanism that would punish Terri or Arthur for breaking their agreement to pool their resources? This is the social contract in a nutshell: an agreement between parties regarding how they will interact with one another, and a mechanism—the sovereign—for punishing violators of that agreement. In this case, neither Terri nor Arthur will end up with all of the Brussels sprouts, but also neither turtle will end up with none at all. Instead, they each get some of what they want and without the risk of being killed or hoodwinked in the process. In this way, rationality and self-interest work together to encourage individuals to join together in a social contract.

However, on occasion, the sovereign created by the social contract—King Yertle in the case of Sala-ma-Sond—may overstep his bounds by acting against the citizens' interests, the protection of which is the whole point of the sovereign's existence. When Mack appeals to the king, telling Yertle that he and his fellow turtles are starving, he is rebuffed:

"You hush up your mouth!" howled the mighty King Yertle.
"You've no right to talk to the world's highest turtle.
I rule from the clouds! Over land! Over sea!
There's nothing, no, NOTHING, that's higher than me!" (Yertle)

This is a problem for Mack: what to do with a tyrannical sovereign. When the sovereign no longer serves the end for which he was created, can you overthrow him? What are the moral reasons one might give for revolution? To address these questions, it may be helpful to turn to that philosopher who was so influential for our own revolutionary history.

To Protect (the Private Property of) Turtles

Men being . . . by Nature, all free, equal and independent, no one can be put out of this Estate and subjected to the Political Power of another, without his own Consent.

—John Locke[4]

John Locke (1632–1704) imagines quite a different world prior to the formation of civil society. Unlike Hobbes's state of nature as a "war of all against all," Locke imagines a state of nature without the conflict induced by scarcity—a state in which individuals have the "freedom to order their actions and dispose of their possessions . . . without asking leave, or depending upon the will of any other man."[5] In Sala-ma-Sond this means that each turtle is free to live without the interference of others regarding her "life, health, liberty, or possessions."[6] In this era before the social contract, we are bound together not by political structures (which only come into existence with the social contract) but by an innate morality and voluntary agreements. Nonetheless, the state of nature, for Locke, "is not a state of license; though man in that state have an uncontrollable liberty to dispose of his person or possessions, yet he has not liberty to destroy himself, or so much as any creature in his possession, but where some nobler use than its bare preservation calls for it."[7]

The opportunity for conflict in Locke's state of nature is pretty much limited to disputes over property. The problem is that there is no authority to which to appeal if we feel we've been wronged. So each of us must seek equity on our own terms. As the parties involved are unlikely to agree regarding what one owes the other, it risks a long-running tit-for-tat feud or even violence. By contracting together to create a civil government, the turtles gain a standardized measure and method for property disputes.

But why is private property so important for Locke? Locke held that the earth was given to all of us for our subsistent use—essentially the earth is a commons to be used by all. Nature's raw material becomes a turtle's private property once that material has been mixed with that turtle's labor—this land becomes hers in the act of tilling, that fruit becomes his by the act of collecting it, etc.[8] As indicated above, this labor theory of value is not unlimited—taking more than one's fair share is theft from the rest of turtlekind. For Locke, this understanding of individuals as proprietors with private property in need of protection is the drive to escape the state of nature and the creation of civil society. We have a natural right to our property and thus need a means to secure it against others.

Civil society then is created via the social contract, but it is a contract designed for the protection of private property, and thus our natural rights. Each contractor surrenders the right to individually protect herself and to individually pursue transgressions and instead places that power in the state creating "one body politic,"[9] in which each member is subject to the will of the majority. With government, the contractors gain a set of laws, judges to adjudicate disputes, and an executive power to enforce those laws. But un-like Hobbes—for whom the formation of the social contract was a one-off event—Locke leaves open the possibility of tearing up the contract. Given that the state was established as a means of protection, if it were to fail to provide for the contractors' lives, liberty, and property, the contractors have a right—perhaps even an obligation—to replace it with a new contract. Yertle has long since given up promoting or respecting the denizens of Sala-ma-Sond's rights. He is no king at all but a morally bankrupt tyrant, and thus ought to be overthrown. According to Locke,

> Whenever the *legislators endeavor to take away, and destroy the property of the people*, or to reduce them to slavery under arbitrary power, they put themselves into a state of war with the people, who are thereupon absolved from any further obedience. . . . [Authority] devolves to the people, who have a right to resume their original liberty, and, by the establishment of a new legislative (such as they shall think fit) provide for their own safety and security, which is the end for which they are in society.[10]

Mack has the right idea; it is time to be rid of King Yertle. But what ought to replace him? What principles of government would best represent all turtle interests? Surely, Mack wants to respect his fellow turtles and their freedom. He doesn't merely want a new king, or to be king himself. Mack is about justice, isn't he?

Free and Rational Turtles

> There is only one innate right, freedom (independence from being con-strained by another's choice), insofar as it can coexist with the freedom of every other in accordance with universal law.
>
> —Immanuel Kant[11]

For Immanuel Kant (1724–1804), rational individuals have an innate freedom—a freedom, it turns out, that can only be preserved within civil society. "Freedom" means something very specific for Kant: the right to choice; that is, to deliberative actions. To speak of "rights," then, is to speak of actions that have an influence over the choices of other rational beings. In this way, the interest of the state isn't so much the welfare of its citizens but rather to guarantee the largest possible amount of self-determination for its citizens. In a sense then, the worst thing that can be done to a rational individual is to make decisions for her; that is, to infantilize her. As Kant puts it, "Any action is right if it can coexist with everyone's freedom in accordance with a universal law, or if on its maxim the freedom of choice of each can coexist with everyone's freedom in accordance with a universal law."[12] So, individual freedom of action amounts to a lack of constraint imposed by the choices of others. The state then acts to constrain choices only if not doing so would result in constraining the choices of others. As such, the state is a necessary condition for—and a means to—securing freedom.

As we are equally free, we are equally subject to the laws of (and opportunities in) the state. The social contract then captures restrictions upon actions available to the state; or, as Kant puts it, the sovereign must "give his laws in such a way that they could have arisen from the united will of a whole people and to regard each subject, insofar as he wants to be a citizen, as if he has joined in voting for such a will."[13] So, it's reason that establishes the social contract, such that no law may come to pass that "a whole people could not possibly give its consent to."[14] On the one hand, consider a law granting access to Sala-ma-Sond's library only to turtles with striped shells: such a law would be unjust as it would be irrational for those without stripes to accept fewer privileges for themselves. On the other hand, imagine a law establishing a tax to build that library. Assuming that the tax is administered equitably, it would be just. Even if a particular turtle objects to financing library construction, it may be being built for legitimate reasons known to the state but not to that individual. That is, if the rational citizen did have full knowledge of the project, she would give her consent.

While the state embodies the social contract as it does with Locke and Hobbes, for Kant the contract is not an instrumental thing resulting from the voluntary, self-interested deal making of individuals. Instead, the agreement is the result of our recognizing the necessary environment for our freedom. In this way, right itself is the basis of the social contract.

Turtles in Veils: Justice as Fairness

And today the great Yertle, that Marvelous he,
Is King of the Mud. That is all he can see.
And the turtles, of course . . . all the turtles are free
As turtles, and, maybe, all creatures should be. (Yertle)

So back to Mack. Given the requirement for some sort of sovereign in order to escape the state of nature, how might Mack know he is getting what the sovereign was created to give him? That is, how might Mack figure out if the kingdom of Sala-ma-Sond is a just social arrangement? And, if it isn't, what can he do about it?

While a contractarian, John Rawls (1921–2002) doesn't share the traditional task of determining the conditions necessary to bring people together into a legitimate civil society; rather, his is an effort to specify conditions necessary for any government to be just (and so legitimate). For Rawls, essentially justice is fairness—and Mack, like the rest of King Yertle's subjects, is not being treated fairly.

Consider Mack, a smallish turtle with a blue-black checkered shell, and Desmond, a large turtle with a hawkish beak. Left to create any sort of social relations they might desire, Mack might create a society in which turtles with solid colored shells are required to carry their checked fellow citizens piggyback style and in which smallish turtles are always given first grazing rights in the nearby clover field. Desmond, on the other hand, might create a civil society in which the large and hawk-beaked are given preferential treatment in hiring or housing. Obviously there is an advantage to selecting principles that favor oneself and those like you. As often, these same principles disadvantage those with attributes, tastes, or characteristics unlike yours. Since it is nigh impossible to call a society just that distributes advantages and disadvantages in such an arbitrary manner as nose shape, Rawls reasons that ignorance of things like our own size and shell color will keep us from selecting the principles of justice in a biased manner.

Rawls does this with a thought experiment called the "original position," an abstracted state of nature that is used to establish the parameters of a just social contract. In this original position, individuals operate under what Rawls calls a "veil of ignorance." This veil provides an epistemological limit such that each individual is not aware of many of those traits that we often take as essential to our individual identities: are you a male or female? Healthy or sickly? Smart or not so much? Individuals behind the veil lack knowledge of their gender, race, disability, age, economic class, etc. That is, the individual does not know if she will be "advantaged or disadvantaged by natural fortune or social circumstances."[15] This ignorance keeps the person from being able to "tailor principles to the circumstances of one's own case."[16] That is, self-interest—stripped of the self's particulars—will generate rules that would justly govern civil society.

Recall Hobbes's claim that we cannot help but pursue our own interests and are disinterested in the welfare of others except in relation to ourselves. By removing any knowledge necessary to pick out one's own interests, Rawls argues that we will select just and fair principles for our society. Moreover, as self-interested "generic human beings" we would each select the same principles: none of us would prefer a principle that enslaved persons under 5'4" since no rational being would choose enslavement and none of us is aware of what our own height will be revealed to be.

Similarly, we can determine if our existing society is or is not just by asking if we would be willing to swap places with any one of our fellow citizens. Consider the gender gap in wages in the United States. On average, women make about seventy-seven cents for each dollar received by a man.[17] While of course a complicated set of social conditions underlie this disparity, all other things being equal, it is difficult to imagine a rational being opting for what is effectively the lesser wage. Under a Rawlsian scheme, this gendered unfairness is a sign that at least this aspect of current American civil society is unjust.

So, for Rawls, justice proceeds out of fairness. That is, we—as disembodied, rational persons—will recognize the inherent unfairness of certain principles of social organization and so not agree to them from under the veil of ignorance. In the original position, we will only accept principles that would be, if not to our advantage, at least not to our disadvantage were we to turn out to be at the bottom of the social hierarchy. If only the Sneetches had been so prescient.

Rawls generates two principles of justice from his thought experiment, "[That] each person is to have an equal right to the most extensive scheme of equal basic liberties compatible with a similar scheme of liberties for others . . . [and that] social and economic inequalities are to be arranged so that they are both reasonably expected to be to everyone's advantage."[18] The just society for Rawls will include a social contract under which there are what we think of broadly as "civil liberties" held equally by all with the equal distribution among the citizens, and if there is any inequality in the socioeconomic standing, it must maximize the benefit to those least well off in the society. For Rawls, the social contract is not a matter of legitimacy of government gained by consent of the governed but instead what sketches out the necessary conditions for a just society of self-interested individuals.

A good society will promote justice among its citizens, but as philosopher Iris Marion Young (1949–2006) points out, justice is not "merely" a matter of fairness in the distribution of resources, rights, opportunities, and so forth, as laid out by Rawls. Rather, "Justice should refer . . . also to the institutional conditions necessary for the development and exercise of individual capacities and collective communication and cooperation."[19] This "enabling concept of justice" requires that the law must act as a guarantor that Mack, Desmond, and, yes, even Yertle have the ability "to develop and exercise their capacities and express their needs, thoughts, and feelings."[20] If Young is correct, a civil society that fails in this role is not just and must be made so.

King and the Law

[All persons] are endowed by their Creator with certain unalienable rights, that among these are Life, Liberty, and the Pursuit of Happiness—That to secure these rights, governments are instituted among men, deriving their just powers from the consent of the governed.[21]

Are we ever justified in defying unjust rule? To answer this, it would be helpful to explain just why we are obliged to obey society's laws at all. Recall that the social contract is a complex set of rules and arrangements to which we agree to be bound in order to gain some set of benefits. Essentially, we gain the benefits of living in a community. We escape from the state of nature and receive a guarantee of certain rights enforced by society's laws. To gain these benefits we agree to follow the laws of the society that makes these benefits possible. In this way we are obliged to follow rules ranging from the speed at which we can drive to not stealing from one another, from how much we pay in taxes to not dumping sewage into the water supply. In this way, under social contract theory there is a strong *prima facie* duty to play according to society's rules.

Now, what if those rules are stacked so that one group of persons within the society is denied the rights enjoyed by all of the rest? Locke argued that by failing to provide for its citizens as required, the state has placed itself in a state of war with them and so must be replaced with a new social contract. Prominent leader of the American civil rights movement, Martin Luther King Jr. (1929–1968), took a slightly different approach—not arguing for a new contract but for the fulfillment of the existing one.

In the Jim Crow South, segregation by race was not merely a despicable social practice, it was also written into the law—laws that the African American population had no voice in forming. The objection was not to the law in general; if it had been, King and his followers would find themselves following the path sketched by Locke. Rather, the objection was to particular laws and practices unjustly targeting African Americans. As King puts it in his "Letter from the Birmingham Jail," the objection was to a culture in which "vicious mobs lynch your mothers and fathers at will," where "hate-filled policemen curse, kick, brutalize and even kill with impunity," and where the color of one's skin systematically limited opportunities for education and employment, leaving some citizens "smothered in an air-tight cage of poverty."[22] The social contract was simply not being honored. Essentially, King's objection is to society's demand that the disadvantaged group accept the same burdens as all other citizens while they are at the same time being denied society's benefits. Resistance to these unjust laws took the form of civil disobedience (sit-ins, marches, boycotts, and the like)—activities that directly violated the unjust law and which would minimally result in the arrest of the lawbreaker. As King claims it, "An individual who breaks a law that conscience tells him is unjust, and who willingly accepts the penalty of imprisonment in order to arouse the conscience of the community over its injustice, is in reality expressing the highest respect for the law."[23] This "respect for the law" is another way of saying respect for the social contract—a respect that demands it be fully honored by all and for all citizens.

King of the Mud

The laws to which King objected came to be for many reasons, but one of the more obvious is that these laws were formed without the consent of all of those to whom they would apply. The less representative the government, the more likely that unjust laws will be made. It is difficult to imagine oppressive racial segregation would be a legal fact in a society in which African Americans had their interests represented in government. While a representative government doesn't guarantee perfect laws, it seems much more likely to avoid gross inequity and unfairness.

Could any form of government be less representative of the interests of the citizens of Sala-ma-Sond than a monarchy—a government by, for, and about the whims of one person? The turtles are hungry, they are tired, and they risk cracking their shells; still King Yertle lifts his hand to command more turtles for his throne. And a smallish turtle at the bottom of the stack, named Mack

Decided he'd had enough. And he had.
And that plain little lad got a little bit mad
And that plain little Mack did a plain little thing.

He burped!
And his burp shook the throne of the king! (Yertle)

With that great shake, Yertle the turtle king plummeted down into the mud of Sala-ma-Sond pond and his fellow turtles laughed, never to be oppressed again.

~

CHAPTER FIFTEEN

Whose Egg Is It, Really? Property Rights and Distributive Justice

Henry Cribbs

Horton the Elephant: "My egg! My egg! Why, it's hatching!"
Mayzie the Lazy Bird: "But it's mine! It's my egg! You stole it from me!
Get off of my nest and get out of my tree!" (Hatches)

In Dr. Seuss's *Horton Hatches the Egg*, the issue of whose egg it is seems settled when the shell finally cracks and an elephant-bird emerges. The spectators appear satisfied by this, even shouting "it SHOULD be like that!" (Hatches). They promptly send Horton the Elephant and the hatchling "home / Happy / One hundred per cent!" (Hatches). However, the issue is not as readily soluble as Seuss makes it out. The story could, and should, continue . . .

The hatchling's half-elephant, but that's not the last word.
It could still be half Mayzie's. It's also half-bird!
We can't cut it in half, because that would be silly,
So we still should be asking, "Whose egg is it, really?"

One might take the case of Horton the Elephant versus Mayzie the Lazy Bird to be a simple legal custody battle. Well, perhaps not so simple. "Completely unprecedented" might be a better way to describe it. However, treating this case as a parental rights question would lead us far afield into tricky metaphysical discussions concerning when a yolk becomes a bird and whether "a person's a person, no matter how small" (Horton) (a question Horton is forced to answer in a separate court appearance). Arguments over ova indeed arise outside the pages of Dr. Seuss, as modern-day divorced couples fight over rights to frozen embryos. However, I would rather avoid such difficulties by thinking of the egg, at least for the moment, as mere property rather than as a potential partridge, for even Mayzie herself uses the term *stole* rather than *birdnapped*, indicating that for her it's a question of property rights, not parental rights. Taken this way, *Horton Hatches the Egg* raises a fundamental question of property rights: How should we decide who owns what?

How would you like for your eggs to be fixed? Scrambled with labor, please! Really well-mixed!

Both petitioners claim property rights to the egg in question. Mayzie, lazy though she is, certainly has a strong claim insofar as she laid the egg in the first place, but Horton has since provided the elephant's share of the work in terms of actual incubation. But how in the world could the egg become Horton's property? One highly influential theory might say it has to do precisely with the work that Horton has done to care for it. In "Of Property," John Locke (1632–1704) explains that if there is anything that an individual owns outright, it's his or her own labor. "Though the earth, and all inferior creatures, be common to all men, yet every man has a property in his own person: this no body has any right to but himself. The labour of his body, and the work of his hands, we may say, are properly his."[1] Indeed, we would have to say that Horton has certainly put a mastodonian effort into incubating the egg, sitting on it for three complete seasons—even enduring a mountain-climbing expedition and an ocean voyage while persevering on his precarious perch.

Locke takes this metaphor of putting a lot of work into something quite literally. "Whatsoever then he removes out of the state that nature hath provided, and left it in, he hath mixed his labour with, and joined to it something that is his own, and thereby makes it his property."[2] By putting work, which is undeniably yours, into something, you make that something yours. But of course one can't just take any old thing and mix a little labor with it to make it yours. Locke explains that this labor-mixing idea does not work for things that are already some other individual's property. It *does* work for things that nature provides. The earth provides certain resources to us all in common, free to any who would take them and make use of them. "[A]ll the fruits it naturally produces, and beasts it feeds, belong to mankind in common, as they are produced by the spontaneous hand of nature; and no body has originally a private dominion, exclusive of the rest of mankind, in any of them, as they are thus in their natural state."[3]

And so the question now becomes whether or not the egg was in its "natural state," in common to everyone, or whether it was already someone's property. Mayzie clearly thinks the egg was already her property before Horton "stole" it. Yet elsewhere in Dr. Seuss eggs seem to be quite easily appropriated as if they were in a state of nature. In *Scrambled Eggs Super!*, Peter T. Hooper travels the world gathering eggs left and right (and even north-east, in the case of the South-West-Facing Cranes) from various fowls to make his famous "Scrambled Eggs Super-dee-Dooper, Special de luxe a-la-Peter T. Hooper" (Scrambled). Some of the birds do seem to mind his taking them, so that he has to rely on sneaky tricks and fleet-footed beasts to get away with the goods, but he never seems concerned that he might be doing anything *wrong*. Hooper considers the eggs he takes to be in their natural state.

By mixing his own labor (along with fifty-five cans of beans, ginger, nine prunes, three figs, parsley, cinnamon, and a clove) with the eggs he has found, Hooper has made them his to enjoy. But when exactly did the eggs become his? When he ate them? When he cooked them? When he raced away with them on his Jill-ikka-Jast? Or when he first picked them up? Locke has an answer, although he speaks of acorns and apples, but his principle applies as well to eggs. "[I]t is plain, if the first gathering made them not his, nothing else could. That labour put a distinction between them and common: that added something to them more than nature, the common mother of all, had done; and so they became his private right."[4] So it seems that as soon as Peter picked up one of those eggs, it became his property.

But Mayzie seems still to have some kind of claim on the egg before Horton comes along and mixes his labor with it. To sort this out, we may first need to look at some important limitations that Locke places on his labor-mixing theory of property.

How much may I have of this wonderful stuff? As long as you leave just as good, and enough.

One of these limits Locke mentions is that no one may take more than his fair share. He explains, "[F]or this labour being the unquestionable property of the labourer, no man but he can have a right to what that is once joined to, at least where there is *enough, and as good, left in common for others*."[5] Peter T. Hooper cannot lay claim to *every* single egg in the world, even if he were to go to all the trouble to collect them. He must leave enough for others. And he cannot simply take the world's sweetest Kweet eggs and leave only the eggs of the Twiddler Owl (which taste "sort of like dust from inside a bass fiddle" [Scrambled]), for everyone else. He must leave not only enough eggs for everyone else but also enough eggs that are as good as what he takes for himself.

The Lorax makes this point quite clear. When the Once-ler chops down one lone Truffula Tree, the Lorax simply wants to know what's going to be done with it, but when the Once-ler starts chopping down four trees at a time, the Lorax explains that the Once-ler's rate of labor mixing has gotten out of hand.

> He snapped, "I'm the Lorax who speaks for the trees
> which you seem to be chopping as fast as you please.
> But I'm also in charge of the Brown Bar-ba-loots
> who played in the shade in their Bar-ba-loot suits
> and happily lived, eating Truffula Fruits.
> NOW . . . thanks to your hacking my trees to the ground,
> there's not enough Truffula Fruit to go 'round.
> And my poor Bar-ba-loots are all getting the crummies
> Because they have gas and no food in their tummies!" (Lorax)

By taking so many trees that the Bar-ba-loots have to go without, the Once-ler has reached the limits of his permissible labor mixing.

By claiming that he speaks for the trees as well as for the Bar-ba-loots, the Lorax also raises another issue. Can nature itself have property rights? If this were so, then it would seem that even resources in their natural state are not considered "in common" to take as we please, since they would be the property of nature itself. Were this true, then no amount of labor that Horton mixes with the egg can make it his. The ecologist Garrett Hardin argues that this notion of nature as "the commons" inevitably leads to there *not* being "enough and as good for others."

> The tragedy of the commons develops in this way. Picture a pasture open to all. It is to be expected that each herdsman will try to keep as many cattle as possible on the commons. . . . [T]he rational herdsman concludes that the only sensible course for him to pursue is to add another animal to his herd. And another; and another. . . . But this is the conclusion reached by each and every rational herdsman sharing a commons. Therein is the tragedy. Each man is locked into a system that compels him to increase his herd without limit—in a world that is limited. Ruin is the destination toward which all men rush, each pursuing his own best interest in a society that believes in the freedom of the commons. Freedom in a commons brings ruin to all.[6]

Hardin claims that a labor-mixing system of property rights that assumes a "commons" provided by nature will eventually lead to injustice. Locke had difficulty in realizing this, for in his day there seemed to be plenty of resources to go around. Back then there was plenty of land available in the so-called New World. He says, "[L]et him plant in some inland, vacant places of America, we shall find that the possessions he could make himself, upon the measures we have given, would not be very large, nor, even to this day, prejudice the rest of mankind, or give them reason to complain."[7] Yet these once "vacant places" weren't truly vacant; they were simply occupied by natives whose system of property rights did not include the concept of individual ownership of land. This view opened them up to easy exploitation by settlers from the so-called Old World who *did* think of land as individual property.

But even if we did consider such "vacant places of America" to be "commons," they are filling up fast—so fast that one country in the Americas has already recognized that unrestricted use of nature's commons may lead to disaster. In September of 2008, Ecuador became the first nation on earth to spell out in its Constitution that nature itself has inalienable rights, including the "right to exist, persist, maintain and regenerate its vital cycles, structure, functions and its processes in evolution."[8] Perhaps there is no "commons" provided for us by nature, after all. Later in Hardin's paper he admits that "our legal system of private property plus inheritance is unjust—but we put up with it because we are not convinced, at the moment, that anyone has invented a better system. The alternative of the commons is too horrifying to contemplate. Injustice is preferable to total ruin."[9]

So the labor-mixing theory seems to be the best we have because we have to have some way of making something ours. Locke points out that otherwise we couldn't even survive because we couldn't even eat without violating someone's (or something's) rights: "The fruit, or venison, which nourishes the wild Indian, . . . must be his, and so his, i.e., a part of him, that another can no longer have any right to it, before it can do him any good for the support of his life."[10] So when Peter T. Hooper yanks an egg out from under the Moth-Watching Sneth in order to scramble up supper, though he might be violating nature's rights, we allow him to do it in order that he (and we) may survive. But remember: after the very last Truffula Tree fell and the Once-ler's business went belly-up he was forced to scrape a living telling stories on the Street of the Lifted Lorax for the measly sum of "15 cents and a nail and the shell of a great-great-great-grandfather snail" (Lorax). Thus, even a farsighted self-interest should tell us that we must be careful not to overexploit nature's commons.

A bird who bites off any more than she chews is
Taking too much, 'cause it's more than she uses.

So we are back to the labor-mixing theory. Mayzie, in fact, had to undergo labor—in something very close to the child-birthing sense—to lay the egg in the first place, and she also did some work of her own in incubating it at the beginning. Indeed, at the beginning of the story, before Horton appears on the scene, she is complaining that "It's *work!*" (Hatches). No amount of labor that Horton adds can take away the labor Mayzie has already contributed. So how could the egg be his?

Locke noted one other limit to labor mixing. If someone takes more than he or she can use, that's also too much. "It will perhaps be objected to this, that if gathering the acorns, or other fruits of the earth, &c. makes a right to them, then any one may ingross as much as he will. To which I answer, Not so. . . . As much as any one can make use of to any advantage of life before it spoils, so much he may by his labour fix a property in: whatever is beyond this, is more than his share, and belongs to others."[11]

If Horton could make the case that Mayzie had taken more than she could use, he might be able to claim the egg should be his. He might appeal to "squatter's rights," or what lawyers call "adverse possession." This is the notion that if a person "squats" on, or takes possession of a property that another person has abandoned and maintains possession for a specific length of time (which varies according to local statutes), then the squatter gains a right to that property. Locke's labor-mixing theory provides justification for this idea because of the fact that one cannot lay claim to more than one can make use of before it spoils. If one person owns a property but is not making use of it and another person *is* making use of it, it makes perfect sense to say that the person who is willing to make use of it may lay claim to it. Even though a piece of land might not actually spoil, if it lies fallow for a year then that year's potential crop production has been wasted. The lost year can never be regained. Squatter's rights arose in part to discourage such wastefulness.

This seems to be what is going on in *Thidwick the Big-Hearted Moose*. Thidwick offers a tiny Bingle Bug a ride on his antlers, but the bug invites more and more creatures aboard to join him, until the poor moose can barely move. Thidwick is big-hearted, of course, and he believes it's his duty to provide hospitality to his guests, so he allows them to remain, even though it means he can't migrate with the rest of his herd, and so he goes hungry and becomes a target for hunters. The creatures in his antlers, however, seem to be invoking squatter's rights rather than the ancient law of hospitality, when they say, "These horns are our home and you've no right to take / Our home to the far distant side of the lake!" (Thidwick). They claim that the antlers are now their property. But this is a misapplication of squatter's rights. A person who takes possession of a property under *permission* of the owner, like a tenant or invited guest, does not gain squatter's rights, because the original owner *is* making use of the property—by choosing to allow someone else to use it.[12]

But can Horton the Elephant appeal to squatter's rights? He has, in fact, been squatting (literally, so he won't crush it) on the egg for almost a year. In most areas, anywhere from five to fifteen years of possession are required before adverse possession can be invoked, so Horton probably hasn't squatted long enough. But even if he had, Mayzie granted him *permission*. Squatter's rights can only be invoked if the squatter has not received permission from the owner. Horton agreed to watch over the egg while Mayzie took a vacation. However, Mayzie has apparently abandoned the egg, for she "Decided she'd NEVER go back to her nest!" (Hatches). Perhaps a court might award squatter's rights to Horton in a clear case of abandonment since he kept the egg from "spoiling."

For Locke, the problem of taking more than one can use before it spoils seems to disappear after the concept of money, "a little piece of yellow metal, which would keep without wasting or decay," is introduced.[13] Money allows one to sell the fruit of one's labor before it spoils, or even to sell one's labor itself. And since money doesn't spoil it seems there should be no limit on how much money one should be allowed to acquire. One can even make use of money after one is dead by leaving it to one's heirs or by leaving specific instructions for its use in a will.

Money ushers in a need for an economic system to organize its transfer because some types of labor appear to be worth more than others. A free-market economy is one method by which one can determine the nominal value of labor or its fruits. Whatever price the buyer and seller are willing to agree upon is its nominal value. Adam Smith distinguishes this nominal monetary value, which can fluctuate with the market, from its *real* value, which is more Lockean in nature. "Labour, therefore, is the real measure of the exchangeable value of all commodities. The real price of every thing, what every thing really costs to the man who wants to acquire it, is the toil and trouble of acquiring it."[14] Smith believes that a market economy will allow self-interest to allocate resources in the best way, and describes an "invisible hand," which is not really a hand at all but the sum total of myriad individual selfish transactions that together guide a society to produce just the right quantity and variety of goods. "By pursuing his own interest he [every individual] frequently promotes that of the society more effectually than when he really intends to promote it."[15]

How should we divvy up all of these bucks?
And what of those folks who are down on their lucks?

But of course the free market can lead to injustices. Sylvester McMonkey McBean, the Fix-It-Up Chappie, is able to make off with every last cent of the Sneetches' money by promoting an artificial demand for the latest Star-Belly fashions, which in no way promotes the interests of society (except, perhaps, by teaching the Sneetches a costly lesson). With a monopoly on belly stars and their removal, the greedy McBean can charge whatever he likes; there is no competition to keep the prices down. McBean engages in price gouging and market manipulation to exploit the star-stricken creatures. Indeed, some such business transactions that are now being called "antisocial" (in the sense that they produce no real goods or jobs for society but just move money around) may be partly responsible for the recent worldwide economic crisis. But while there may well be individual instances of injustice and transactions that are detrimental to society, Smith contends that in the long run the "invisible hand" of the free market will promote society's overall interest.[16]

However, such injustices may be enough to trigger a revolution. In Seuss's *I Had Trouble in Getting to Solla Sollew*, the narrator falls in with a chap with a One-Wheeler Wubble, who offers him a ride. But when the Wubble needs pulling the narrator is stuck doing all the work while the Wubble chap sits back with nothing to do but to pick which road to take.

> "Now, really!" I thought, "this is rather unfair!"
> But he said, "Don't you stew. I am doing my share.
> This is called teamwork. I furnish the brains.
> You furnish the muscles, the aches, and the pains . . ."
> Then he sat and he worked with his brain and his tongue
> And he bossed me around, just because I was young. (Trouble)

Alhough this seems to the narrator to be rather unfair, there may be an excellent reason why some jobs that appear to be much less work get much more pay (or in this case, better perks, like being able to ride in the Wubble instead of pulling it). The "brain and tongue" work that the Wubble chap does may require certain skills that are in high demand but short supply. It may have taken the Wubble chap years of training to learn the safe paths through the steep mountain trails. Because it took a great deal of time and hard work to learn the highly skilled profession of Wubble driving, it may indeed be fair for the chap to ask the narrator, in return, to furnish the muscles, aches, and pains. After all, muscles, aches, and pains are probably in much more plentiful supply than highly skilled brains, and hence would be cheaper in the free market. Plus, the chap *owns* the Wubble, presumably having bought it as an investment hoping to gain some return from it. By risking his own capital, he deserves to make a profit if he can. Indeed, a capitalist economy can't function without such entrepreneurs.

Still, inequalities like this can lead to a disgruntled labor force. If labor, according to the labor-mixing theory, is what produces property, then it would seem the labor force should wind up quite wealthy as a result. However, due to unfair exploitation by those like McBean and the Wubble-chap, property may wind up being distributed quite differently. If the people doing the largest share of the work, who are the creators of all the wealth, are not being compensated adequately for their labor, the situation can lead to revolution. This, in essence, is what is described in the *Communist Manifesto*, that claims such a revolution is inevitable as the proletariat, or working class, become further alienated from the fruits of their labor.[17] Seuss illustrates (literally) just such a revolution with a plain little turtle named Mack.

Yertle the Turtle King is king of all that he can see, but he wants to see more so that he can rule more. To that end, he enlists the aid of his fellow turtles in the Sala-ma-Sond pond to build his throne higher so that he can see farther. They throw themselves into the task by stacking their own bodies higher and higher so that Yertle may sit higher and higher. King Yertle gets a wonderful view. All the turtles' labor winds up generating quite a bit of property for him. But a plain little turtle speaks up from the very bottom of the massive turtle stack:

"I know, up on top you are seeing great sights,
But down at the bottom, we, too, should have rights.
We turtles can't stand it. Our shells will all crack!
Besides, we need food. We are starving!" groaned Mack. (Yertle)

Eventually, if the proletariat is not seeing the results of its hard work to the point of not even having their basic needs met while management and the owners reap all of the rewards for doing very little, then the labor force will revolt, or will at least have the moral authority to do so.

Communist revolutions indeed broke out in many parts of the world during the past century, creating societies based in theory (if not in practice) on the idea that instead of property being distributed through a free market based on the value of one's own labor, property should be distributed "from each according to his ability, to each according to his needs!"[18] However, the end of the Cold War and the opening of capitalist markets to many of these former communist regimes, including the former Soviet Union and China, suggest that Smith's invisible hand is a more successful, if not always just, method of distributing goods in a society.

But such revolutions, regardless of their ultimate success, suggest that property rights may require redistribution at some point, for a couple of reasons. First, for practical purposes, in order to make sure such revolutions do not happen, some method of making sure that the labor force is not overexploited may be needed. So even a devout free-market capitalist like McBean should at least recognize that taking care of the basic needs and rights of the labor force is imperative to avoid a violent revolution, and thus rich capitalists should be willing to redistribute some of their wealth to those less fortunate. But it's not just about prudence and practicality. While a laissez-faire free-market economy may be an efficient way to promote society's best interest overall, it's not always just. There are compelling moral reasons besides enlightened self-interest to make sure that basic needs are met and basic rights are respected. Simple ownership rights may, in some cases, be overridden by higher moral values, such as the rights of everyone to life, liberty, and the pursuit of happiness. If the labor force is starving and is forced to work under oppressive conditions, then it seems that rights to both life and liberty are being ignored. So we need a framework of distributive justice that can acknowledge and allocate property rights while at the same time recognizing that some property might need to be reallocated to fulfill other moral imperatives. Property is not an absolute right—there are limits, and sometimes redistribution is morally demanded. One prominent theory of distributive justice is that of John Rawls (1921–2002), who invokes a principle of "justice as fairness."[19]

Rawls argues that to decide a fair method of distribution, we must put ourselves in what he calls the "original position":

> This original position . . . is understood as a purely hypothetical situation characterized so as to lead to a certain conception of justice. Among the essential features of this situation is that no one knows his place in society, his class position or social status, nor does anyone know his fortune in the distribution of natural assets and abilities, his intelligence, strength, and the like. . . . The principles of justice are chosen behind a veil of ignorance. This ensures that no one is advantaged or disadvantaged in the choice of principles by the outcome of natural chance or the contingency of social circumstances.[20]

The idea is to consider what kind of system of justice we would endorse if we did not know what our place in society would be. If I am in fact a Star-Bellied Sneetch, I might for selfish reasons endorse a society in which those with stars get more benefits than those with bare bellies. But if I had to choose *before* I knew whether I would have a star on my belly or not, then I would certainly choose a more equitable division of goods.

So the trick is to put ourselves, hypothetically, in the position of not knowing anything about ourselves ahead of time in order to decide the fairest way of distributing goods. We wouldn't know, for instance, if we would be born into poor families or would become disabled sometime during our lives or if we might not be quite talented enough to achieve a higher-paying, skilled job. Since any of us might wind up in such situations, we would probably agree to a society that ensures that all have at least their basic needs met, such as food, clothing, shelter, and perhaps education and health care, and a society in which all have both the liberty and opportunity to better themselves.

This doesn't necessarily mean everyone gets an equal share of everything. We would probably be willing to allow some inequalities to exist, if those inequalities wind up helping the less fortunate along with the more fortunate. For instance, since a relatively free market provides the incentive of increased wealth to hard workers and innovative entrepreneurs, a free market encourages the production of more goods, which ultimately means more for society as a whole, although it does mean that some people will earn more than others. So we might accept such inequalities since a high tide floats all boats. However, in the original position we also realize that some accident might befall us during our lives or that we might be born less clever, less capable of hard work, or simply not lucky enough to be born into wealthy, successful, or otherwise privileged families. We would have to consider the possible outcome of being disadvantaged or otherwise historically disenfranchised. So we would want to make sure that some goods get redistributed to those who may not benefit from a free-market economy. Especially since not all people are equal in the eyes of the free market and so often one's chances of success hinge on characteristics beyond one's control. This means that while we might wind up with something approximating a free market, which acknowledges property rights, we would probably also agree to a method of redistributing wealth in order to have some basic safety nets built in to ensure that everyone has at least their minimum needs met and rights guaranteed, as well as a somewhat level playing field in order to achieve equal opportunity.

If we didn't know whether we were going to wind up as Mayzie or Horton, what kind of system of distributive justice would we choose? Would it be the kind of system in which Horton the hard-working elephant gets the egg, or Mayzie the lazy mother bird? Before we answer, we must also remember that we could wind up in the place of the newly hatched elephant-bird.

He who thinks he has all of the answers is dumb
But asking hard questions can often bring wisdom.

The question, "Whose egg is it, really?" has no clear answer. In several of his works, Dr. Seuss has raised questions of property and distributive justice in a way that even a child can understand. How should goods be distributed in a society? What is a fair division of labor? How should markets be regulated? How should environmental concerns affect property rights? Are children property? In many cases Dr. Seuss has deliberately left such questions hanging.

Another somewhat famous philosopher similarly kept asking questions while never giving answers. In ancient Greece, Socrates taught his listeners to constantly question what they were told. Although this practice led to his being sentenced to death by the people of Athens for the crime of "corrupting the youth" (i.e., teaching them to think for themselves), Socrates became immortalized in Plato's dialogues.

Seuss, too, deserves our thanks for continuing this long tradition of corrupting the youth. One of the many great things about Seuss is that while his wit, poetry, and art make him eminently accessible to children, he raises issues with which philosophers have wrestled for centuries and which still perplex adults today. Children (and adults) reading him may not find answers, but at least Seuss has them thinking about the questions.

〜

CHAPTER SIXTEEN

It's Not Personal . . . It's Just Bizzyneuss: Business Ethics, the Company, and Its Stakeholders

Matthew F. Pierlott

Just as people cannot live without eating, so a business cannot live without profits. But most people don't live to eat, and neither must businesses live just to make profits.

—John Mackey, Whole Foods Market CEO[1]

At one time it was the social responsibility of anyone addressing the topic of business ethics to admit the apparent oxymoronic nature of the subject. "Business ethics? Isn't that a bit like vegan hamburgers?" Fortunately, the very idea of applying moral thinking to business is no longer presumed misguided. That is not to say cynicism with regard to the moral conduct of businesspeople has died. The past decade has certainly seen its share of corporate scandals, from the Enron and WorldCom fiascos that, with a plethora of other creative accounting disasters, began the decade to both the financial crisis and the BP oil catastrophe glupping up the Gulf that closed it out. While all of these events have certainly contributed to the cynicism, they also have underscored the importance of taking business ethics seriously.

A fundamental issue in business ethics is determining to whom a company has a responsibility. It's fundamental because so many other conversations in business ethics (although not all) must presuppose some model or other, and it appears that there are two competing perspectives on the issue that divide our thinking. One is known as the "stockholder" or "shareholder model," and the other is the "stakeholder theory" of the modern corporation. In this chapter, we will examine the two basic perspectives and then explore the different responsibilities a business might have to different sets of stakeholders, with the help of Dr. Seuss, of course.

Taking Stock of the Stakeholders
and the Stakes for the Stockholders

So, what criteria must a company meet to be a "good" company? One way to answer this is to recognize that the evaluation of something depends on the function it performs. This follows the method of the Greek philosopher, Aristotle (384–322 BCE), who said:

> [E]very virtue or excellence both brings into good condition the thing of which it is the excellence and makes the work of that thing be done well; e.g., the excellence of the eye makes both the eye and its work good; for it is by the excellence of the eye that we see well. . . . Therefore, if this is true in every case, the virtue of man also will be the state of character which makes a man good and which makes him do his own work well.[2]

The specific excellence of something is determined by its proper functioning. Aristotle saw natural functions as the illustration of this idea, but it applies to artifacts, too. A good axe is a sharp axe, because a sharp axe chops wood better than a dull one. We can also apply this notion to organizations, like companies.

Well, what is it that a company is supposed to do? One position that has had a lot of ideological influence is famously associated with the Nobel Prize–winning economist, Milton Friedman. This view is often called the "stockholder" or "shareholder" theory of the firm. Friedman argues that a business serves a social good by seeking profit, since the free-market system transforms these individual efforts into results that benefit society as a whole.[3] Competition in the market incentivizes ingenuity and greater efficiencies, which translates into better quality and lower prices for end users and more profits for entrepreneurs and investors. Further, having more capital available allows for more investment and development, meaning more jobs and the opening of new markets. Oh, the magical things they can do on street Wall. Everyone wins, with investors being the winning-est winners of all.

The important moral concept here is the idea of a property right. If I own something, I am free to use it as I wish, provided my use doesn't interfere with the basic rights and freedoms of others.[4] Obviously, then, if I employ you with the expectation that you'll work to make as much money for me as possible, you owe it to me to maximize my profit. By accepting employment, you're trading your right to make decisions as you see fit according to your own value system—at least while you are "on the clock." You are free to reject the deal or to walk away later within the terms of the deal, but under the deal, you have a role responsibility to earn a profit for me. If you wish to do something for someone else, do it on your own time and with your own money (that you can get from me by making a profit for me). Using your employee role to accomplish other goals is tantamount to theft. Shareholder theorists assert that overall this system is best for society as a whole.

On the other side of the issue, there is a view that recognizes that businesses are a complex of human relationships and that the reduction of all interests to those of the owners is illegitimate. The American philosopher R. Edward Freeman is credited with articulating this view, known as stakeholder theory, and is often anthologized in business ethics texts right along with Friedman.[5] Stakeholder theory is used in a variety of senses, though, with myriad articulations. Thus, the claims about how it contrasts or converges with shareholder theory are harder to assess than might appear in standard presentations of them (including this one).[6] For present purposes, though, I only wish to provide a thumbnail sketch of the normative use of the stakeholder theory to open up the dialogue about the extent of the responsibilities of decision makers in a company, publicly traded or not.

Basically, the stakeholder theory recognizes that management of a company has the moral obligation to consider the interests of all of those who have a stake in the company's activities and that their competing interests must be negotiated in some way. As much as their employer may want them to continue Zizzer-Zoofing, the five foot-weary salesmen must get some sleep after a day of pushing Zizzer-Zoof seeds, which nobody wants because nobody needs (Sleep). If the employer insists that their sales are too low and they must work longer hours, they can respond with the claim that having no time to sleep will endanger their health (the salesman's interest) and leave them with less internal resources to pitch the unneeded seeds (the long-term profit interest of the employer). The shareholder model may accept the second reason as legitimate, but not the first. Within the stakeholder model all competing claims have to be evaluated, then prioritized or balanced. Property rights are one important consideration but don't necessarily trump the variety of other claims that might emerge.

Each group generally has different interests and expectations and so develops a different perspective on what makes the company a good company (just consider the different perspectives of the Lorax and the Once-ler, as we will in detail below). Obviously, the owners' interests play a central role. Yet, the interests of employees and managers, clients and customers, suppliers, the local community, social groups, the environment, future generations, and so on may also place legitimate claims on the activity of the company. Even in the absence of someone able to voice those interests, those interests exist and lay a moral claim on the business activity. Without the Lorax, the Bar-ba-loots and Swomee-Swans still have a legitimate claim worth considering. All of these various interests place a heavy burden on the corporation or business, and it's in practice impossible to meet all of the demands satisfactorily. Making the choices of how to prioritize and meet as many of the obligations as possible in an effective way is the challenge for business and political leaders.

There are two important things to note here. First, shareholder theory would allow a CEO to consider the interests of other stakeholders, but only in an instrumental way.[7] Treat the customers well, but only to the extent necessary to increase profits. Only the law can serve as a legitimate constraint on profit maximization. Second, stakeholder theory would admit profit as a central goal, but primarily instrumentally. Friedman put it this way: "Maximizing profits is an end from the private point of view; it is a means from the social point of view."[8] Profit allows the corporation to thrive and continue to create value for a variety of stakeholders. Stockholders also have a legitimate claim to expect a return on their investments, and so the CEO will value profit in its own right, but she would not feel the need to *maximize* profit at the expense of other values, as Friedman suggests.

What this opens up is the requirement for decision makers within a company to retain their sense of *personal* moral responsibility in their roles and to recognize the many stakeholders as *persons* as well. Generally speaking, with respect to stakeholder theory, it is when a company fails to respect a group of people by at least weighing their interests or by weighing them far too lightly that one might claim the company acted wrongly. In the next three sections, let's look at how Seuss comments on these stakeholder relationships in commerce, starting with the relationship between a business and its customers.

Caveat Emptor: "No, You Can't Teach a Sneetch"

So, we've all heard the expression: Buyer Beware! Is this a bit of prudential advice, or an attitude of justification for convention? If the former, no problem. I would advise anyone to use caution with others when money is on the line, since all of us give in to temptation sometime. But sometimes this phrase is used as a justification: "I'm not wrong for having cheated you . . . you should've known better."[9] The good Doctor presents us with a perfect illustration in Sylvester McMonkey McBean, the "Fix-It-Up Chappie" from "The Sneetches."

So the Sneetches are divided into two social classes, Plain-Belly and Star-Belly, with those with "stars upon thars" as the dominant class. Besides being a wonderful allegory about the social construction of class and the role fashion plays in it, the poem provides a great example of the exploitation and manipulation of consumer desires. McBean swings into town with a machine to print stars on bellies, allowing second-class Sneetches to appropriate the appearance of first-class Star-Bellies for a small fee. Unable to maintain class domination without a means to discern class membership, Star-Bellies now desire a new way to differentiate themselves. McBean has a "Star-*Off* Machine" to do the trick, and soon he has all of the Sneetches filing in and out of his two machines. Once he has taken all of their money, he leaves the Sneetches confused on the beaches, laughingly exclaiming, "They never will learn. No. You can't teach a Sneetch" (Sneetches).

But before we look at McBean more closely, let's consider a prevalent principle in ethics. Immanuel Kant famously argued that morality is grounded on a fundamental command built into the nature of every rational being, the *categorical imperative*.[10] Something like the Golden Rule, the categorical imperative requires an agent to act in way that can be universalized, insisting on equality among rational agents; respecting the inherent dignity of all others. One formulation of the command states: "So act that you use humanity, whether in your own person or in the person of any other, always at the same time as an end, never merely as a means."[11] It's okay to use someone as long as you do so in a way that is respectful. The idea of a contract can be understood as a mutually beneficial agreement to use another person. One person sells and another person buys, each getting what they want from the other, each being used for the other's purpose. But so long as they are equals and the transaction occurs on a level playing field between free actors, it's all okay.

So, did McBean use the Sneetches in a way that recognized their own moral worth, their dignity? Should we view the Fix-It-Up Chappie's activity as respecting Sneetch interests, or should his activity be viewed as manipulative and using the Sneetches merely as means to his own end, without any regard for them as ends in themselves—that is, as dignified beings? McBean provided a desired service to the Plain-Bellies, and then another desired service to the Star-Bellies. At no point did he misrepresent his service, and he did not create the desires in the consumers. We might say that he created an environment to exploit the desires of the Sneetches for his own profit, but the word *exploit* might smuggle in a moral condemnation that we need to justify. If the Sneetches got what they wanted at the time of purchase, didn't McBean provide them a valuable service by making them happier? McBean can't be blamed if it didn't last. If a consumer regrets a purchase later, does that mean the provider took advantage?

Of course, we know that McBean exploited the Sneetches, because we heard him laugh at their sorry state. He knew all along how this would turn out, with Sneetches penniless and confused. He wasn't providing a valuable service to the consumers; he was undermining the value of his product after its sale. Think of the nationwide conversion to digital television broadcasting that began on June 12, 2009. The FCC fined Sears, Wal-Mart, Best Buy, and others in 2008 for failing to provide proper labels to inform customers buying analog TVs that they would need to purchase additional equipment to maintain full use of the product after the transition.[12] Regardless of the merits of the FCC's claim, the intention is clear: if true, consumers are unwittingly being sold a product whose value will soon plummet. Whenever a provider of a service or good knowingly undermines the value of that service or good after its purchase, or pushes the service or good well aware of some upcoming event that will undermine the value, that provider is exploiting the consumer.

McBean's behavior illustrates the inadequacy of simply using consumer desire as a justification for one's treatment of the consumer. Note that Friedman's view must condone McBean, since he profited greatly. The Sneetches should have had better laws, I guess. Oddly, the Friedmanite view encourages society to generate more legal regulation and interference in the free market, which is counter to its goal of securing a free market. In order to protect children from manipulative and harmful advertising, the European Union issued the 2007 Audiovisual Media Services Directive (amending an 1989 directive aimed solely at television advertising), which in Article 3e.1(g) requires member states to regulate media service providers, ensuring that:

> [A]udiovisual commercial communications shall not cause physical or moral detriment to minors. Therefore they shall not directly exhort minors to buy or hire a product or service by exploiting their inexperience or credulity, directly encourage them to persuade their parents or others to purchase the goods or services being advertised, exploit the special trust minors place in parents, teachers or other persons, or unreasonably show minors in dangerous situations.[13]

Such strong legislation serves to restrain the unscrupulous activity of those few (one hopes) in the marketplace who would exploit children for profit. One could ask whether exploiting inexperienced or credulous adults is somehow morally acceptable. If we think not, then McBean might find himself in a European court.

The stakeholder view would conclude differently about McBean's status as a moral agent. A good company provides a good or service that benefits its consumers. If a company undermines the value of its product in order to sell something else, or if it manipulates or produces desires to sell a product that would otherwise be less desirable, then we can see the company dealing in merely "apparent" goods. Just as one would despise an eye that creates illusions, we should reject companies offering services that exploit our needs and desires, rather than meeting them.

Whenever we consider the relationship between business and the consuming public, we should ask whether business activity is meant to serve the public good or whether individual consumers are merely the instruments for the higher business agenda of profit. McBean preyed upon the Sneetches, just as Bernie Madoff preyed upon his investors. The laws didn't need to be in place to make Madoff's activity immoral, and the apparent lack of Sneetch laws doesn't make McBean's activity less exploitative. But a company's responsibilities don't stop with its consumers. Companies are also capable of mistreating the employees that make it successful.

Take This Job and Love It

Another relationship to examine is between the company and its employees. There has always been tension between the owner's desire to increase profits by fetching labor at lower costs and the laborers desire to earn good wages and benefits. Some recognize all the worker protections now enjoyed in countries like the United States are the result of organized labor's historic struggles. Some view unions as protecting lazy and less competent workers and illegitimately demanding compensations that business simply can't afford. However one feels about the balance of interests in mainstream cases, it's difficult to maintain that human beings aren't being exploited when the working conditions reach the extreme. In such cases, we use the word *sweatshop* to connote our moral condemnation.

A sweatshop has been defined by the U.S. General Accounting Office as a "business that regularly violates both safety or health and wage or child labor laws."[14] Typically, people debate about whether some workplace is a sweatshop when conditions of health, safety, employment, or compensation are far enough beneath some minimal standard that one side views the situation as severely exploitative. In the postindustrial United States, there exists now the stereotype that sweatshops are mainly located in China and Southern and Southeast Asia. But the United States has its own share, too. Just in July of 2008, a factory in Queens was found to have cheated workers of $5.3 million, while coercing employees to lie about their pay and working conditions to state officials.[15] Wherever they occur, sweatshops serve as the extreme case of undervaluing the contribution of the worker.

Most students of philosophy will encounter Karl Marx's critique of capitalism and his arguments why labor is exploited. Briefly, Karl Marx (1818–1883) saw capitalism as an economic form that emerged for various historical reasons and would pass for others. It would pass because it's a system that sets one class against another. In this case, it allows capitalists, who own the means of production, to appropriate the surplus value that a laborer generates above the value needed for the worker to subsist. Workers, who cannot afford to hold out without work for long, find themselves competing for less meaningful jobs and for lower wages. And the better the workers become at their task, the less valuable that work becomes, since the employer will come to expect greater productivity while keeping wages low. Ultimately, workers find that both the nature and the product of their work are owned by another who profits from their exertion. So, even if the conditions are not sweatshop conditions, under a Marxist perspective workers are exploited because one class uses its property rights to profit from the labor of another class that has no real choice but to work for those who own the means of production. Capitalism is thus seen as inherently, morally problematic.

But the undervaluation of labor can also be explained and condemned as illegitimate within a capitalist framework.[16] Largely, the internal moral legitimacy of capitalism rests on the absence of chronic monopolistic conditions. If one can point to structures of power within the political and economic system that serve as monopolistic or near-monopolistic forces over labor, one can make the charge that labor is undervalued from within capitalism itself. Given the influence wielded by multinational corporations and the various giants that dominate a given industry (e.g., Wal-Mart, among retailers), it is not difficult to make the claim that such forces are at play and skew the price of labor from the natural price Adam Smith would expect to emerge in a truly competitive market.

Avoiding the larger ideological pictures, however, one could opt to develop a Seussian theory of exploitation. The good Doctor provides some insight into how employees might be undervalued in his classic *If I Ran the Circus*. Morris McGurk is a young entrepreneur with big ideas for the lot behind Sneelock's Store. McGurk imagines his friend, Sneelock, will help out with "doing little odd jobs" like selling balloons and lemonade. As McGurk imagines even grander and grander ideas to implement, he imagines poor old Sneelock doing harder and harder jobs. Sneelock must carry a big cauldron of hot pebbles, have arrows shot at apples on his head, roller skate down a shoot littered with cacti, tame a ferocious Spotted Atrocious and wrestle a Grizzly-Ghastly, lie under cars racing over ramps, get spouted back and forth between two whales, and dive 4,692 feet into a fishbowl. To be sure, if he pulls it off, McGurk would have quite an amazing circus. Who wouldn't pay to see it?!

What is interesting is McGurk's nonchalant attitude toward the overworking and endangering of poor Sneelock in light of his visionary quest to bring about a greatly improved service to his potential consumers. Over and over, McGurk assumes Sneelock's willingness, because "he likes to help out," and he'll even be "delighted" and "love it." Indeed, "He'll be a Hero." McGurk is under the impression that his workers share his vision and are willing to do all the work and run all the risks to make his vision a reality:

> My workers *love* work. They say, "Work us! Please work us!
> We'll work and we'll work up so many surprises
> You'd never see half if you had forty eyeses!" (Circus)

Of course McGurk depends on those workers, since he doesn't know how to train deer to jump simultaneously through each other's antlers. But he's sure Sneelock can train them. And how will Sneelock safely dive into that fishbowl? McGurk says:

> He'll manage just fine.
> Don't ask how he'll manage.
> That's his job. Not mine. (Circus)

McGurk rejects responsibility for the feasibility and reasonability of his expectations. It is precisely this kind of washing of one's hands that allows a systematic "legitimation" of exploitation. And given the fact that most nonunion jobs in the United States are covered by the employment-at-will doctrine, an employer can simply cite the employee's ability to quit if she's dissatisfied as a justification for ridiculous demands and taxing conditions. The idea that workers are "free" to leave or stay is often used for a defense in the cases of sweatshops overseas.

In a well-anthologized 1997 article, Ian Maitland argues that humanitarian concerns over working conditions in sweatshops are misplaced and acting on them by interfering with the market might do more harm than good.[17] The basic point is that "sweated" workers in foreign countries often are paid far better than their home standards, so these factory jobs are very desirable. Further, attempts to improve the worker's situation will likely have the opposite effect, since there will always be trade-offs between the number of jobs and the amount of compensation and between improving standards and encouraging foreign development.

Maitland argues that workers voluntarily accept these working conditions. But surely this is because they are desperate and don't have better alternatives. Aristotle distinguishes between the purely *voluntary* action and the *mixed* action:

> Something of the sort happens also with regard to the throwing of goods overboard in a storm; for in the abstract no one throws goods away voluntarily, but on condition of its securing the safety of himself and his crew any sensible man does so. Such actions, then, are mixed, but are more like voluntary actions; for they are worthy of choice at the time when they are done, and the end of an action is relative to the occasion. . . . Such actions, therefore, are voluntary, but in the abstract perhaps involuntary; for no one would choose any such act in itself.[18]

Aristotle makes clear that some actions are done voluntarily in the sense that one selects the course of action out of the available alternatives but that none of the alternatives are genuinely worthy of choice. Isn't Maitland banking on confusing these two concepts? After all, if a tyrant threatened to kill my family if I did not perform some action, I would "voluntarily" opt to perform the action. But we would call this a situation of coercion (as would Aristotle), not freedom. In the present case, a company decides to outsource labor to a foreign factory, and the workers voluntarily choose to work there. But they're not being given a better choice! True, this isn't coercion in the sense we just saw, since the tyrant causes the limited alternatives to be such as they are. In the case of sweatshops, some given company is not usually responsible for the poverty and corruption in some other country (at least directly), but they are often seeking workers in a desperate climate. Taking advantage of this is not some moral act of social responsibility. Imagine if Poor Sneelock had no other choice but to work for McGurk or let his ailing family slowly starve to death. Could we honestly say he voluntarily wrestled that Grizzly-Ghastly?

Maitland's caution about the unintended consequences of humanitarian intervention should give us pause. But using the difficulty of addressing a situation as a justification for the practice is morally suspect. If a company contracts work out to a foreign factory, that company takes on the responsibility to ensure a sustainable living wage and decent working conditions for those workers. Otherwise, the company has decided to become involved in such a way as to take advantage of the disadvantage of others. Outsourcing labor while maintaining a sustainable living wage will quite often still be cost cutting for the company, but it won't place profit maximization above treating its employees abroad with respect and dignity.

While it would be a mistake to naïvely believe that pointing out moral responsibilities is sufficient to solve the situation, justifying inaction is a recipe for the sometimes detestable status quo. While the solutions are surely complex and less than ideal, the idea that it is justifiable to place workers under harsh conditions for the sake of profit and cheaper prices for the consumer should be scrutinized. We should ask ourselves if we are not being something like McGurk, letting our vision of a thriving business blind us to the condition of the laborers whose work realizes the vision and secures our standard of living.

So far we have briefly examined the ideas that a company ought to respect its consumers and employees. Both are important stakeholders in a company. While the list of potential stakeholders is quite long, we have time to extend our consideration out just a bit to include one more, the environment within which we all must work and live.

The Sustainable Balance between the
Green of a Dollar and the Green of a Tree

A final relationship we can explore is that between a company and the environment and the tension between profits and protection of resources. The Seussian parable of *The Lorax* is the obvious choice.[19] The Once-ler, now hiding away in the desolate land of his creation, tells us of his entrepreneurial adventure producing Thneeds from Truffula Trees. Thneeds are multipurpose objects that symbolize all consumer desire in a single product, while Truffulas represent an essential link in the ecochain. As the Once-ler's enterprise grew and environmental damage mounted, the various species went away, and the tree-hugging Lorax continuously failed to convince the Once-ler to alter his practice.

The story ends without much redemption for the Once-ler, the Once-ler defiantly carrying on business as the very last Truffula falls. The Once-ler's business is gone because the material resources are depleted, and the environment lies polluted and barren. Now the Once-ler, a recluse in his dilapidated buildings, sells his story for fifteen cents, a nail, and a great-great-great-grandfather snail's shell. The only glimmer of hope is the last Truffula Seed that the Once-ler passes on to the boy so that he can grow back the forest. The Once-ler warns, "Unless someone like you cares a whole awful lot, nothing is going to get better. It's not" (Lorax). Even here the Once-ler does not work to fix his own mess but passes on the responsibility to the young boy, presumably symbolic of the future generations who will bear the burden of our present environmental negligence.

So does a business have a special obligation toward the environment? Well, first, is the environment the kind of thing one can have an obligation toward? One might argue so, but it is perhaps easier to defend the claim that one has an obligation toward some beings that depend on the environment. If a tree doesn't feel pain, chopping it down might not violate the tree in any morally interesting way. On the contrary, if the last Bar-ba-loot family needed its shade and fruits, then perhaps I owe it to them not to chop the tree down. Of course, those most reluctant to admit that there is intrinsic value in nature will include animals as lacking intrinsic value. Think of the view that pets are really just property. So, we might only owe it to human beings (or at least similar kinds of beings) not to chop down the tree, since some human beings may derive some good from the existence of Bar-ba-loots. In fact, we find a spectrum of views regarding moral obligations to nonhuman nature. On the one side, some will see an inherent worth in living things, and perhaps even in special nonliving features of nature.[20] In the middle, we see varying degrees of inclusion based on morally relevant properties, like being able to feel pain or being rational. On the other end, we find those who see only instrumental value in things and beings other than moral persons like humans.

While these differences are important in determining how one will act with regard to environmental dilemmas, we can simply allow that having an obligation toward the environment might be shorthand for at least having obligations to respect the environment for the sake of other persons. This allows us to postpone that larger philosophical debate for the moment. Now we can easily say that humans do have some obligation toward the environment and can ask whether businesses are like us in this respect.

One scholar, Norman Bowie, argues that businesses don't have any special responsibility to the environment, only to uphold the law. Businesses are meeting consumer preferences, so environmentalists should only expect businesses to become greener if consumers desire greener products. Bowie informs us that "[b]usiness will respond to the market. It is the consuming public that has the obligation to make the trade-off between cost and environmental integrity."[21] This echoes the Once-ler's declaration that it's only someone else (besides those in business) caring an awful lot that can save the environment. While we are seeing shifts in the direction of proactive consumer choice nowadays, it's hard to distinguish genuinely "ecofriendly" businesses from mere "greenwashed" ones. A "greenwashed" business or product is simply one that has been marketed to seem "ecofriendly," when in fact it has little to no environmental advantages. Think of BP's marketing campaign to establish itself as an environmental leader, when its core business is fundamentally at odds with environmental concerns. Nonetheless, from Bowie's perspective, it is really up to consumers to keep making the difference.

One could object to Bowie by noting that the market may not be able to truly reflect consumer preferences about the environment. Like so many public goods, individuals may prefer to have others bear the cost of protecting the environment while they enjoy its benefits. Market failures of this type, Bowie points out, are supposed to be remediated by the government, which is why business does have the obligation to uphold the law. Consumers can voice within the political arena those preferences that the market doesn't register. As a consequence, Bowie notes (as we noted in our discussion of the Sneetches) the inconsistency of businesses claiming this Friedmanite stance while simultaneously using corporate money and influence to interfere with politics. Likewise, the power of consumers is significantly limited when businesses monopolize various sectors of the economy, thus limiting consumer choice for necessary or highly valued goods, such as energy, food, and transportation.

Again, while certainly there are responsibilities across the board, the idea that a company can simply pass the buck to consumers and politicians compartmentalizes the human activity of commerce. Decision makers within a company are in the best position to determine how to minimize environmental impact of their specific commercial activity and coordinate with peers to remove pressures to ignore environmental concerns. On a shareholder model, however, a company should only bother with environmental concerns to the extent that such energies would increase profits, for example, for public relations purposes or for marketing. Providing merely the appearance of being an environmentally conscious company (or greenwashing one's not-so-ecofriendly products) can be just as effective as actually attending to issues of pollution, habitat protection, or sustainability. The idea that the goal of business is profit maximization at the expense of any value unprotected by law not only condones but also encourages businesses to externalize the costs of environmental impact. Externalizing costs occurs when the cost of some business activity is not carried by the business or its customers, but by some external party. Imagine a factory upstream from a town that pollutes the town's water supply to make its products. If the town taxes residents to run a water treatment plant instead of requiring the factory to clean the water at a cut into profit, a decrease in employee wages, or an increase in prices for its customers, then one component of the cost to produce the factory's product (namely, the cleanup of polluting by-products) has been externalized. The Friedmanite view encourages businesses to comply with legal standards as minimally as possible and externalize environmental costs to distant stakeholders in both present and future generations. If we don't embrace the activities of the Once-ler, then we can't embrace the shareholder model.

Who Heard a Who?

In conclusion, business ethics is a field of inquiry and debate among fairly divergent views. I have offered some Seussian thoughts to lend support for taking account of multiple stakeholders over washing managers' and owners' hands of responsibility. Consumers should be treated fairly and with an aim to offer them something of genuine value, not just because profit is to be had by doing so but also because business activity is one that takes place among persons who owe each other such respect. Similarly, employees should be fairly compensated and provided with dignified work environments, not just because doing so will keep up productivity but because they are persons who deserve proper treatment. Finally, the environment itself deserves to be respected, if not for its own sake, then at least for the sake of all of those persons who live within it. There are obviously more stakeholder groups that we can identify, but the general approach should now be clear.

To be fair, though, there are larger and more complicated political, economic, and social issues at play, and perhaps the followers of Friedman are right to restrict the role responsibility of a businessperson to making profits. My worry is that defining one's role in business narrowly will externalize these moral concerns to be dealt with on a societal and global political level (perhaps meaning they will not be attended to properly). To be sure, defining one's role broadly results in having to make even more complicated business decisions, perhaps making one more vulnerable to less scrupulous competitors. Yet, even though attending to profit and competitive advantage is crucial, commerce is a human activity. It emerges among human beings and affects human beings, as well as the environment we all live in. The myth that business is impersonal does ideological work, making immorality seem acceptable and moral deliberation inappropriate. Abolishing that myth opens up the requirement for decision makers within a company to retain their sense of *personal* moral responsibility in their roles and to recognize the many stakeholders as *persons* as well. Acknowledging as much makes managing a company a morally weighty activity. The morally responsible manager admirably pursues profit in the most beneficial and least harmful way, gathering her creative resources and leadership skills to navigate the challenges. By comparison, it reveals profit-maximizing managers to be merely the adolescent McGurks, devious McBeans, and self-destructive Once-lers that we could all do without.

CHAPTER SEVENTEEN

~

Speaking for Business, Speaking for Trees: Business and Environment in *The Lorax*

Johann A. Klaassen and Mari-Gretta G. Klaassen

Questions about the role and responsibilities of business in adult society are not, generally speaking, addressed in the stories of Dr. Seuss. Perhaps, if we stretch the topic a bit, *If I Ran the Zoo* and *If I Ran the Circus* could be read as a child's understanding of how adults can and should act in the world—but both are obviously written from the child's perspective and show the limits of even a child's imagination when applied to the problems of adult life. This means that *The Lorax* is unusual among Dr. Seuss's works in two respects: first, it is a story told by an adult to a child, from the adult's point of view; and second, it is one of a very few stories that Dr. Seuss admitted having begun with a clear moral in mind.[1] In *The Lorax*, the main character, the Once-ler, tells his story to an unnamed child: a story of how he built a business and destroyed an ecosystem in the process, despite the interventions of the Lorax, who "speaks for the trees." The book ends hopefully, with the Once-ler asking for the child's help to restore that environment—*almost* hopefully, we should say, as it is not entirely clear that the child is actually willing to participate or that any amount of effort will restore the land, water, and air.

In this chapter, we will examine the three questions we think drive this book—questions that ride a fine line between business ethics and environmental ethics. First, what IS a "Thneed"? It's the product that the Once-ler produces in his factory, "a Fine-Something-That-All-People-Need!"—an object that has so many uses that it is really, to all extents and purposes, useless.

However, people still buy it, perhaps due to a sudden fad. Or, in other words, when we buy things like Thneeds, do we consume too much? Second, is the Once-ler really so focused on the growth of his business that he cannot see the destruction he is causing? The Lorax warns the Once-ler, pointing out the harms that his factory is doing as it grows—but these warnings do not cause him to reconsider his environmental policies but rather to shrug off the problems. Or, in other words, are there alternatives to economic growth? Third, why does the Once-ler ignore the long-term sustainability of his business? It seems he forgets that there are a finite number of Truffula Trees, and doesn't plant any new ones. He allows the resources the business relies on to run out; his business is ruined, and the local environment has been permanently altered. Or, in other words, can attention to a longer time frame have positive impacts on both business and the environment? Such questions lie at the intersection of business ethics and environmental ethics—and might be seen as central to understanding our place on the planet.

Do You Need a Thneed?

The Once-ler begins his story by describing a beautiful place full of interesting animals, clean water, and fresh air—and, most importantly to him, Truffula Trees. The "Truffula tufts" are full of a soft fiber that the Once-ler knows he can knit into . . . well, a "Thneed." This is an indescribable item with more "uses" than could ever be realistically useful.

> It's a shirt. It's a sock. It's a glove. It's a hat.
> But it has *other* uses. Yes far beyond that.
> You can use it for carpets. For pillows! For sheets!
> Or curtains! Or covers for bicycle seats! (Lorax)

From the production of the very first Thneed it seems fairly clear that the Thneed has no real use or value. It's important to keep an open mind when reading a Dr. Seuss book, but we find it hard to imagine an object that could fulfill all these tasks and still be comfortable or practical while being used for any of these functions. The Lorax speaks for all of us, it seems, when he says that the Once-ler won't sell a single Thneed. But immediately the Lorax is proven wrong. "For, just at that minute, a chap came along, / and he thought that the Thneed I had knitted was great. / He happily bought it for three ninety-eight" (Lorax). And although it seems that Thneeds become incredibly popular, we never do find out what they're really any good for . . . just that people think that they're "great." The popularity of the Thneed, despite its uselessness, prompts us to ask a key question: are there some products that should not be made? Philosophically speaking, this question is usually turned around: Are there moral limits to our freedom to consume? Might there be some things that we should not want to buy? Many of us hope to follow Thoreau's dictum and "simplify, simplify"—and we have probably all seen bumper stickers urging us to "live simply, that others may simply live" (a maxim attributed to Mahatma Gandhi). But why should we?

Drawing from the 2004 Worldwatch Institute report, Joseph DesJardins puts consumption patterns into stark perspective:

> The wealthiest 25% of the world's population consumes 58% of the energy, 45% of the meat and fish, 84% of the paper, and 87% of the vehicles, and accounts for 86% of the total private consumer expenditures. In contrast, the world's poorest 25% consumes 24% of the energy, 5% of the meat and fish, 1% of the paper, and less than 1% of the vehicles, and accounts for only 1.3% of the total private consumer expenditures.[2]

Americans and Western Europeans make up a large part of the wealthiest quarter of the world's population, and DesJardins argues that this huge disparity shows that we "consume too much" in three fundamental ways.[3]

First, our consumption patterns—the habits born of our "work and spend cycle"—are not in our best interests, so we consume too much "in a practical sense." We are more likely to be obese, more likely to labor under a crushing debt load, and less likely to describe ourselves as happy than the rest of the world. Dr. Seuss doesn't really tell us much about the practical impact of Thneed purchases on the chaps who buy them; because we understand something of how fads work, though, we might guess that some people are driven to distraction (at least!) by their lack of a Thneed, especially once all of their friends have them. Second, our consumption patterns drive and are reinforced by an unequal and unjust allocation of scarce natural resources, so we consume too much "in an ethical sense." Americans spend more on cosmetics every year than it would cost to provide basic education to all the children in the poorest parts of the world; Americans and Europeans, counted together, spend more on pet food every year than it would cost to provide basic health care and food to those same children. Dr. Seuss doesn't really address this issue either, and we don't hear anything about the other uses to which the money spent on Thneeds might have been put—but it seems to us that the uselessness of Thneeds would mean that just about any other use would have been better, really. Third, our consumption patterns drive production practices that threaten to destroy the natural environment, so we consume too much "in an environmental sense."

This essay was written during the unfolding of one of the worst environmental disasters the world has ever known, the Deepwater Horizon oil disaster in the Gulf of Mexico. It seems clear to us that our desires to use more and more fossil fuels are doing more harm than good. Once he sells his first Thneed, the Once-ler immediately hires a work force and builds a factory to make Thneeds on an industrial scale in the middle of nowhere, without any apparent thought for the environmental impact of his actions (to which we'll return below).

Just before his initial description of the Thneed, the Once-ler assured the Lorax of his good—or at least not *bad*—intentions: "'Look, Lorax,' I said. 'There's no cause for alarm. / I chopped just one tree. I am doing no harm. / I'm being quite useful. This thing is a Thneed'" (Lorax). And it's hard to object, really, to the Once-ler's claim, since Thneeds haven't yet had a chance to have a practical impact on the society or to have an ethical impact on the distribution of scarce resources, and the environmental impact of cutting down and using up one Truffula Tree probably really is so small as to be "no harm," or not enough of a harm to be particularly concerned about. But once the Once-ler brought many of his relatives to his factory, where they all knitted Thneeds, the impact of Thneed consumption begins to be felt quickly.

Now, consumption in and of itself is not necessarily morally problematic, and DesJardins admits as much: "What we might call 'smart consumption' or 'good consumption' recognizes the many good reasons there are to consume and seeks to distinguish good from bad consumption."[4] Bad consumption, clearly, is the "too much" consumption that we have discussed in the previous paragraphs; what could good consumption be? DesJardins has only a brief suggestion: "One does not sacrifice by consuming less if what one consumes is better."[5] Although DesJardins doesn't refer to it directly, we think that his drawing this distinction is meant to pick up on the work of Mark Sagoff. In "Do We Consume Too Much?" Sagoff argues that at least some of our worries about our rate of consumption are unfounded: various ecologically minded prognosticators have been predicting impending human and ecological disasters (food shortages, energy shortages, and the like) at least since the seventies, none of which have come about. Instead, Sagoff argues, we find ourselves detached and distanced from one another, from our homes and communities, and from the natural world around us by the impacts of our consumption patterns.[6]

Rather than urge less consumption, Sagoff (like DesJardins) recommends a smarter approach to consumption:

> The alternative approach suggests not so much that we consume less but that we invest more. Environmentalists could push for investment in technologies

that increase productivity per unit of energy, get more economic output from less material input, recycle waste, provide new sources of power, replace transportation in large part with telecommunication, and move from an industrial to a service economy.[7]

In short, in this sort of a view, consumption itself isn't a particular problem: our economic system can continue to produce the things we'd like to consume—but it should be done better, using fewer resources and less energy, as it rolls along. It's not a problem, really, for us to desire Thneeds, as long as their production processes are (or become) environmentally benign. But, as we discover, the Once-ler's factory is anything but benign.

Must Business Grow?

Like many business owners before him the Once-ler quickly begins to focus on "biggering" his business. Unfortunately, as it grows the Once-ler's business requires more and more Truffula Trees.

> Now, chopping one tree
> at a time
> was too slow.
> So I quickly invented my Super-Axe-Hacker
> which whacked off four Truffula Trees at one smacker.
> We were making Thneeds
> four times as fast as before! (Lorax)

In cutting down so many Truffula Trees, the Once-ler has incurred the wrath of the Lorax. The Lorax goes on to state the plight of the Brown Bar-ba-loots, who are running low on their native food source, Truffula Fruits. This could be a good first sign to the Once-ler: if there's a Truffula Fruit shortage, and the Bar-ba-loots have to find somewhere else to live, then there are probably not enough Truffula Trees for the Once-ler to continue production at his present pace. So why does he continue? Does he simply not care?

In fact, we think that this is one of the first questions to occur to a child when reading *The Lorax*: Why did the Once-ler mess up the place he admired?[8] Before the Once-ler begins making Thneeds, there is no doubt that he does admire the Truffula Tree grove. So why does he allow his drive to make his business bigger overwhelm his concern for his local environment? The answer seems to be, simply put, *money*. The Once-ler isn't particularly concerned by the plight of the Bar-ba-loots: although he says he feels badly that they must leave, he is able to ignore the Lorax for the time being. Instead, his exclusive focus turns to his business:

> I meant no harm. I most truly did not.
> But I had to grow bigger. So bigger I got.
> I biggered my factory. I biggered my roads.
> I biggered my wagons. I biggered the loads
> of the Thneeds I shipped out. I was shipping them forth
> to the South! To the East! To the West! To the North! . . .
> I went right on biggering . . . selling more Thneeds.
> And I biggered my money, which everyone needs. (Lorax)

The sudden popularity of Thneeds may have surprised the Once-ler at first, but it seems that he was ready to take advantage of it by rapidly increasing production—and to increase it with unsubtle marketing, since on the side of the wagons, as they depart the factory, we can see the Once-ler's unsubtle message: "You Need a Thneed!"

As we discussed with consumption, economic growth is not, in itself, morally problematic. In large parts of the world, people are struggling to survive, and economic development would clearly improve their lot. But these last two sentences illustrate a common conceptual confusion, which we think is very important to keep clear: "economic growth" and "economic development" are not the same. Herman Daly has long urged that we make a sharp distinction: "We can simply distinguish growth (quantitative expansion) from development (qualitative improvement), and urge ourselves to develop as much as possible, while ceasing to grow."[9] But what could it mean to have an economy that doesn't grow?

Economic orthodoxy would have us believe that a company or an economy that does not continually move forward, growing at every moment, will starve and die. To intentionally limit growth, particularly by imposing strict environmental regulation, would on such a view mean a sort of retreat from economic activity—which would itself mean a worldwide and permanent contraction of the sort that would wreck everyone's standard of living. But this line of thinking has faded in recent years, as mainstream economists looked closely at the actual result of environmental regulation and found that they are "not only benign in their impacts on international competitiveness, but actually a net positive force driving private firms and the economy as a whole to become more competitive in international markets."[10] Or it could be that the idea of "limiting growth" could mean holding the total of economic activity in the global economy exactly at current levels. This would imply a strange kind of stagnation, in which the world's standard of living would gradually converge on a level lower than the developed world currently enjoys but higher than the extreme poverty so prevalent around the world. It seems unlikely that very many people in the developed world would be excited by the prospect of transferring wealth to others, even if it meant that the suffering of others was largely eliminated.

Joseph DesJardins, following Daly, argues that there's a third way:

> The alternative to economic growth is economic development, not economic stagnation. . . . True economic *development* must encourage targeted economic growth in those areas in which human well-being can be promoted in ecologically sustainable ways and a decrease in those economic activities that degrade the earth's biosphere.[11]

Shifting from "more" to "better," in other words, can allow our economy to continue to move forward without the environmental and social dangers of using up more and more of the planet's resources. With some things—Thneeds, for instance—it's hard to see quite how we could substitute gains in quality for gains in quantity. The Once-ler seems to be stuck in a bind. Having created something for which there seems to be an almost insatiable demand (a demand that he helped create), he doesn't have any incentive to do anything more than produce *more* of the same old Thneeds he knows he can sell. And he doesn't stop to wonder if perhaps the increased production of Thneeds from his factory has done any harm until it's too late.

Selling the Last of the Truffula Trees

The Lorax returned to show the Once-ler more of the environmental damage that the Thneed factory had caused—air pollution, in the form of "smogulous smoke," had driven off the Swomee-Swans; and water pollution, in the form of "Gluppity-Glupp" and "Schloppity-Schlopp," had driven off the Humming-Fish. Blame for the plight of the Swomee-Swans and Humming-Fish is laid clearly at the feet of the Once-ler, but he still doesn't seem to get it.

> Well, I have my rights, sir, and I'm telling *you*
> I intend to go on doing just what I do!
> And, for your information, you Lorax, I'm figgering
> on biggering
>
> and BIGGERING
>
> and BIGGERING
>
> and **BIGGERING**,
>
> turning MORE Truffula Trees into Thneeds
> which everyone, EVERYONE, *EVERYONE* needs! (Lorax)

But the Once-ler's tirade was interrupted—at that moment, a machine chopped down the last Truffula Tree. Without the raw material it needs, the Thneed factory was suddenly shut down, and all of his relatives left.

In his pursuit of quick wealth, the Once-ler has entirely used up the single natural resource on which his business depended and destroyed the natural environment in which the business was located. In one respect, that's not particularly surprising—the initial creation of the Thneed was little more than a whim, it seems, and the business was built on the faddish demand for Thneeds. But in another respect, it's emblematic of much of modern business, in that an emphasis on short-term results—the quick biggering of his business—blinds the Once-ler to long-term issues, putting long-term success out of reach. If only the Once-ler had heard of "sustainability"!

There has been a lot of discussion of "sustainability" in the decades since *The Lorax* appeared.[12] At first glance, it's a relatively simple idea: sustainability is simply something's ability to sustain itself, of course, usually indefinitely. But we quickly run into difficulties, as the Once-ler's example shows: the continued, sustained growth of the Thneed factory is not compatible with the continued, sustained existence of the Truffula Tree forest. The most widely cited discussion of sustainability is that of the World Commission on Environment and Development, also known as the Brundtland Commission, which offers this definition: "Sustainable development is a development that meets the needs of the present without compromising the ability of future generations to meet their own needs."[13] Most contemporary economists, it seems, point to this sort of "intergenerational equity" as a fundamental part of any discussion of sustainability, and most appear to agree that the general stock of capital is the best way to measure this, so that "a development is called sustainable when it leaves the capital stock at least unchanged," if not increased.[14]

In this sense, the Once-ler is operating in a sustainable way when he turns the last of the Truffula Trees into Thneeds: the total stock of capital is increased. Sure, the local ecosystem has been wrecked, and all that remains of the indigenous flora and fauna are "Grickle-grass" and crows, but the Once-ler and his family got "mighty rich," so the natural capital of the area was transformed into Thneeds, a factory, and money, and the society's total capital was (apparently) increased. Some senses of sustainability are narrowly focused on measures of wealth, and their conditions appear to be satisfied if there is as much or more capital tomorrow as there was yesterday. Other measures of societal and environmental well-being are left out of the picture, unless they can be expressed in terms of "stock of capital."

The strongest forms of sustainability, on the other hand, ask that we look not only at the *value* of our stock of capital but also at the *context* for the accumulation or use of each type of capital. Think again of the Thneed factory: it seems clear that the factory is at least less valuable (if not completely valueless) once the last Truffula Tree is cut down. Suddenly, in order to determine whether or not a course of action (say, improving our Truffula-cutting equipment) is sustainable in the strong sense, we need to look past the sum of the value of the factory and the Thneeds; we need to investigate the size of the current Truffula Tree population, its rate of reproduction, the minimum size of a healthy population, the impact of the factory's emissions on the forest's health. . . . In short, when we use the strongest definitions of sustainability, a vastly more complicated set of variables comes into play.

In 1990, Herman Daly offered what are now known as the "Daly Rules" for the sustainable use of natural capital:

1. Renewable resources (fish, forests, soils, groundwaters) must be used no faster than the rate at which they regenerate;
2. Nonrenewable resources (mineral ores, fossil fuels, fossil groundwaters) must be used no faster than renewable substitutes for them can be put into place;
3. Pollution and wastes must be emitted no faster than natural systems can absorb them, recycle them, or render them harmless.[15]

Others are seeking to extend these rules to other forms of capital, so that the same kind of analyses can be performed on them as well.[16] Sustainability, then, assumes that we can have a broad accounting of a variety of different kinds of capital, holds that some of these forms of capital are not substitutable for one another, and requires that we leave our stocks of all these different forms of capital intact (if not improved) for the next generation. In building and biggering his business, the Once-ler has given no evidence of concern for the future at all. Any more attentive businessman would certainly have noticed that his raw material was being used up faster than it could replace itself, and an environmentally conscious businessman might even have worried about the long-term sustainability of his entire operation. Could the Once-ler have produced Thneeds in a sustainable way? We're not certain—but he certainly could have done better than he did.

The Lorax: Speaking for Trees

Is it odd that this chapter has focused so much on the actions of the Once-ler and their consequences to the near exclusion of the Lorax himself? After all, the book's title is *The Lorax*, but he has only made a couple of quick appear-ances. So, as the nameless narrator asks at the outset:

> What *was* the Lorax?
> And why was it there?
> And why was it lifted and taken somewhere
> from the far end of town where the Grickle-grass grows? (Lorax)

The Lorax appears with a "*ga-Zump!*," leaping out of the stump of the first Truffula Tree that the Once-ler cut down, and introduces himself: "'I am the Lorax. I speak for the trees. / I speak for the trees, for the trees have no tongues'" (Lorax). Later, we find out that he is also caretaker for the Brown Bar-ba-loots and responsible for sending off the Swomee-Swans and the Humming-Fish. Does the idea of having someone to speak for the trees seem unusual to you?

Most philosophers who teach classes on environmental ethics seem to find that the idea of speaking for trees is at least vaguely familiar. Some may attribute this to having read *The Lorax* to their kids at bedtime, but others will think of Christopher D. Stone's influential essay, "Should Trees Have Standing? Toward Legal Rights for Natural Objects,"[17] which is reprinted in most environmental ethics textbooks. Stone argues that we should, within the context of our legal system, "give legal rights to forests, oceans, rivers and other so-called 'natural objects' in the environment—indeed, to the natural environment as a whole."[18] To give a Truffula Tree grove, for example, the kind of legal rights that Stone envisions would require finding ways (a) for the trees to go to the courts on their own behalf, (b) because of some injury to themselves, and (c) in order to get benefits for themselves. It seems that (b) and (c) here are fairly easy to understand—if the Once-ler cuts down part of the grove, it is injured, and a court could step in to prevent the Once-ler from cutting down more trees and to cause him to plant some new trees in the grove to make it whole. But how could the Truffula Trees go to the courts themselves? They can't speak for themselves, after all. But Stone points out that there are a wide variety of things that we recognize as having legal rights, which similarly can't speak for themselves:

> Corporations cannot speak, either; nor can states, estates, infants, incompe-tents, municipalities, or universities. Lawyers speak for them. . . . One ought, I think, to handle the legal problems of natural objects as one does the problems of legal incompetents[:] . . . those concerned with his well-being make such a showing to the court, and someone is designated by the court with the author-ity to manage the incompetent's affairs.[19]

In the case of the Truffula Trees, it seems that the Lorax designated himself the guardian *ad litem* of the trees, animals, and all—though rather than take the Once-ler to court, he tries to appeal to the Once-ler's environmental conscience, to no avail.[20]

Once the last Truffula Tree had been cut, the Once-ler's family all packed up and left, leaving the Once-ler with an empty factory . . . and the Lorax. The Lorax also leaves, suddenly, and without any overt comment: "The Lorax said nothing. Just gave me a glance . . . / just gave me a very sad, sad backward glance . . . / as he lifted himself by the seat of his pants" (Lorax). The Once-ler discovers that on the "small pile of rocks" from which the Lorax lifted himself was one word, "unless"—which the Once-ler simply doesn't understand. Years pass, and the factory crumbles away; but with the appearance of an unnamed child, the Once-ler finally understands the meaning and importance of the Lorax's parting message.

UNLESS someone like you
cares a whole awful lot,
nothing is going to get better.
It's not. (Lorax)

The Once-ler then gives the child the last of the Truffula seeds with the hope that a new Truffula forest can be planted, and maybe the Lorax and all the other animals will come back. Is this a hopeful ending? We're not really sure: on the one hand, the nameless child *appears* to be interested enough to follow through on the Once-ler's request; on the other, even if he does go and plants the single seed, there's no guarantee that a new forest will result. It seems to us that the odds are stacked pretty heavily against the revival of the Truffula forest and the return of the Lorax and all the animals . . . but we're not quite ready to give up hope.

What Do *You* Think? Will the Lorax Come Back?

Most readers seem to think of *The Lorax* as an environmental book—and it is, but it's much more than that. Dr. Seuss gives us loving descriptions of "that glorious place" and its plants and animals and is clearly distraught at the harms done to them all. But what seems to be seldom recognized is that this book is also about the rights and responsibilities of businesses with regard to the natural environment. In this chapter, we've highlighted some key issues we think Dr. Seuss wanted his readers to consider when they read this story: Are there ethical limits to economic consumption? Can we replace our current focus on economic growth with a new emphasis on economic development? And can attention to the concept of long-term sustainability have positive impacts on both business and the environment? Dr. Seuss seems to have had some answers in mind when he wrote *The Lorax*, and his idea of the Lorax himself as someone who can "speak for the trees" might show us a way to address serious conflicts between business and the environment going forward—but, most importantly to us, this beautifully written and drawn book captures our attention and gets us thinking about these questions for ourselves.

CHAPTER EIGHTEEN

~

Dr. Seuss Meets
Philosophical Aesthetics

Dwayne Tunstall

I can imagine some philosophers of art glancing at this chapter and thinking: Dr. Seuss is a well-known children's book author, but for goodness sake, not a serious artist or aesthetic theorist. Choose someone more serious. Choose someone more scholarly. Just choose someone else. Besides, aren't you contributing to the ghettoization of the field in the mainstream English-speaking philosophical community by introducing people to philosophical aesthetics using Dr. Seuss?

After getting reacquainted with some of the advertisements, children's picture books, political cartoons, television adaptations of his picture books, and paintings Seuss created over the course of his lifetime, I realized that Seuss's artworks are just the sort of art objects I should use to introduce people to philosophical aesthetics. Perhaps by introducing people to aesthetics using Dr. Seuss, they will see that philosophical aesthetics is not an esoteric discipline. Rather, philosophical theories of art can help people better appreciate artworks, some of which they've been acquainted with since childhood. After all, learning to better appreciate artworks enables us to be more sensitive to how the arts teach us to see the world differently than we normally would see it. For example, being mesmerized by the vivid reds of the Cat in the Hat's hat and the bow tie worn by a cute humanoidlike cat takes us away from our everyday concerns. Reading books like *The Cat in the Hat* allows us to imagine ourselves watching an anarchist cat having fun juggling, violating virtually any and every household rule he can violate, causing trouble wherever he goes, yet cleaning up after himself once his fun is done. Exercising our imaginations this way is worthwhile in itself. Learning to appreciate things that exercise our imaginations in this manner is also worthwhile. If introducing people to aesthetics using Dr. Seuss further marginalizes philosophical aesthetics from the mainstream English-speaking philosophical community, then so be it. Introducing more people to philosophical aesthetics is worth that risk.

As a sign of respect to my colleagues in the field, I will introduce philosophical aesthetics using two of the more influential philosophies of art: Monroe Beardsley's aesthetic theory of art and Arthur Danto's philosophy of art. In addition, I will introduce a third influential aesthetic theory: cultural criticism. Yet I won't use perhaps the most well-known theory of cultural criticism in the field, namely, Theodor W. Adorno's aesthetic theory. Rather, I use Philip Nel's cultural studies approach to interpreting Dr. Seuss's work.

Why Is Dr. Seuss's Art, Art: Beardsley's Aesthetic Theory of Art

I have just taken it for granted that Dr. Seuss's work *is* art. But what makes his work *art*? This question became an urgent one for me as I looked at many of his surrealist oil paintings, his ink drawings, and his fanciful sculptures of exotic Seussian animals, done in a faux-taxidermy style. One painting in particular grabbed my attention: *Every Girl Should Have a Unicorn*. In this painting Seuss places an apparently nondescript and naked girl on a Seussian unicorn. She rides her unicorn on a green-blue hill. She is surrounded by wild vines, painted in fluid, curving lines. These vines—painted in rich vibrant blues, reds, oranges, pinks, yellows, dark blues, and greens—dance across the painting, intersecting randomly. This painting appears to be a landscape in the artistic style of what Jon Agee calls "Seussism." Here is Agee's dictionary-esque definition of this Seussy artistic style: "Seussism (*Soos-izm*), n. Fine Arts. A style of art characterized chiefly by a grandubulous sense of ornamentation and color, where exotic, snergelly architecture twists, turns and schloops into countless grickelly filigrees and flourishes, and rippulous shapes loom about in space as if they were some kind of new-fangled noodles let loose in zero gravity."[1]

Yet, Seussism does not seem to fit the image of what most nonartists consider to be art. Most nonartists think that art should be the beautiful, realistic representation of a person, thing, or event. If this is the case, then what makes *Every Girl Should Have a Unicorn* art? How can we call this painting art? Is it just because Dr. Seuss painted it?

I think Beardsley's aesthetic theory of art can help us answer these questions. Before we see how Beardsley's aesthetic theory of art lets us answer this question, though, we should learn more about it. Like other philosophies of art, Beardsley's aesthetic theory aims to offer a philosophical definition of art. But such a definition is not meant simply to describe how people normally use the word *art* in their everyday conversations. Rather, a philosophical definition of art aims to provide the necessary and sufficient conditions for an object to be classified as an art object. In other words, a philosophical definition of art aims to answer the question: What criteria must objects satisfy in order to be classified as artworks? This question is important if for no other reason than because philanthropies and governments who fund the arts need to be able to identify which objects and projects are, in fact, art.

Beardsley's aesthetic theory of art is built on his definition of art. In *Art as Aesthetic Production*, he proposes the following definition of art: "An artwork is something produced with the intention of giving it the capacity to satisfy the aesthetic interest."[2] Of particular importance is his emphasis on satisfying the aesthetic interest. When an artist produces something, she aims to not only produce an artwork but also consciously desires and intends to produce an object capable of evoking an aesthetic experience in those who encounter it. When having an aesthetic experience, the one appreciating the work experiences it "independent of any expectation of the use or consumption of those objects that might in turn be dependent upon the possession of the objects."[3] Beardsley explains what it means to have an aesthetic experience this way:

> [When we receptively] view, listen to, contemplate, apprehend, watch, read, think about, peruse, and so forth an artwork . . . we find that our experience (including all that we are aware of: perceptions, feelings, emotions, impulses, desires, beliefs, thoughts) is lifted in a certain way that is hard to describe and especially to summarize: it takes on a sense of freedom from concern about matters outside the thing received, an intense effect that is nevertheless detached from practical ends, the exhilarating sense of exercising powers of discovery, integration of the self and its experiences.[4]

To have such an experience requires us to have an intense experience where the different features or components of an object are unified into a coherent pattern.[5] We can have such intense experiences by looking at Seuss's artwork, especially his oil paintings.

Take Seuss's painting, *Cat Carnival in West Venice*,[6] for example. This painting figures a humanoid Seussian cat wearing an absurd and elongated hat on its head. The cat, male I presume, also wears a handsome suit as he leads a lady down a red, blue, and grayish-blue flight of stairs. The stairs descend into darkness. The lady is shaped like a petite, porcelain figurine. She wears what appears to be an elegant dress perfect for a carnival in West Venice; it resembles a nineteenth-century dress with a flowing ruffled train. She also wears what appears to be an elaborate, almost-translucent headpiece on her grayish-blue hair. Thick, vibrant lines take up the entire right side of the painting. Once these elements are seen together, an alluring scene emerges before our eyes. As we look at Seuss's painting, we are transported from our everyday reality to a magical scene. We witness a handsome cat walking a pretty lady down a flight of stairs, perhaps on their way to a carnival in West Venice.

We can now see how Beardsley's aesthetic theory would explain why Seuss's *Every Girl Should Have a Unicorn* would be art. Just like *Cat Carnival in West Venice*, this painting transports us from our everyday reality into a surreal scene. We are transfixed by the intersecting, curving lines dancing across a dark background. We are surprised by the nondescript, naked girl riding a unicorn in the lower right-hand corner. Almost hiding there, she playfully rides the unicorn as it walks down a green-blue hill.

We can also use Beardsley's aesthetic theory to see how Seuss's children's books are artworks. Take Seuss's first children's book, *And to Think That I Saw It on Mulberry Street*. In this book Seuss's illustrations convey the story line at least as much as the actual text and lets children who can't read follow along. His illustrations let the readers' imaginations roam free as they lose themselves in Dr. Seuss's world. The surreal scenery, the absurd characters, the almost doodlelike, unfinished quality of its characters—all these features lead the reader to imaginatively fill in the gaps; to let their eyes wander around the page and tie everything together in a flowing narrative. This style remained a prominent feature of Seuss's children's picture books from the late thirties well into the sixties.

What also makes Seuss's children's books artworks is his efficient and economical use of language, language that is understandable to young children. For example, *The Cat in the Hat* uses only 237 different words to create "a fast-paced, intriguing tale with vivid characterization, eliciting a high degree of reader participation. . . ."[7] This efficient and economical use of language is coupled with rhyming couplets, nonsensical words, and a playful arrangement of words. These stylistic features are further coupled with his tendency to ink his strong lines boldly to offset the often unfinished quality of his illustrations. Taken together, these stylistic features were what enabled

Seuss to create books that made it easy for children and adults alike to have aesthetic experiences while reading them. Beardsley's aesthetic definition of art gives us a means of accounting for how Seuss's style can invoke aesthetic experiences in his readers.

Beardsley's aesthetic definition of art seems fine since it allows us to explain why Seuss's paintings and children's books are artworks. However, his definition of art entails at least two things that many philosophers of art and art critics are not willing to accept. First, some art critics and philosophers of art are not willing to accept that very young children can create art, regardless of how bad it might look, as long as that child creates it spontaneously. Second, many art critics and philosophers of art are not willing to admit that well-done forgeries are artworks in their own right. Yet sometimes forgeries appear to be works of art in their own right. One example of this phenomenon is when Dr. Seuss painted a faux-modernist painting in the mid-fifties. Seuss's parody of modernist art began when his friend Edward Longstreth, a patron of the La Jolla Museum of Art and a lover of modern art, gave him a condescending lecture about modern art. He decided to trick his friend by concocting a story about a great Mexican modernist named Escarobus. He then told Longstreth that he owned five original Escarobus paintings. Upon hearing that news, Longstreth asked to see one of Seuss's Escarobus paintings. Since none existed at the time, Seuss had to create them from scratch. So in one night, Seuss created the first original Escarobus using the following method: He "peeled the wood off a soft pencil, scraped the lead lengthwise across art paper, dipped small hunks of bread in the vodka he was drinking, and dragged the soggy bread across the paper. Next he painted [Lady] Godivas on the smudges, bisecting and trisecting them so that it was impossible to tell that they were naked ladies."[8] Longstreth liked the first Escarobus painting so much that he purchased it for $550 and wanted to buy the other four original paintings. Seuss's first wife had to stop him from playing along with Longstreth and selling him the "remaining" four. I take this incident as evidence that a forgery can be considered a work of art in its own right.

Why Seuss's Art Is Art: Danto's Philosophy of Art

Even though many of the consequences of accepting Beardsley's aesthetic theory are fine, there is a consequence of Beardsley's aesthetic theory that I think we should reject. That is, his theory would occasionally require us to regard some things that are normally considered artworks as being nonart. Indeed, it sometimes would require us to regard some artworks that are epoch-making artworks as nonart. For example, Michel Duchamp's *Fountain* (1917) would be an epoch-making artwork that would no longer be considered art if we accepted Beardsley's aesthetic theory. I think this is a sufficient reason to introduce a second philosophy of art that can account for things like Duchamp's ready-mades being artworks. So we now turn to Arthur Danto's philosophy of art.

Danto's philosophy of art is built on an insight he had in the early sixties; namely, that evoking an aesthetic experience is neither a necessary nor sufficient condition for an object to be art. This would allow us to claim that Duchamp's *Fountain* is an artwork. He reaches this conclusion by studying the philosophical significance of the pop art movement of the sixties. As Danto attended the exhibit of Andy Warhol's boxes in New York, he noticed that the *Brillo Box* Warhol created was visually indistinguishable from the large Brillo boxes used to ship Brillos from the warehouse to the supermarket. Both boxes had attention-grabbing, aesthetically pleasing designs; yet only Warhol's *Brillo Box* was considered art.

That fact led Danto to reject the idea that evoking an aesthetic experience is a necessary condition for an object to be art. Danto has dedicated most of his philosophical career after the sixties to formulating a philosophical definition of art that would admit that two outwardly indistinguishable objects could have different statuses—one could be considered art whereas the other could not be.

Danto's insight is the result of his idiosyncratic art history.[9] For Danto, art history began in the fifteenth century when some Renaissance art critics claimed that the arts are essentially mimetic activities. That is to say, the goal of the arts is to represent people, events, and things as realistically as possible. The visual arts became the paradigm for the arts because they seemed to represent people, events, and things more realistically than the nonvisual arts. This visual paradigm of artistic excellence is identifiable with the theory of art called representationalism.

Modernism, in terms of artistic representationalism, began in the 1880s when photographs and later movies could depict reality better than any painting in terms of realistic representation. For many artists and art critics, art became a means of representing how artists interpreted reality or expressed a reality that can't be represented mimetically. Such a concept of art opens the door for many types of nonrepresentationalist art movements (e.g., Dadaism and Cubism).

Until the emergence of pop art in the sixties, the future of art (at least in the United States and those non-U.S. art communities influenced by the New York art scene of the fifties) was abstract expressionism, as practiced by the New York School of painting in the fifties. Representatives of abstract expressionism of this time period included Jackson Pollock, Willem de Kooning, Yves Klein, Barnett Newman, Mark Rothko, and Robert Mother-well. It seemed as though abstract expressionism had "defeated" the remaining remnants of realism in painting by the fifties, hence supplanting the over six hundred years of Renaissance paradigms in painting where artworks were evaluated by how well they realistically represented someone or something.

Danto contends that the pop art movement had ended the modern period of the visual arts and hence thwarted the future envisioned by abstract expressionists and modern art theorists such as Clement Greenberg. Moreover, the pop art movement ended art history itself; it did so by teaching people that there is no overarching purpose to art. That movement taught us that the nature of art had nothing to do with better embodying any particular purpose. Of course, this means that no art form or art movement is better than any other. What is left for art and artists after the end of art history is an endless permutation of movements and styles.

When it comes to the philosophy of art, Danto is a historicist and essentialist with respect to the concept of art.[10] Danto is confident that there are necessary conditions that, when combined together, are sufficient for an object to be a work of art. Two of these necessary conditions are (1) that an object must have content, or be about something, and (2) the content expressed by that object is embodied using material mediums. Yet, Danto thinks that we have not been able to formulate a definitive list of these necessary conditions due to the historically indexical nature of the arts. For example, pop art as a style of painting was not imaginable for artists living in the thirteenth century. Indeed, according to Danto, the very idea of being an "artist" was not imaginable in the thirteenth century. Yet pop art is a recognized style of painting today because we live in a historical and sociocultural milieu where Cubist paintings are recognized as legitimate artworks.

When we examine Seuss's *And to Think That I Saw It on Mulberry Street* from the standpoint of Danto's historicist and essentialist philosophy of art, we can better appreciate just how important historical and social context is to determining whether (and when) an object can be interpreted to be a work of art. *And to Think That I Saw It on Mulberry Street* was originally not recognized as being a legitimate children's picture book. Twenty-seven publishers rejected the manuscript that eventually became the book during the winter of 1936–1937.[11] Many of the characters in this book appeared to be unpolished, in fact almost unfinished; sketches and doodles of mythical childhood creatures playing with frumpy people. It took one of his Dartmouth classmates, Mike McClintock, introducing him to the president of

Vanguard Press, James Henle, and an editor of that press who later became its president, Evelyn Shrifte, to find a receptive publisher.[12] Once Vanguard Press decided to take a risk and publish Dr. Seuss's unconventional children's picture book, some critics acknowledged that Dr. Seuss had written and illustrated a legitimate and worthwhile work. One memorable review of Seuss's first book shows how it was accepted into the realm of legitimate children's picture books: "Highly original and entertaining, Dr. Seuss' picture book partakes of the better qualities of those peculiarly American institutions, the funny papers and the tall tale. It is a masterly interpretation of the mind of a child in the act of creating one of those stories with which children often amuse themselves and bolster up their self-respect."[13]

So, until the community of children's literature writers, critics, and librarians recognized his style of writing and illustrating children's books as permissible, Seuss was not recognized as a publishable children's book writer. It probably did not hurt that Seuss's illustrations resembled impressionist and surrealist paintings that had become legitimate artistic styles in the United States during the decade or so prior to the publication of his first children's book. It also didn't hurt that his style integrated elements associated with the cartoons and parodies popular during the twenties and thirties. After all, he began his artistic career as a satirist and cartoonist, beginning with his work for his Dartmouth College humor magazine, the *Jack-o-lantern*, and later for several magazines including *Judge*, *Life*, and *Liberty Magazine*. It would've been natural for him to retain those features of parodies that kept readers' attention—for example, mocking people by imitating their mannerisms in a humorous fashion. And this style was most prominent in his political cartoons and parodies, especially ones intended to convince people of the foolishness of the U.S. isolationist policies prior to the attack on Pearl Harbor and later to promote the U.S. war effort during World War II, published in *PM* from January 1941 until June 1942.

Yet his artistic style forecloses the possibility that any of his artworks could ever fit the classic model of artworks. That is to say, none of his artworks were truly beautiful.[14] Take the hundreds of fictional characters Seuss drew: the Zooks, the Zax, Yertle the Turtle, the Grinch, the Sneetches, Gertrude McFuzz, and so forth. Some of them might have been cute, but none of them were beautiful if what we mean by *beauty* is either (1) the aesthetic pleasure we experience by appreciating an elegant design or (2) the aesthetic property possessed by an object that evokes disinterested pleasure in us. And even when Seuss sought to draw alluring, beautiful human bodies, for example, the seven naked protagonists in his early book for an adult audience, *The Seven Lady Godivas*, he was unsuccessful. Apart from the curvatures meant to represent a woman's breasts and hips, their bodies were as neutered and sexless as any of his nonhuman fictional characters.

Danto's philosophy of art reminds us that sometimes *when* someone creates an object determines whether that object can be a work of art. In Seuss's case, if he had attempted to write his children's books prior to the thirties, his books probably wouldn't have been considered art. They would have not lived up to the expectations, say, of middle-class European American parents living in the United States during the 1820s. These parents would have expected children's stories to teach their children moral lessons. These parents would have expected children's book authors to be moral tutors to their children, not playful compatriots. In other words, reading children's stories would have primarily been exercises in moral education.

This approach to writing children's stories was never Seuss's approach to writing children's books, however. When he began writing children's books, he responded to editors who rejected *And to Think That I Saw It on Mulberry Street* for lack of a clear moral message by saying to his wife: "What's wrong with kids having fun reading without being preached at?"[15] And even when Seuss wrote polemical books, he privileged exercising children's imaginations over giving them clear-cut moral lessons.[16] And we all should be thankful that in the late thirties there was a publisher willing to flaunt the conventions of American children's books and bet on a first-time children's book author who actively protested the bland moralism of American children's literature.

Nel on Dr. Seuss, the Cultural Critic

Nel's cultural studies approach is the third and last aesthetic theory I would like to discuss. Unlike Beardsley and Danto, who are philosophers of art, Nel is a scholar of children's literature and American studies who has written a book-length study on Seuss, *Dr. Seuss: American Icon.* In that book, Nel incorporates several different analytical methods into his approach, including formalism, historicism, art history, and biographical criticism. After all, Seuss's artistic career cannot be described exhaustively by any single analytical method. His artistic career is too multifaceted for such a reductionist approach. Imagine describing the artistic career of someone who was, among other things, a satirist, a cartoonist, a documentary filmmaker who won the Academy Award for Best Documentary in 1948, a script writer for two films and two television programs on art and museums for the Ford Foundation in the forties and fifties, a children's writer, and winner of a Pulitzer Prize in 1984 using just one analytical method. Something of his artistic career would be excluded.

We should admit that this section is not meant to explore Dr. Seuss the artist in all his complexity. Rather, this section is meant to introduce how Seuss's work comes out when we view it using Nel's cultural criticism approach to aesthetic theory. For our purposes we can limit our application of Nel's approach to an examination of how Seuss's concerns about communism, fascism, racism, environmental pollution, and U.S. policies in the Cold War "inspired him to write activist books like *Horton Hears a Who!*, 'The Sneetches,' *The Lorax*, and *The Butter Battle Book*."[17] I regard *The Lorax* and *The Butter Battle Book* as being the two books where Seuss engaged in cultural criticism most effectively—with *The Lorax* being a compelling critique of crass U.S. consumerism and its blind desire to maximize profit at all costs,[18] and *The Butter Battle Book* being a thoughtful critique of the Reagan administration's nuclear deterrence policy.

The Lorax is an explicitly polemical work. Seuss wrote it desiring to awaken people from their indifference to impending environmental disasters, but not by argument and statistics. Rather, he has them imagine that they are witnessing the telling of a tale about a once idyllic, beautiful land; a land whose natural bounty and biodiversity was to be envied. It once had green grass, a blue pond, clean clouds, Truffula Trees and Truffula Fruit, Brown Bar-ba-loots, and the Lorax. The Once-ler recounts how he contributed to the devastation of the environment in his desire to earn ever more money producing and selling Thneeds. Chopping down the Truffula Trees was no problem. Polluting the pond and sky with toxic smoke from the factory was no problem. Whatever it took for the Once-ler to maximize profits was fine until all that was left was an ecological wasteland.

After reading *The Lorax*, one gets a sense that the Once-ler is a parody of the salesperson who sacrifices himself and everything around him for momentary wealth and only acquires a conscience when it's apparently too late. As for the polemical stance taken by Seuss in *The Lorax*, I think the *Newsweek* review of the television version of *The Lorax* sums it up well: *The Lorax* was "a hard-sell ecological allegory, stabbing mainly at big business through a deceptively gentle blend of gorgeous colors, superb animation, and a rippling imagery of words and pictures."[19] The same could be said about the original picture book. It is not surprising that *The Lorax* became associated with the environmentalist movement, and it still fits well within the contemporary sustainability movement.

The Butter Battle Book is Seuss's allegory of the arms race between the United States and the former Soviet Union during the Cold War. It's also a cautionary tale of how an escalating arms race between two states with sophisticated weaponry could really end in mutually assured destruction. The Yooks and the Zooks, the symbolic stand-ins for the United States and the former Soviet Union, have been engaged in a long-standing feud. This feud is over a particular custom—how people should butter and eat their bread. The Yooks prefer to eat their bread butter-side up, whereas the Zooks prefer to eat their bread butter-side down. Each group thinks the other eats their bread wrongly. Moreover, their rival's custom is a threat to their entire way of life. At first they had a few low-level skirmishes along the wall that separates their towns. Over time, though, these skirmishes convince each side to develop ever more sophisticated weaponry. The one-upmanship between the Yooks and the Zooks continue until they both develop the Bitsy Big-Boy Boomeroo, a bomb with enough destructive force to destroy an entire town. The book ends with a general from each side holding a Bitsy Big-Boy Boomeroo, posturing on the wall separating their towns.

Seuss wrote *The Butter Battle Book* as a protest of the Reagan administration's escalation of the nuclear arms race with the former Soviet Union. This book originated from his concern that "a democratic government could impose 'such deadly stupidity' on people like him who were so opposed to nuclear proliferation."[20] He thought that the Reagan administration's policy had the very real potential of causing another world war. This time, though, a world war could mean the end of human civilization, given that each superpower had enough nuclear weapons to annihilate every population center in the world. We can interpret the cliffhanger ending of *The Butter Battle Book* as being Seuss's means of getting people to question the legitimacy and even sanity of the Reagan administration's nuclear deterrence policy.

Nel's cultural criticism approach gives us the theoretical framework necessary to identify at least two reasons Seuss's criticism of capitalism run amok, pollution of the environment, and nuclear deterrence is ironic yet effective. First, Seuss began his professional career as a cartoonist for the very successful and lengthy Flit insecticide campaign. As the brainchild of the "Quick, Henry, the Flit!" advertising campaign, he had an intimate working relationship with one of the most influential corporations in the United States at the time, Standard Oil. Perhaps it was Seuss's familiarity with advertising and large corporations that made his criticisms of crass U.S. consumerism and laissez-faire capitalism so compelling. Second, by the time Seuss wrote his books criticizing influential tendencies in U.S. society he had become a well-known and respected children's author. That status enshrined him as an icon and supposed purveyor of bourgeois U.S. cultural sensibilities. Having an icon of bourgeois U.S. cultural mores and sensibilities, one whose books middle-class parents read to their children, criticize the status quo must have been a warning siren, indeed. The sometimes satirical nature of Seuss's art allows him to dwell in these ironies and take full advantage of them.

Ending the Tale

As we have seen in this chapter, Beardsley's aesthetic theory of art, Danto's philosophy of art, and Nel's cultural criticism approach are three ways people can decide what makes something a work of art. We applied each of these theories to Dr. Seuss's children books and oil paintings. Beardsley's aesthetic theory contended that Seuss's works are artworks because they were created with the purpose of invoking an aesthetic experience in us whenever we appreciate them. Danto's philosophy of art reminded us that *when* Seuss wrote his children's books and painted his oil paintings matters a lot in determining whether they will be considered works of art. Nel's cultural criticism approach got us to admire Seuss's talent for conveying meanings in illustrations and verse, especially in his later activist books. It also allowed us to appreciate Seuss's ability to use irony and allegory to criticize U.S. bourgeois culture while being one of its representatives.

As you revisit Dr. Seuss's children's books and maybe acquaint yourself with his paintings for the first time, see if any of these aesthetic theories helps you better appreciate Seuss's art. If so, then this chapter is a success. If not, don't give up philosophical aesthetics, altogether. Perhaps there is another aesthetic theory out there that might better suit your taste.[21]

~

Notes

Chapter 1

1. Plato, *The Apology of Socrates*, trans. C. D. C. Reeve (Indianapolis: Hackett Publishing, 2002), 22d–e.

2. See Plato, *Euthydemus* 278e; *Symposium* 204e–205a; *Republic* 6.505d–e. All citations and quotations from Plato (except from the *Apology*) are from *Plato: Complete Works*, ed. John M. Cooper (Indianapolis: Hackett, 1997).

3. In Plato's dialogues, Socrates argues that all people do what they believe at the time to be best at *Meno* 77b–78b and *Protagoras* 352c–358e. See also *Gorgias* 466b–468e.

4. Plato, *Apology* 30b.

5. Socrates critiques the conventional Greek cultural education at some length in Plato's *Republic*, Books 2 and 3 in particular. He takes aim at political rhetoric in the *Gorgias*, arguing that public speakers and political leaders in general are nothing more than shameful flatterers, telling people what they want to hear to advance their own selfish ends (462c–465e). Later in the dialogue, he argues that music, poetry, and drama—the keystones of Greek cultural life—are just different forms of flattery and rhetoric, aimed at the gratification of the soul without regard to what is best for it (501d–502e).

6. Plato, *Apology* 38a.

7. Plato, *Laches*, in *Plato: Complete Works*, ed. John M. Cooper (Indianapolis: Hackett Publishing, 1997), 187e–188a.

8. Plato, *Laches* 190e.

9. Plato, *Laches* 191a–c.

10. Plato, *Laches* 192c.

11. Plato, *Laches* 192d.

12. Plato, *Laches* 195a.

13. Plato, *Laches* 199e.

14. Plato, *Apology* 22d–e.

15. Plato, *Apology* 30a.

16. Several characters in Plato's dialogues espouse different versions of this worldview, including Polus and Callicles in the *Gorgias* and Thrasymachus in the *Republic*. In each case, the character describes his ideas as a matter of common sense.

17. For this argument, see *Gorgias* 474b–480a, 482a–c, 492d–500a; *Republic* 4.441c–445a; *Theaetetus* 173c–177b.

18. See Richard Layard, *Happiness: Lessons from a New Science* (New York: Penguin, 2005); Daniel Gilbert, *Stumbling on Happiness* (New York: Vintage Books, 2005); Ed Diener and Robert Biswas-Diener, *Happiness: Unlocking the Mysteries of Psychological Wealth* (Malden, Mass.: Blackwell, 2008).

19. Plato, *Crito* 46b.

20. Plato, *Phaedo* 85c–d.

Chapter 2

1. Arthur Schopenhauer, *The World as Will and Representation*, Volume I, trans. E. F. J. Payne (New York: Dover Publications, 1969), 275.

2. Schopenhauer, *The World as Will and Representation*, Vol. I, 309.

3. Schopenhauer, *The World as Will and Representation*, Vol. I, 312.

4. Schopenhauer, *The World as Will and Representation*, Vol. I, 313.

5. For a more positive assessment of *Oh, the Places You'll Go!* see Benjamin Rider, "Oh, the Places You'll Go! The Examined, Happy Life," in the present volume.

6. The wise man could easily be an allusion to the ascetic St. Simeon Stylites the Elder or any other pillar hermit. These ascetics chose to respond to the suffering of this life by mortifying the flesh and denying all bodily urges and desires.

7. See Plato's *Phaedo* (118a). The reference is to the practice of sacrificing a cock to Asclepius. Cocks were traditionally sacrificed to Asclepius by the ill

who were seeking a cure. Socrates' reference on his deathbed seems to imply that he views death as a "cure" to the disease of existence.

8. Arthur Schopenhauer, *The World as Will and Representation*, Volume II, trans. E. F. J. Payne (New York: Dover, 1966), 605.

9. Friedrich Nietzsche, *The Gay Science: With a Prelude in Rhymes and an Appendix of Songs*, trans. Walter Kaufmann (New York: Vintage Books, 1974), 177.

10. Friedrich Nietzsche, *Thus Spoke Zarathustra: A Book for All and None*, ed. Adrian del Caro and Robert Pippin, trans. Adrian del Caro (Cambridge: Cambridge University Press, 2007), 99.

11. Nietzsche, *The Gay Science*, 272.

12. Nietzsche, *The Gay Science*, 92.

13. Nietzsche, *The Gay Science*, 113.

14. Nietzsche, *The Gay Science*, 252.

15. Friedrich Nietzsche, *Twilight of the Idols, or How to Philosophize with a Hammer* in *The Anti-Christ, Ecce Homo, Twilight of the Idols, and Other Writings*, ed. Aaron Ridley and Judith Norman, trans. Judith Norman (Cambridge: Cambridge University Press, 2007), 157.

16. See Nietzsche, *The Gay Science*, 273–74.

17. Nietzsche, *Thus Spoke Zarathustra*, 17.

18. Nietzsche, *The Gay Science*, 228.

19. Nietzsche, *The Gay Science*, 232.

20. Nietzsche, *Twilight of the Idols*, 229.

Chapter 3

1. *Pontoffel Pock and His Magic Piano/Pontoffel Pock, Where Are You?* (TV 1980), *Seuss Celebration* (DVD: Universal Studios). Further references will occur in the text as (Pock).

2. See Karl Marx, "Economic and Philosophical Manuscripts," in *Marx: Early Political Writings*, ed. and trans. Joseph O'Malley with Richard A. Davis (Cambridge: Cambridge University Press, 1994).

3. Karl Marx, "Ökonomisch-philosophische Manuskripte," in *Marx/Engels Gesamstausgabe (MEGA)*, eventually 114 conceptual volumes. Erste Abteilung, Band 2 (Berlin: Dietz, 1972), 369.

4. G. W. F. Hegel, *Introductory Lectures on Aesthetics*, trans. Bernard Bosanquet, ed. Michael Inwood (New York: Penguin Books, 1993), 36.

5. Karl Marx, "Ökonomsiche Studien (Exzerpte)," in *Marx/Engels Gesamstausgabe (MEGA)*, eventually 114 conceptual volumes. Erste Abteilung, Band 3 (Berlin: Dietz, 1972), 549.

6. Karl Marx, "The German Ideology" in *Marx: Early Political Writings*, ed. and trans. Joseph O'Malley with Richard A. Davis (Cambridge: Cambridge University Press, 1994), 142.

7. Marx, "The German Ideology" in *Marx: Early Political Writings*, 86.

8. See Erich Fromm, *The Sane Society* (New York: Owl Books, 1990), 67.

9. See Fromm, *The Sane Society*, chapter 3, A–E.

10. See Erich Fromm, *Escape from Freedom* (New York: Owl Books, 1994), chapter 4.

11. Max Horkheimer, *Eclipse of Reason* (New York: Oxford University Press, 1947), 141.

12. Max Horkheimer and Theodor W. Adorno, *Dialectic of Enlightenment*, trans. John Cumming (New York: Herder and Herder, 1972), 137.

13. The rash of "depression" may be more illustrative of the fact that society is not meeting people's needs than that there is something wrong with people.

14. Theodor Adorno, "Culture Industry Reconsidered" in *The Adorno Reader*, ed. Brian O'Conner (Oxford: Blackwell, 2000), 235.

Chapter 4

1. David Abel, "Secret Life Steals a Promising Future," *Boston Globe*, January 24, 2004, www.boston.com/news/local/articles/2004/01/24/secret_life_steals_a_promising_future/ (May 20, 2010).

2. Plato, *Apology* in *Five Dialogues*, trans. G. M. A. Grube (Indianapolis: Hackett, 1981), 31 (26c).

3. Plato, *Apology*, 32–33 (27c–d).

4. See, for example: *Bullshit and Philosophy*, ed. Gary L. Hardcastle and George A. Reisch (Chicago: Open Court, 2006); also, Kimberly A. Blessing and Joseph J. Marren, "Bullshit and Political Spin: Is the Medium the Massage?," and Andrew Sneddon, "Bullshitting Bullshitters and the Bullshit They Say," in *The Daily Show and Philosophy*, ed. Jason Holt (Malden, Mass.: Blackwell, 2007).

5. Harry G. Frankfurt, *On Bullshit* (Princeton, N.J.: Princeton University Press, 2005), 61.

6. Lying is a narrower concept than deception, since lying in some way involves propositions, spoken or written, while one can deceive in ways that do not involve assertions at all (e.g., wearing camouflage). Both concepts, though, are rife with philosophical perplexities, and coming up with uncontroversial definitions of either is a difficult task. For a nice overview and bibliography for further research, see James Edwin Mahon, "The Definition

of Lying and Deception," *Stanford Encyclopedia of Philosophy*, plato.stanford
.edu/entries/lying-definition/ (May 20, 2010).

7. If one does not include honestly representing one's intellectual process
and product to others as I do in (5), then a liar could even be said to have
intellectual integrity. She might lack moral integrity, but not necessarily
intellectual integrity. A bullshitter, though, doesn't care about his own intellectual integrity.

8. While related to bullshit, the idea of deluding oneself with what one
wants to be true is closer to the concept of "truthiness" now popularized by
satirist Stephen Colbert. For several papers addressing the concept, including my own "Truth, Truthiness and Bullshit for the American Voter," see
Stephen Colbert and Philosophy, ed. Aaron Schiller (Chicago: Open Court,
2009).

9. Harry G. Frankfurt, *On Truth* (New York: Knopf, 2006), 99–101.

Chapter 5

1. Charles Sanders Peirce, *Philosophical Writings of Peirce*, ed. Justus Bu-
chler (New York: Dover, 1955), 10.

2. Peirce, *Philosophical Writings*, 28.

Chapter 6

1. Yes, yes. There are *real* catfish and *real* dogfish swimming around in
our world, but these hardly resemble the Seussian creatures that share their
names.

2. Plato, *Theaetetus* 201d–210a.

3. See for instance, what has come to be known as "the Gettier problem,"
a counterexample to the claim that knowledge is merely justified true belief,
in Edmund Gettier's "Is Justified True Belief Knowledge?" in *Analysis*, v. 23
(1963), 121–23.

4. René Descartes, *Meditations on First Philosophy*, trans. Elizabeth S. Hal-
dane (Cambridge: Cambridge University Press, 2003), 70.

5. Including, presumably, the claim that global skepticism is true!

6. John Locke, *Essay Concerning Human Understanding*, II.viii.10 (Oxford:
Oxford University Press, 1975), 135.

7. Marco is also the protagonist of Dr. Seuss's *And to Think That I Saw It
on Mulberry Street*.

8. George Berkeley, *A Treatise Concerning the Principles of Human Knowledge* (Indianapolis: Hackett, 1982), 30.

9. Berkeley suggests that this uniformity exists because the universe is held together by God's continuous, perfect perceiving. While consistent with epistemological idealism, introducing a supernatural being probably requires even more of an explanation than what its introduction is intended to explain.

10. From the Latin meaning "from the one before."

11. From the Latin meaning "from the one after."

12. René Descartes, *Discourse on the Method* in *Philosophical Writings of Descartes*, Vol. 1 (Cambridge: Cambridge University Press, 1985), 127.

13. The analytic-synthetic distinction has been a focus of many philosophers and schools of thought, most notably in Immanuel Kant's *Critique of Pure Reason* and more recently in the work of the Logical Positivists. Others have rejected the distinction as untenable; see for instance W. V. O. Quine's 1951 essay "Two Dogmas of Empiricism."

14. Robin May Schott, *Discovering Feminist Philosophy* (Lanham, Md.: Rowman & Littlefield, 2003), 56.

15. Immanuel Kant, *Critique of Pure Reason*, trans. Norman Kemp Smith (New York: St. Martin's, 1965), 93 [A 51/B 75].

16. Friedrich Nietzsche, *The Birth of Tragedy and the Genealogy of Morals*, trans. Francis Golffing (New York: Doubleday, 1956), 255–56.

17. Jalal al-Din Rumi, *Tales from Masnavi*, trans. A. J. Arberry #71. Retrieved from www.khamush.com/tales_from_masnavi.htm#The%20Elephant (August 1, 2010).

18. W. V. O. Quine, "Epistemology Naturalized" in *Ontological Relativity and Other Essays* (New York: Columbia University Press, 1969), 69.

Chapter 7

1. Jean-François Lyotard, *The Postmodern Condition: A Report on Knowledge*, trans. Geoff Bennington and Brian Massumi (Minneapolis: University of Minnesota Press, 1984), xxiv.

2. Lyotard, *The Postmodern Condition*, 81.

3. Lyotard, *The Postmodern Condition*, xxiii.

4. Immanuel Kant, *Critique of Pure Reason*, trans. Norman Kemp Smith (New York: St. Martin's Press, 1965), 635 [A805/B833].

5. Kant, *Critique of Pure Reason*, 29, xxx.

6. You now know more about Kant than 99.9 percent of the population including, unfortunately, my students.

7. Simone de Beauvoir, *The Second Sex*, trans. and ed. H. M. Parshley (New York: Vintage Books, 1974), 301.

8. See Michel Foucault, *The History of Sexuality Volume I: An Introduction*, trans. Robert Hurley (New York: Vintage Books, 1990).

9. Jean-François Lyotard and Jean-Loup Thebaud, *Just Gaming*, trans. Wlad Godzich (Minneapolis: University of Minnesota Press, 1985), 43.

10. Lyotard and Thebaud, *Just Gaming*, 100.

Chapter 8

1. See Frantz Fanon, *Black Skin, White Masks* (New York: Grove Press, 1967).

2. Richard H. Minear, "Yertle, Hitler, and Dr. Seuss" in *Your Favorite Seuss: A Baker's Dozen by the One and Only Dr. Seuss*, ed. Janet Schulman and Cathy Goldsmith (New York: Random House, 2004), 190.

3. See Martin Buber, *I and Thou*, trans. Walter Kaufmann (New York: Touchstone-Simon and Shuster, 1970).

4. Peggy McIntosh, "White Privilege and Male Privilege," in *Oppression, Privilege, and Resistance: Theoretical Perspectives on Racism, Sexism, and Heterosexism*, ed. Lisa Heldke and Peg O'Connor (Boston: McGraw-Hill, 2004), 320.

5. Fanon, *Black Skin, White Masks*, xiv–xv.

6. Sandra Bartky, "On Psychological Oppression" in *Oppression, Privilege, and Resistance: Theoretical Perspectives on Racism, Sexism, and Heterosexism*," ed. Lisa Heldke and Peg O'Connor (Boston: McGraw-Hill, 2004), 31.

7. Bartky, "On Psychological Oppression," 26.

8. Joyce Mitchell Cook, quoted in Bartky, "On Psychological Oppression," 24.

9. Bartky, "On Psychological Oppression," 24.

10. Paulo Freire, *Pedagogy of the Oppressed, 30th Anniversary Edition* (New York: Continuum, 2000), 44.

11. Freire, *Pedagogy of the Oppressed*, 44.

12. This inability to be heard is an example of what Jean-François Lyotard refers to as the *Differend*, a direct result of one's voice not being communicable or audible in the authoritative or grand narrative. See Jean-François Lyotard, *The Differend: Phrases in Dispute*, trans. Georges Van Den Abbeele (Minneapolis: University of Minnesota Press, 1988). For a discussion of this issue in the present volume see Jacob M. Held, "On Beyond Modernity, or Conrad and a Postmodern Alphabet."

13. Martin Luther King Jr., "Letter from Birmingham City Jail," in *A Testament of Hope: The Essential Writings and Speeches of Martin Luther*

King, Jr., ed. James M. Washington (San Francisco: Harper San Francisco, 1986), 290.

14. King, "Letter from Birmingham City Jail," 290.

15. Emma Lazarus, "New Colossus," in *Favorite Poems, Old and New*, ed. Helen Ferris (New York: Doubleday-Delacorte, 1957), 448.

16. The Universal Declaration of Human Rights does receive criticism as being too Western due to its emphasis upon individual autonomy. For a detailed discussion, see Sor-Hoon Tan's *Confucian Democracy: A Deweyan Reconstruction* (New York: SUNY Press, 2004).

17. John Dewey, "Creative Democracy: The Task before Us" in *The Essential Dewey, Vol. 1: Pragmatism, Education, Democracy*, ed. Larry A. Hickman and Thomas M. Alexander (Bloomington: Indiana University Press, 1998), 341.

18. Dewey, "Creative Democracy: The Task before Us," 342.

19. Anthony Weston, *A 21st Century Ethical Toolbox*, 2nd ed. (New York: Oxford University Press, 2008), 29.

Chapter 9

1. Mary Midgley, "Trying Out One's New Sword," in *Contemporary Moral Problems*, 9th ed., ed. James E. White (Belmont, Calif.: Thomson Wadsworth, 2009), 38.

2. For an interesting discussion on relativism, especially the notion that moral truths are only "true for me," as well as relativism being a cowardly response to ethical inquiry, see Norman Melchert, *Who's to Say? A Dialogue on Relativism* (Indianapolis: Hackett, 1994).

3. Immanuel Kant, *Groundwork of the Metaphysics of Morals*, trans. and ed. Mary Gregor (Cambridge: Cambridge University Press, 1998), 53 [4:448].

4. See Immanuel Kant, *Critique of Practical Reason*, trans. and ed. Mary Gregor (Cambridge: Cambridge University Press, 1997), 26–27 [5:29–30].

5. Immanuel Kant, *Lectures on Ethics*, eds. Peter Heath and J. B. Schneewind, trans. Peter Heath (Cambridge: Cambridge University Press, 1997), 246 [29:631].

6. Kant, *Groundwork of the Metaphysics of Morals*, 42 [4:435–36].

7. Immanuel Kant, *The Metaphysics of Morals*, trans. and ed. Mary Gregor (Cambridge: Cambridge University Press, 1996), 209 [6:462].

8. Kant, *Lectures on Ethics*, 229 [29:605].

9. Immanuel Kant, *Fundamental Principles of the Metaphysic of Morals*, trans. T. K. Abbott (Buffalo, N.Y.: Prometheus Books, 1987), 49.

10. Kant, *Fundamental Principles of the Metaphysic of Morals*, 58.

11. John Stuart Mill, *Utilitarianism* (Ontario: Broadview Press, 2000), 14.

12. Mill, *Utilitarianism*, 18.

13. For a good discussion of the Good Life and Dr. Seuss, see Benjamin Rider, "Oh, the Places You'll Go! The Examined, Happy Life," in the present volume.

14. Aristotle, *Nicomachean Ethics* in *The Complete Works of Aristotle*, Vol. 2, ed. Jonathan Barnes (Princeton, N.J.: Princeton University Press, 1984), 1743 [1103b24].

15. Thanks to Ron Novy for offering helpful comments on an earlier draft of this chapter.

Chapter 10

Thanks go to Jacob Held for offering insightful commentary on an earlier draft of this essay.

1. A similar interpretation of Kant's basic ethical ideas can be found in Alan Donagan, *The Theory of Morality* (Chicago: Chicago University Press, 1977). Furthermore, it is not uncommon for philosophers to offer revisions to the theories of other philosophers; this is so even for philosophers of Kant's stature. The idea is that by refining theories that are already quite plausible, philosophers move closer and closer to the truth (which *is* out there).

2. Horton does, however, utter this sentence in the 2007 motion picture adaption of *Horton Hears a Who!*

3. Immanuel Kant, *Foundations of the Metaphysics of Morals*, 2nd ed., trans. Lewis White Beck (New York: Library of the Liberal Arts, 1990), 38.

4. Kant believed that, from this formulation, he could also derive obligations against suicide, to develop one's latent but natural talents, and to offer aid to those in need. Regarding the last, see Kant's *Foundations of the Metaphysics of Morals*, 40. Scholars are divided about whether Kant's derivations are completely successful.

5. Immanuel Kant, "On a Supposed Right to Lie from Altruistic Motives," in *Critique of Practical Reason and Other Writings in Moral Philosophy*, ed. and trans. Lewis White Beck (Chicago: University of Chicago Press, 1949), 348.

6. This sort of dilemma is sometimes expressed via an actual historical situation. Dutch fishermen attempted to smuggle Jews to England during World War II. Sometimes Dutch fishing boats would be stopped by a Nazi patrol boat. A Nazi officer would inquire of the Dutch fisherman where he was headed and who was on board. If you were the fisherman (and assuming no third alternative), what would you do? Should you lie to the officer to protect the life of

innocent people or answer the question honestly, knowing that the innocents in your cargo hold will undoubtedly die a horrible death at Auschwitz?

7. For example, Russ Shafer-Landau comments: "Kant does not need to defend the existence of absolute moral duties. His philosophy can, for instance, justify lying to the inquiring murder. Kant's hatred of lying made him overlook a crucial element of his own view—namely, that the morality of action depends on one's maxim." *The Fundamentals of Ethics* (New York: Oxford University Press, 2010), 157. See also James Rachels, *The Elements of Moral Philosophy*, 4th ed. (New York: McGraw-Hill, 2003), 122–27.

8. Kant, *Foundations of the Metaphysics of Morals*, 46.

9. There is also a sense in which persons, by willfully choosing to not uphold their ethical obligations, fail to respect their own inherent dignity. This entails that we have moral duties to ourselves and not merely to other persons, which (some argue) is another controversial feature of Kant's view.

Chapter 11

1. For an account of relativism, utilitarianism, Kantian ethics, and Aristotle's virtue ethics see Jacob M. Held and Eric N. Wilson, "What Would You Do If Your Mother Asked You? A Brief Introduction to Ethics," in the present volume. For a different assessment of Kant's ethics see Dean Kowalski, "Horton Hears You, Too! Seuss and Kant on Respecting Persons," in the present volume.

2. John Dewey, *Human Nature and Conduct* in *The Middle Works of John Dewey*, Vol. 14, ed. Jo Ann Boydston (Carbondale: Southern Illinois University Press, 1983), 150.

3. See Sartre's famous monograph *Existentialism Is a Humanism*; it is included in many anthologies.

4. Dewey, *Human Nature and Conduct*, 194.

5. John Dewey with James Tufts, *Ethics* in *The Later Works of John Dewey*, Vol. 7, ed. Jo Ann Boydston (Carbondale: Southern Illinois University Press, 1985), 285.

6. Dewey, *Ethics*, 295.

Chapter 12

1. Kant, Immanuel. *Groundwork for the Metaphysic of Morals*, ed. and trans. Allen Wood (New Haven, CT: Yale University Press, 2002), 46.

2. Hume, David, *A Treatise of Human Nature* (New York: Penguin, 1984), 462.

3. Hume, *A Treatise of Human Nature*, 463.

Chapter 13

1. John Locke, *Two Treatises of Government*, ed. Peter Laslett (Cambridge: Cambridge University Press, 1960), 287–89.

2. Robert Nozick, *Anarchy, State, and Utopia* (New York: Basic Books, 1974), 290–92.

3. For example, in James Buchanan and Richard Wagner, *Democracy in Deficit: The Political Legacy of Lord Keynes* (Indianapolis: Liberty Fund, 2000), 105–6. Buchanan is referring here to democratically mandated deficit spending in particular, but the insight applies to any other government policy—see James Buchanan and Gordon Tullock, *The Calculus of Consent* (Ann Arbor: University of Michigan Press, 1962), esp. 131–45.

4. I am grateful to Jacob Held for helpful comments on this essay, and to Daniel Schmutter for prompting me to read *Thidwick* from a public-choice perspective.

Chapter 14

1. Hobbes, Thomas, *Leviathan*, ed. Richard Tuck (Cambridge, UK: Cambridge University Press, 1991), 96.

2. Hobbes, *Leviathan*, 88.

3. Hobbes, *Leviathan*, 89.

4. John Locke, *Second Treatise of Government*, ed. C. B. Macpherson (Cambridge: Hackett, 1980), 52.

5. Locke, *Second Treatise of Government*, 8.

6. Locke, *Second Treatise of Government*, 9.

7. Locke, *Second Treatise of Government*, 9.

8. For an additional account of Locke's theory of property and distributive justice generally, see Henry Cribbs, "Whose Egg Is It, Really? Property Rights and Distributive Justice" in the present volume.

9. Locke, *Second Treatise of Government*, 13.

10. Locke, *Second Treatise of Government*, 111.

11. Immanuel Kant, *The Metaphysics of Morals*, ed. and trans. Mary Gregor (Cambridge: Cambridge University Press, 2003), 30.

12. Kant, *The Metaphysics of Morals*, 24.

13. Immanuel Kant, "On the Common Saying: That May Be Correct in Theory, but It Is of No Use in Practice," in *Practical Philosophy*, ed. and trans. Mary Gregor (Cambridge: Cambridge University Press, 1999), 297.

14. Kant, "On the Common Saying," 297.

15. John Rawls, *A Theory of Justice*, Revised Edition (Cambridge, Mass.: Harvard University Press, 1999), 16.

16. Rawls, *A Theory of Justice*, 16.

17. "Women's Earnings Fall: U.S. Census Bureau Finds Rising Gender Wage Gap," Institute for Women's Policy Research, media release, August 27, 2004, retrieved October 2010.

18. Rawls, *A Theory of Justice*, 53.

19. Iris Marion Young, *Justice and the Politics of Difference* (Princeton, N.J.: Princeton University Press, 1990), 40.

20. Young, *Justice and the Politics of Difference*, 39, 40.

21. The Declaration of Independence of the United States.

22. Martin Luther King Jr., "Letter from the Birmingham Jail," April 16, 1963, www.law.umkc.edu/faculty/projects/ftrials/conlaw/mlkjail.html. (November 1, 2010).

23. King, "Letter from the Birmingham Jail."

Chapter 15

1. John Locke, *Second Treatise of Government* in *Classics of Moral and Political Theory*, 2nd ed., ed. Michael L. Morgan (Indianapolis: Hackett, 1996), 748.

2. Locke, *Second Treatise of Government*, 748.

3. Locke, *Second Treatise of Government*, 748.

4. Locke, *Second Treatise of Government*, 749.

5. Locke, *Second Treatise of Government*, 748, my emphasis.

6. Garrett Hardin, "The Tragedy of the Commons," in *Science* (December 13, 1968).

7. Locke, *Second Treatise of Government*, 751.

8. Cyril Mychalejko, "Ecuador's Constitution Gives Rights to Nature" in *OpEdNews* (September 26, 2008).

9. Hardin, "The Tragedy of the Commons."

10. Locke, *Second Treatise of Government*, 749.

11. Locke, *Second Treatise of Government*, 749.

12. For further discussion of Thidwick and property rights, especially the right over one's own body, see Aeon J. Skoble, "Thidwick the Big-Hearted Bearer of Property Rights," in the present volume.

13. Locke, *Second Treatise of Government*, 751.

14. Adam Smith, *An Inquiry into the Nature and Causes of the Wealth of Nations* (London: Methuen & Co., 1776), bk. 1, ch. 5, para. 1.

15. Smith, *Wealth of Nations*, bk. 4, ch. 2, para. 9.

16. For a more in-depth discussion of the responsibilities of business toward other people's interests, see Matthew F. Pierlott, "It's Not Personal . . . It's Just Bizzyneuss: Business Ethics, the Company, and Its Stakeholders," and Johann A. Klaassen and Mari-Gretta G. Klaassen, "Speaking for Business, Speaking for Trees: Business and Environment in *The Lorax*," in the present volume.

17. Karl Marx and Friedrich Engels, "Manifesto of the Communist Party," in *Marx/Engels Selected Works*, Vol. 1 (Moscow: Progress Publishers, 1969), 98–137.

18. Karl Marx, *Critique of the Gotha Program*, ed. C. P. Dutt (New York: International Publishers, 1966), 10.

19. John Rawls, *A Theory of Justice*, Revised Edition (Cambridge, Mass.: Harvard University Press, 1999), 10.

20. Rawls, *A Theory of Justice*, 11.

Chapter 16

1. See Mackey's contribution to the debate, subtitled "Putting Customers Ahead of Investors" in "Rethinking the Social Responsibility of Business," *Reason* 37, no. 5 (October 2005), 28–32.

2. Aristotle, *Nicomachean Ethics* II.6, trans. W. D. Ross, classics.mit.edu/Aristotle/nicomachaen.2.ii.html (May 20, 2010).

3. For the condensed and oft-anthologized expression of this view, see: Milton Friedman, "The Social Responsibility of Business Is to Increase Its Profits," *New York Times Magazine* (September 13, 1970), 122–26.

4. For further discussions of property see Aeon J. Skoble, "Thidwick the Big-Hearted Bearer of Property Rights," and Henry Cribbs, "Whose Egg Is It, Really? Property Rights and Distributive Justice" in the present volume.

5. In order to keep these thinkers and their theories straight, I offer this Seussian pneumonic device: "While Freeman is free to take stock of the stakeholders, for Friedman, it's freedom that's at stake for the stockholders."

6. For an articulation of Freeman's standard version, see E. Freeman and D. Reed, "Stockholders and Stakeholders: A New Perspective on Corporate Governance," in *Corporate Governance: A Definitive Exploration of the Issues*, ed. G. Huizinga (Los Angeles: UCLA Extension Press, 1983). For an articulation of differing contexts in which it's invoked, see T. M. Jones and A. C. Wicks, "Convergent Stakeholder Theory," *Academy of Management Review* 24, no. 2 (April 1999), 206–21. For a nice overview of the historical development of the debate see H. Jeff Smith, "The Shareholders vs. Stakeholders Debate," *MIT Sloan Management Review* (Summer 2002), 85–90.

7. See Friedman's contribution to the debate, subtitled "Making Philan-
thropy Out of Obscenity," in which he sees talking about other stakeholders'
interests as mere rhetoric, where acting on them must always contribute to
the bottom line or be avoided: "Rethinking the Social Responsibility of Business," in *Reason*, vol. 37, no. 5 (October 2005), 28–32.

8. Friedman, "Rethinking the Social Responsibility of Business," 28–32,
30.

9. For a perfect example in business ethics literature, arguing that deception in business negotiations is moral because it is conventionally expected,
see: Albert Carr, "Is Business Bluffing Ethical?," *Harvard Business Review* 46
(1968), 143–53.

10. For a more in-depth treatment of Kantian ethics see Dean A. Kowalski, "Horton Hears You, Too! Seuss and Kant on Respecting Persons," in
the present volume.

11. Immanuel Kant, *Groundwork of the Metaphysics of Morals*, ed. and
trans. Mary Gregor (Cambridge: Cambridge University Press, 1998), 38.

12. Jim Puzzanghera, "Retailers Fined over Digital TV," *Los Angeles Times*,
April 11, 2008, articles.latimes.com/2008/apr/11/business/fi-tv11 (May 20,
2010).

13. Directive 2007/65/EC of the European Parliament and of the Council
of 11 December 2007, *Official Journal of the European Union* L 332/27-45, 40.
www.ivir.nl/legislation/eu/2007_65_EC.pdf (May 20, 2010).

14. U.S. GAO Report, *GAO/HRD-88-130BR: "Sweatshops" in the U.S.:
Opinions on Their Extent and Possible Enforcement Options* (U.S. General
Accounting Office, 1988), /archive.gao.gov/d17t6/136973.pdf (May 20,
2010).

15. Steven Greenhouse, "Apparel Factory Workers Were Cheated, State
Says," *New York Times*, July 24, 2008, N.Y./Region section, www.nytimes
.com/2008/07/24/nyregion/24pay.html (May 20, 2010).

16. See Horace Fairlamb, "Adam Smith's Other Hand: A Capitalist Theory of Exploitation," *Social Theory and Practice* 22, no. 2 (1996), 193–223.

17. Ian Maitland, "The Great Non-debate over International Sweatshops," *Ethical Theory and Business*, 6th ed., ed. Tom Beauchamp and Norman Bowie (Upper Saddle River, N.J.: Prentice Hall, 2001), 593–605.

18. Aristotle, *Nicomachean Ethics* III.1, trans. W. D. Ross, classics.mit.edu/
Aristotle/nicomachaen.3.i.html (May 20, 2010).

19. For a further discussion of the relation between business and the environment see Johann A. Klaassen and Mari-Gretta G. Klaassen, "Speaking
for Business, Speaking for Trees: Business and Environment in *The Lorax*,"
in the present volume.

20. For example, W. Michael Hoffman, "Business and Environmental Ethics," *Business Ethics Quarterly* 1 (1991), 169–84.

21. Norman Bowie, "Morality, Money, and Motor Cars," in *Business, Ethics, and the Environment: The Public Policy Debate*, ed. W. Michael Hoffman, Robert Frederick, and Edward S. Petry Jr. (Westport, Conn.: Quorum Books, 1990), 93.

Chapter 17

1. "Every once in a while I get mad. The Lorax . . . came out of my being angry. The ecology books I'd read were dull. . . . I was out to attack what I think are evil things and let the chips fall where they might." Jonathan Cott, "The Good Dr. Seuss," in *Of Sneetches and Whos and the Good Dr. Seuss: Essays on the Writings and Life of Theodor Geisel*, ed. Thomas Fensch (Jefferson, N.C.: McFarland, 1997), 118.

2. Joseph R. DesJardins, *Business, Ethics, and the Environment: Imagining a Sustainable Future* (Upper Saddle River, N.J.: Prentice Hall, 2007), 125.

3. See DesJardins, *Business, Ethics, and the Environment*, 125–29.

4. DesJardins, *Business, Ethics, and the Environment*, 124–25.

5. DesJardins, *Business, Ethics, and the Environment*, 124.

6. Mark Sagoff, *The Economy of the Earth: Philosophy, Law, and the Environment*, 2nd ed. (New York: Cambridge University Press, 2008), 110–36.

7. Sagoff, *The Economy of the Earth*, 113.

8. One of the downsides to having a philosopher father is that such seemingly simple questions can prompt long answers . . . or long conversations. One of the upsides of being a philosopher father is that such long answers can, when applied carefully and at the proper moment, shorten the bedtime book-reading obligation considerably.

9. Herman Daly, *Beyond Growth: The Economics of Sustainable Development* (Boston: Beacon Press, 1996), 28.

10. Adam Jaffe, Steven Peterson, Paul Portney, and Robert Stavins, "Environmental Regulation and the Competitiveness of U.S. Manufacturing: What Does the Evidence Tell Us?" *Journal of Economic Literature* 33 (March 1995), 133.

11. DesJardins, *Business, Ethics, and the Environment*, 10.

12. Much of this section is based on the discussion of sustainability from Johann A. Klaassen, "Sustainability and Social Justice," forthcoming in *Responsible Investment in Times of Turmoil*, ed. Wim Vandekerckhove, et al. (Springer Verlag).

13. Gro Harlem Brundtland and the World Commission on Environment and Development, *Our Common Future* (Oxford: Oxford University Press, 1987). "Development" in this context means economic and social growth: increasing economic activity, to be sure, but also thereby reducing unemployment, poverty, and social inequalities as well.

14. Frank Figge, "Capital Substitutability and Weak Sustainability Revisited: The Conditions for Capital Substitution in the Presence of Risk," *Environmental Values* 14, 186. Notice the resemblance between this formulation and the "Lockean" proviso: the requirement that we leave "as much and as good" available for others, if our appropriation of property is to be justifiable. See John Locke, *Two Treatises of Government*, ed. Mark Goldie (London: Everyman, 1689/1924), 128.

15. Herman E. Daly, "Toward Some Operational Principles of Sustainable Development," in *Ecological Economics*, Vol. 2, No. 1 (April 1990), 1–6.

16. See, for example, discussions of "social capital" in Donella Meadows, *Indicators and Information Systems for Sustainable Development: A Report to the Balaton Group* (Hartland Four Corners, Vt.: The Sustainability Institute, 1998), and Joseph Lewandowski and Gregory Streich, "Democratizing Social Capital: In Pursuit of Liberal Egalitarianism," *Journal of Social Philosophy* 38 (2007), 588–604.

17. Christopher D. Stone, "Should Trees Have Standing? Toward Legal Rights for Natural Objects," *Southern California Law Review* 45(2) (1972), 450–501. Citations here will be made to the latest reprinting, in Christopher D. Stone, *Should Trees Have Standing? Law, Morality, and the Environment*, 3rd ed. (Oxford: Oxford University Press, 2010).

18. Stone, *Should Trees Have Standing?*, 3.

19. Stone, *Should Trees Have Standing?*, 8.

20. There is a remarkable coincidence in timing between Stone's influential article and Dr. Seuss's *The Lorax*. Dr. Seuss's book first hit bookstore shelves on August 12, 1971, according to the official website of Random House and Dr. Seuss Enterprises (www.seussville.com/lorax/). In the introduction to his book, Stone says he had the initial idea for his article in a class in the fall of 1971, had planned out the bulk of the article by October 1971, and published it in the spring of 1972 (*Should Trees Have Standing*, xiii). Now, we certainly can't say that Stone got his idea from Dr. Seuss, but it seems odd to find that he has never addressed the similarities, as far as we can tell. In fact, Stone seems to find it strange, even inexplicable, that some of the responses to his article in the academic and public press were written in rhyme. We can't decide whether Stone's expressions of

perplexity, and his steadfast refusal to talk about Seuss, are meaningful or merely disingenuous.

Chapter 18

1. Jon Agee, "The 500 Cats of Theodor Geisel," *Los Angeles Times Book Review*, Book Review Holiday Special Section (December 3, 1995), 22.

2. Monroe C. Beardsley, "Monroe C. Beardsley: An Aesthetic Definition of Art," in *The Nature of Art: An Anthology*, 2nd ed., ed. Thomas E. Wartenberg (Belmont, Calif.: Thomson Wadsworth, 2007), 232.

3. Paul Guyer, "The Origins of Modern Aesthetics," in *Blackwell Guide to Aesthetics*, ed. Peter Kivy (Malden, Mass.: Blackwell, 2004), 20.

4. Beardsley, "Aesthetic Definition," 232.

5. See Monroe C. Beardsley, *Aesthetics: Problems in the Philosophy of Criticism*, 2nd ed. (Indianapolis: Hackett, 1981), 470.

6. Theodor Seuss Geisel, *The Secret Art of Dr. Seuss*, with an introduction by Maurice Sendak (New York: Random House, 1995), 60.

7. Gary D. Schmidt, "Playing to the Audience: A Critical Look at Dr. Seuss," *Children's Literature Association Quarterly* 16.1 (Spring 1991), 41.

8. See Philip Nel, *Dr. Seuss: American Icon* (New York: Continuum, 2004), 206, note 17.

9. See Arthur C. Danto, *After the End of Art: Contemporary Art and the Pale of History* (Princeton, N.J.: Princeton University Press), esp. chapters 2 and 7.

10. See Danto, *After the End of Art*, chapter 11.

11. Judith Morgan and Neil Morgan, *Dr. Seuss and Mr. Geisel: A Biography* (New York: Da Capo, 1995), 81.

12. Morgan and Morgan, *Dr. Seuss and Mr. Geisel*, 82.

13. Quoted in Morgan and Morgan, *Dr. Seuss and Mr. Geisel*, 84.

14. See Arthur C. Danto, *The Abuse of Beauty: Aesthetics and the Concept of Art* (Chicago: Open Court, 2003), chapter 1.

15. Morgan and Morgan, *Dr. Seuss and Mr. Geisel*, 81.

16. Nel, *Dr. Seuss: American Icon*, 38. Nel reminds us that Seuss believed that his nonsensical verse helped children develop a much-needed sense of humor. Surely, developing a sense of humor might help children develop into moral adults. But Seuss seemed to think developing their moral character was secondary to developing their imaginations, which would enable them to make sense of what Seuss called "this sordid world."

17. Nel, *Dr. Seuss: American Icon*, 14.

18. For discussions of the relation between business and the environment and the responsibility of businesses to interests outside of themselves see Johann A. Klaassen and Mari-Gretta G. Klaassen, "Speaking for Business, Speaking for Trees: Business and Environment in *The Lorax*," and Matthew F. Pierlott, "It's Not Personal . . . It's Just Bizzyneuss: Business Ethics, the Company, and Its Stakeholders," respectively, in the present volume.

19. Morgan and Morgan, *Dr. Seuss and Mr. Geisel*, 223.

20. Morgan and Morgan, *Dr. Seuss and Mr. Geisel*, 249.

21. If none of the aesthetic theories covered in this chapter appeal to you, I recommend: Noël Carroll, *A Philosophy of Mass Art* (Oxford: Oxford University Press, 1998) or Denis Dutton, *The Art Instinct: Beauty, Pleasure, and Human Evolution* (New York: Bloomsbury, 2009).

Index

~

The Menagerie: Author Biographies

Thomas M. Alexander is a professor at Southern Illinois University, Carbondale. He is mainly known as a Dewey scholar, but he also teaches classical philosophy and has an active interest in Buddhism and Native American culture. He grew up in New Mexico. His father was also a professor of philosophy, as was his father.

Randall E. Auxier teaches philosophy at Southern Illinois University, Carbondale. He lives with four very creative but temperamental cats and one similarly talented spouse. Only Dr. Seuss could possibly come up with a suitable rhyme for his last name, but he enjoys thinking about what sort of creature might bear the name of a Snauxier.

Henry Cribbs serves on the editorial board for *Nimrod International Journal of Prose and Poetry* at the University of Tulsa, pens a monthly column for *Redstone Science Fiction*, and in his spare time publishes poetry about Schrödinger's cat. He taught logic, ethics, rhetoric, and poetics for several years at the University of South Carolina before deciding he could better corrupt the youth if he taught those subjects to actual youths. Now he masquerades as a high school English teacher somewhere in Oklahoma not very far from Flobbertown, where he forces his students to read Seuss alongside Shakespeare and Sophocles and strives to make every day a Diffendoofer Day.

Anthony Cunningham is professor of philosophy at St. John's University in Collegeville, Minnesota. He is the author of *The Heart of What Matters: The Role for Literature in Moral Philosophy.* He works in ethics, with a special interest in literature, and has published in the *American Philosophical Quarterly,* the *Journal of Value Inquiry, Mind,* and *Ethics.* Fortunately, he has never even thought about stealing Christmas, not a bit, not a sliver.

Jacob M. Held is assistant professor of philosophy at the University of Central Arkansas. He has written extensively at the intersection of philosophy and popular culture, having coedited (with James South) *James Bond and Philosophy: Questions Are Forever* (Open Court, 2006) and contributed to volumes on the Beatles, South Park, and *Watchmen,* to name a few. He has also written more "respectable" academic pieces on topics such as Kant, Marx, obscenity law and free speech, and applied ethics. He currently spends the majority of his time avoiding Hakken-Kraks and Poozers and trying to ignore that there is a 1 and ¼ percent chance he won't succeed.

Tanya Jeffcoat is an instructor of philosophy at the University of Central Arkansas, where she teaches courses on American pragmatism, feminism, and world philosophies. Her recent writing has focused on John Dewey, ecological individualism, sustainability, and issues in diversity—all of which are currently looking for academic homes. When she's not dreaming of Truffula Trees, Brown Bar-ba-loots, and Swomee-Swans, she's trying to convince her students that nothing will get better unless we start caring a whole awful lot.

Johann A. Klaassen is vice president of Managed Account Solutions for, and a member of the Investment Committee of, First Affirmative Financial Network, LLC. He earned a BA in liberal arts (the Great Books Program) from St. John's College in Santa Fe, New Mexico, and a PhD in ethics and social philosophy from Washington University in St. Louis. His scholarly articles have appeared in such journals as *Philosophy and Literature, Journal of Social Philosophy,* and *Journal of Value Inquiry;* he has presented papers to international conferences in Helsinki, Las Vegas, and Washington, D.C., among others. He is particularly fond of Scrambled Eggs Super-dee-Dooper-dee-Booper, Special de luxe a-la-Peter T. Hooper—but will happily accept a plate of green eggs and ham.

Mari-Gretta G. Klaassen is a student at Palmer Ridge High School in Monument, Colorado, where she focuses her studies on literature and drama. She is coauthor, with Johann A. Klaassen, of "Humiliation and Discrimination:

The Role of Shame in the Politics of Difference among the Sneetches of Dr. Seuss." She does not own, nor does she want, a Thneed.

Dean A. Kowalski is currently an associate professor of philosophy at the University of Wisconsin-Waukesha. He is the author of *Classic Questions and Contemporary Film: An Introduction to Philosophy* (2005) and has edited and contributed essays to three popular culture and philosophy books: *The Philosophy of* The X-Files (2007, paperback 2009), *Steven Spielberg and Philosophy* (2008), and *The Philosophy of Joss Whedon* (2011). He has also contributed essays to *James Bond and Philosophy*, *The Philosophy of Martin Scorsese*, and *Homer Simpson Goes to Washington*.

Ron Novy is lecturer in philosophy and the humanities in the University College at the University of Central Arkansas. He has contributed to volumes on Batman, supervillains, Iron Man, Green Lantern, and the forthcoming *Spider-Man and Philosophy*. Ron teaches a number of seminar courses that begin with the letter "M" and spends much of his time reminding freshmen that philosophy begins with imagination. He grew up on Mulberry Street.

Matthew F. Pierlott is assistant professor of philosophy at West Chester University of Pennsylvania. His research interests center on moral agency, ethical theory, and applied ethics, specifically business ethics. He has become active in philosophy and pop culture literature, contributing to *Stephen Colbert and Philosophy* (Open Court, 2009) and *Fashion and Philosophy* (Wiley, 2011). For his contributions to this book he shamelessly employed his young children as research assistants, paying them nothing and keeping them up way past their bedtime.

Benjamin A. Rider is assistant professor of philosophy at the University of Central Arkansas. He has written about Plato's views about moral and philosophical education as well as on other topics in ancient philosophy and applied ethics. He probably spends more time than is healthy examining his life and trying to get others to do the same.

Aeon J. Skoble is professor of philosophy and chair of the Philosophy Department at Bridgewater State University in Massachusetts. He is the coeditor of *Political Philosophy: Essential Selections* (Prentice Hall, 1999), author of *Deleting the State: An Argument about Government* (Open Court, 2008), and editor of *Reading Rasmussen and Den Uyl: Critical Essays on Norms of Liberty* (Lexington Books, 2008), and has written many essays in both scholarly and popular journals. In addition, he writes widely on the intersection of philosophy and popular culture, including such subjects as *Seinfeld*, *Forrest Gump*, *The Lord of the Rings*, superheroes, film noir, Hitchcock, Scorsese, science fiction, and baseball, and is coeditor of *Woody Allen and Philosophy* (Open Court, 2004), *The Philosophy of TV Noir* (University Press of Kentucky, 2008), and the best-selling *The Simpsons and Philosophy* (Open Court, 2000). He cannot read with his eyes shut.

Dwayne Tunstall is assistant professor of philosophy at Grand Valley State University. He is the author of *Yes, But Not Quite: Encountering Josiah Royce's Ethico-Religious Insight* (Fordham University Press). His academic publications have covered a wide range of topics, including Africana educational theory, African American philosophy, Gabriel Marcel's religious existentialism, social and political philosophy, twentieth-century American idealism, transcendental pragmatism, and the teleological suspension of philosophy. Writing about Dr. Seuss is just his current side gig.

Eric N. Wilson is a recent graduate of philosophy and linguistics at the University of Central Arkansas. Prior to working with Jacob M. Held he acted as an assistant editor for *STANCE: International Undergraduate Philosophy Journal*, deciding to test the waters of academic philosophy firsthand. Most of his time there was spent mulling over papers in epistemology and philosophy of mind. Currently Eric is enjoying a stay in the Waiting Place, but he won't be there long. He's just that type of guy.